NEWBURY HOUSE PUBLISHERS, Inc

Joshua A. Fishman
*University Research Professor
of Social Sciences*

Yeshiva University

BILINGUAL EDUCATION

*An
International
Sociological
Perspective*

With an Appendix by

E. Glyn Lewis
Wales

Library of Congress Cataloging in Publication Data

Fishman, Joshua A
   Bilingual education.

   Bibliography: p.
   1. Education, Bilingual. I. Title.
LC3715.F57   371.9'7   76-17561
ISBN 0-88377-056-3

Cover design by Lois Jefferson Kordaszewski

NEWBURY HOUSE PUBLISHERS, Inc.

Language Science
Language Teaching
Language Learning

68 Middle Road, Rowley, Massachusetts 01969

Printed in the U.S.A.   First printing: September 1976
                                       5 4 3 2 1

This volume, begun in the fall of 1972, while I was Visiting Professor of Sociology of Language at the Hebrew University, Jerusalem, and completed in first draft by the fall of 1974, a year after I had returned to my permanent base at Yeshiva University in New York, is such an example of the benefits of international cooperation that I am even more eager than is usually the case to acknowledge the assistance I have received.

The grant from the Division of Foreign Studies, DHEW-USOE,* which made possible the research upon which this volume is based, would not have been obtained without the assitance of Dean Joseph B. Gittler, of the Ferkauf Graduate School of Yeshiva University; his assistant, Mrs. Silvia Brick; and the Vice-President for Financial Affairs of Yeshiva University, Dr. Sheldon E. Socol. Their cooperation and attention with respect to an application submitted by a faculty member who was many thousands of miles away was truly heartwarming.

Many colleagues and bilingual educators familiar with local realities all over the world helped obtain the data that this volume reports. Literally hundreds wrote long letters and filled out complicated questionnaires in reply to my inquiries. As a result, it is clearly impossible to mention them all by name here. Hopefully this volume will be some small recompense for their time and this paragraph an indication of my appreciation for their priceless assistance.

A smaller group of distinguished associates served as a "voluntary cabinet" throughout the many months of efforts to obtain worldwide data relative to bilingual education of a kind never before located or systematized. Among those whose help was most crucial were William Mackey, Richard Tucker, Jose P. Rona, and John Macnamara of Canada; Thomas Kellahan of Ireland; Glyn Lewis of Wales; Albert Verdoodt of Belgium; Andrée Tabouret-Keller and Charlotte Borga of France; G. E. Malherbe of the Republic of South Africa; and Rudolph Troike, Bernard Spolsky, Charles Ferguson, Vera John, Vivian Horner, and Avengelos Afendras of the United States. To all of them I wish to express my gratitude and indebtedness.

---

*See: Final Report, Contract OECO-73-0588, September 1974: *A Sociology of Bilingual Education,* Joshua A. Fishman, Principal Investigator.

ACKNOWLEDGMENTS

An even smaller number of research assistants and consultants served valiantly in helping to obtain, process, and analyze the data reported in this volume. It is literally true that without them this volume would not have been possible. Lee Strunin, Marvin Langsam, Dina Nehemias, Nava Avinun, Thea Reeves, David Fishman, Gertrude Schweid, Joyce Gleit, and Peter Rothenberg as research and secretarial assistants on the one hand, and Robert Cooper, Norman Grover, and Mendel Hoffman as technical consultants and associates on the other, worked often against great odds, and always across several continents. Their unparalleled willingness to do so must be mentioned here for all to note.

I must mention two members of the Division of Foreign Studies, Carl Epstein and Julia Petrov, whose encouragement and understanding, particularly in the few periods of difficulty that every project inevitably runs into, made this whole undertaking an unusually enjoyable and rewarding one. It is a pleasure indeed to encounter dedicated public servants such as these and to acknowledge their productive assistance.

The final draft of this volume, a complete "rethink" and rewrite of the original report to the Division of Foreign Studies, DHEW-USOE, has benefited considerably from the frank comments and criticisms of my students, from the painstaking advice of colleagues (particularly Judith Guskin, Heinz Kloss and Robert L. Cooper), and from the additions and corrections submitted by school personnel on all continents to whom copies of the original report had been sent. To one and all, my heartfelt gratitude for their assistance to me and for their contribution to bilingual education.

Joshua A. Fishman
Institute for Advanced Study
Princeton, New Jersey

September 1975/Tishrey 5736

Acknowledgments		iv
Preface		viii

Part I *POINT OF VIEW*

I. Bilingual Education is Good for the Majority Group *Language and Culture in the Global Community* 3

II. Bilingual Education is Good for the Minority Group *The Third Century of Non-English-Language Maintenance and Non-Anglo Ethnic Maintenance in the U.S.A.* 11

III. Bilingual Education is Good For Education *Bilingual Education, What and Why?* 23

IV. Bilingual Education is Good for Language Teachers and Language Teaching *Bilingual Education and the Future of Language Teaching and Language Learning in the U.S.A.* (with Robert L. Cooper) 32

Part II *INTERNATIONAL FINDINGS*

V. *Will Foreign Languages Still Be Taught in the Year 2000?* 47

VI. *Worldwide Perspective on Bilingual Education* 52

VII. *The Nations of the World: Some Social and Economic Characteristics* 77

VIII. *The International Sociology of Bilingual Secondary Education: Empirical Findings and Theoretical Implications* 94

IX. *International Socioeducational Perspective on Some Uncomfortable Questions about Bilingual Education* 108

CONTENTS

Part III   *APPENDICES*

1.   *Thumbnail Sketches of Ten Bilingual Schools
     Outside of the United States*   127

2.   *Comments on Recent References*   136

3.   *Bilingualism and Bilingual Education: The Ancient
     World to the Renaissance* (E. Glyn Lewis)   150

4.   *Consolidated Bibliography*   201

This is a partisan volume. Not only is it unabashedly in favor of bilingual education, but it is strongly in favor of a certain context for bilingual education: a context that values it as *enrichment* for one and all, rather than merely as *compensation* for down-and-out minorities or as a *group-maintenance* opportunity for reawakening ones. I have written this book because I want to bring this view, and the data and reasoning on which it is based, to teachers, teacher-trainees, educational administrators, a wide variety of other educational specialists, and educationally concerned laymen, for all of whom *bilingual education* is a matter of rapidly growing interest. This book is, in part, polemic and passionate in tone. I hope I will be pardoned for feeling deeply and for communicating feelings and values in addition to information and conclusions. I believe it is my duty as an empirical researcher to do the former as well as the latter because bilingual education urgently requires not only attention and understanding but also sympathy, assistance, and dedication.

In the United States, interest in bilingual education has become particularly marked only in the past five or six years. However, in that brief period astounding changes have taken place with respect to the *climate* vis-à-vis bilingual education, as well as with respect to its *substance* in terms of students, teachers, curricula, and funds. There has been a mushrooming of interest and experimentation, much of it uninformed and almost all of it inexperienced, underbudgeted, and uncertain insofar as stability is concerned. Nevertheless, excitement and foment and eagerness and hopefulness and need all count for a good deal in the world of education, where very little is fully "nailed down" in the sense of definitive and detailed expertise. Thus, it is into this American context of widespread and growing interest in bilingual education that I would like to introduce several ingredients . . . some of them cognitive and some of them affective and conative . . . that have seemed to me to be regrettably underpresented heretofore. Furthermore, it is also my hope that educators the world over will consider the views and findings presented here to be of value and of interest. Indeed, it is my fond and fundamental hope to lead bilingual educators in the U. S. A. and elsewhere to consider themselves to be a *single* community of interest, each learning from the other and correcting each other's experimental and attitudinal limitations.

PREFACE

Bilingual Education Is Not Merely for Heterogeneous Populations

One of my major messages in this volume is that bilingual education is "good for everybody" and, particularly, for the relatively homogeneous and monolingual populations of the world, be they citizens of large or small nations. Indeed, the full fruits of bilingual education may yet be savored most satisfyingly in nations pursuing Type A self-definitions (see Fishman, 1969), that is, in the nations viewing themselves as reflecting but a single, unifying Great Tradition; precisely because they need not be propelled toward bilingual education by vexing internal pressures for rudimentary intergroup communication and amelioration of grievances. This is not to say that nations adopting Type A self-definitions are in any way as homogeneous as they pretend. Indeed, they commonly have many linguistic and cultural minorities, which, although they may have adopted multiple-membership and self-identities that tie them symbiotically to the majority and to each other, can still provide sensitive and sensible starting points for bilingual education for all.

When Type A national self-definitions coincide with Languages of Wider Communication (e.g., English, Russian, French, Spanish, Arabic, Chinese, etc.), it is particularly desirable to provide as many students as possible with bilingual education in order to emphasize one crucial lesson: that mankind is not all of one cloth and that reality is not entirely according to the seemingly ubiquitous home-fashioned mold. Of course, this is also vital when Type A self-definitions coincide with rather small languages on the world scene (e.g., Hebrew, Hungarian, Thai, or Turkish), particularly if these have only recently "arrived" themselves as vehicles of independent government and higher education and are therefore still in the grip of traditional conflict with even less powerful languages "below" them and with more powerful languages "above" them (Fishman, 1972d). "God save us from former slaves who have become kings." A history of former deprivation may be hard to forget; harder, indeed, than a history of former plenty. Nevertheless, the smaller, less powerful nations of the world ultimately must and do adapt, like it or not, at least to the more powerful cultures that flood in upon them. It is the "great powers," and the "near-great," "would-be great," and those who have joined them via de-ethnification and re-ethnification, who are always less willing and less likely to "try on another pair of glasses," to broaden their exposure to other views and approaches, to see themselves as others see them, to attend to any drummers but their own. Thus, it is primarily to *their* educational personnel—and particularly to the Anglo-American components among them—that this volume is addressed. *They* need bilingual education more than they know; and only if *they* come to believe in and implement such education for themselves and for their monolingual charges will bilingual education really come into its own and attain its unique humanizing and civilizing potential.

Bilingual Education Is Not Merely for Poor or Dislocated Populations

I have shown previously and elsewhere (Fishman, 1968) that linguistic heterogeneity, on a worldwide scale, is not necessarily related either to economic disadvantage or to ethnic disagreement. Nevertheless, like all fundamental untruths, the putative relationship between these three variables continues to be believed, suspected, imagined, and rumored far beyond my own weak ability to set aright. Nevertheless, I have continued the "good fight" in the present volume by providing worldwide perspective on bilingual education. Although I realize full well that more and better information is not enough to overcome the disinclination of most teachers and laymen (and most humans of whatever background) to confront the tried and traditioned untruths that comfort us, I nevertheless continue to believe that more and better information is of some help in shaking up all establishments, whether personal or societal. Of course, other dynamic factors must also be called upon: political sophistication and political clout (Fishman, 1970a); organizational ability and changes in the climate of opinion related to other, more pervasive concerns (Fishman, 1973a, and Chapter V of this volume). But, in each of these connections more and better information must also be called into play for truly effective action. It is this faith in the ultimate usefulness of accurate knowledge and expertise which comforts me as I note the totally unnatural, shameful and, indeed, slanderous relationship between bilingual education and poverty or other societal dislocation which is still *required* by much of the Bilingual Education legislation in the United States.

It is my hope that the international and diachronic perspective provided by this volume will persuade readers whose only prior association with bilingual education is in terms of "those poor Chicanos" or "those unfortunate Puerto Ricans" that they have thus far been in touch with only a very small and atypical part of the bilingual education "elephant." The "entire beast" is, indeed, a multisplendored thing and as a whole, it is by no means related to poverty or to social disorganization of any kind, as is shown by the bilingual education experience of Wales, Singapore, the Soviet Union, and the better upper-class schools throughout the word. Bilingual education is of several *different kinds,* with widely *different purposes,* serving a great variety of needs. It is wrong to identify it with any one of these kinds, purposes, and needs. It is particularly unfortunate for Americans to do so at a time when bilingual education in our country is still in its infancy and when many kinds, purposes, and needs urgently need to be explored if bilingual education in the United States is to become the serious educational alternative or option that it deserves to be and that it successfully is elsewhere.

Bilingual Education Is Not Merely a Recent Psychological Approach for the Improvement of Elementary Instruction

Most of the evidence, controversy, and speculation with respect to bilingual education have concentrated upon psychological dimensions and upon the elementary level of instruction. Although a variety of topics has been examined (bilingual education and intelligence, bilingual education and academic achievement, bilingual education and communicative/linguistic competence, bilingual education and affective/affiliative development, bilingual education and attitudes toward schooling), they are mostly viewed within the context of the learners' early educational career and in terms of psychoeducational considerations. The time has come to transcend both of the above limitations, particularly since they are both arbitrary and restrictive from the point of view of the need for and the reality of bilingual education itself.

Like all education, indeed, like all sociolinguistic behavior of whatever kind, bilingual education functions within a social context which includes schoolwide, communitywide, regionwide, nationwide, and even international dimensions and ramifications (Fishman, 1972e). Bilingual education does not merely serve individual children or involve parents and teachers as individuals; it serves community needs, pursues societal goals, is constrained by organized opposition, is fostered by organized support, and, in the end, helps *create* communal, regional, and international realities, in addition to *responding* to such. Not to be alert to such dimensions and realities is tantamount to being blind to a good half of the phenomena that constitute bilingual education in its entirety.

The same is true with respect to the ill-advised restriction to the elementary level in connection with the bulk of the attention given to bilingual education. Not only does no such restriction obtain in reality, when we view bilingual education in worldwide and diachronic perspective (Verdoodt, 1969 and 1971; Welbes, 1975), but it is not even valid with respect to the U. S. A. itself. Even given the extreme recency of bilingual education in its current incarnation in the U. S. A. (for earlier manifestations of bilingual education, see Fishman and Nahirny, 1964 and Fishman, 1966), there are already dozens of programs operating at the junior and senior high levels (not to mention the small but growing number of college and university programs of this type, e.g., Pedersen, 1975). Furthermore, many *more* postprimary bilingual education programs are to be expected in the U. S. A. during the next few years, as more and more graduates of our many current bilingual programs at the elementary level arrive at junior and senior high schools. There is bound to be increased call for secondary bilingual education, and the time to begin preparing for such programs, at least conceptually and curricularly, and, if possible, also experimentally, is now. Without such preparation now we will once more need to go through the painful educational process of building and repairing the "bilingual ship" at the very same time that it is already storm-tossed on the high seas.

Unlike most other countries of the world, the U. S. A. has an extensive and all-inclusive system of secondary education. This fact must make us all the more interested in bilingual education at that level. If bilingual education at the secondary level can be as common as it is in other countries, notwithstanding the elitist nature of secondary education in some of them, how can we possibly justify virtually ignoring it in our own midst, given our own more democratic and representative commitments?

Our blunders with respect to bilingual education are self-imposed and self-defeating. It is high time that we removed them and looked at the secondary level as well as at the elementary.

Bilingual Education Is Not an Endless Hassle

Bilingual education is growing rapidly in the U. S. A., but it is surrounded by problems. Every beginning is hard, and a beginning that requires new societal structures is hardest of all. Since most bilingual education in the United States is relatively new, it suffers from lack of community consensus (minority support and minority opposition often being more marked than mainstream support and opposition), lack of trained teachers, lack of perfected curricula, lack of clear goals, lack of validated language models, and above all, lack of information. In the past decade some $300,000,000 have been spent in the U. S. A. on bilingual education with less than ten percent being allocated for research. Doubtless, the total amount to be allocated over the next decade will be even larger, and regrettably the amounts allocated for research may even be proportionately smaller. Is it any wonder that parents are confused, teachers uninformed, and administrators undecided?

Given the foregoing, is it any wonder that bilingual education does not always "pan out" well; that it cannot pay off all the contradictory promises foolishly made on its behalf; that the necessary structural reorganization of education has not yet caught up with court orders or legislative mandating on behalf of bilingual education; that the few knowledgeable and experienced people available are still frequently prevented from working with educational and community leaders on the development of sound educational programs? Do not the birth pangs of bilingual education parallel the birth pangs of other highly touted panaceas in American education, many of which have since vanished from the scene and been forgotten with few regrets?

It is my hope to provide a perspective by means of which bilingual education can become and remain a permanent feature of the American educational landscape. We should realize that bilingual education is working well in schools all over the world, its goals so well articulated that they can be achieved; we should realize that the communities that engage in it are unified and peaceful, not *despite* bilingual education but *because* of it; we should realize that the parents, children, teachers, and administrators involved in it are well pleased with it; and, above all, we should note that desired cognitive, affective, and societal goals are achieved through bilingual education. In short, bilingual education in the U. S. A. must mature into a healthy and happy socioeducational endeavor, taking off from a solid base of empirical and theoretical information. Others have made a go of bilingual education before, and we, in the U. S. A., can do it too. Let us not permit bilingual education to "self-destruct" in a decade like the countless educational fads of former years. Bilingual education is not a fad or gimmick. We need information and perspective and conviction to make it work, and we need them every bit as much as we need the time, the money, and the manpower that are so much more frequently mentioned.

The Time Is Now

The time for a reexamination of bilingual education is now, before it is overtaken by the consequences of its own embattled popularity. The Bilingual

Education Act has recently been revised and refunded. Within a few years it will again come up for congressional deliberation. The Ethnic Heritages Act has slowly begun to be implemented and desperately requires reliable and increased funding. An interest in ethnic studies has swept over our colleges and universities, leaving behind untold programs, courses, and clubs anxious for a permanent place in the academic sun. The Cabinet Committee on the Spanish-Speaking is increasing its activity. The Supreme Court's Lau vs. Nichols decisions (1973), prompted by developments on our West Coast, and the Aspira vs. New York City Board of Education consent-ruling (1974), responding to developments on our East Coast, have both made bilingual education an educational option that must be seriously considered by every school district in which there are children whose English is deficient. At the same time a new view of bilingual education is gaining ground, namely, that bilingual education need not be entirely compensatory or minority-group-oriented, but that it can also be a type of "alternative education" for mainstream children. Over three dozen training programs for bilingual teachers have recently gotten under way at master and doctoral levels, many with the help of newly appropriated federal training and dissemination funds. A national association for bilingual education has been organized. National and international conferences on bilingual education have already been convened and are scheduled for the future on an annual basis. The Civil Rights Commission has endorsed bilingual education (*New York Times,* July 28, 1975, p. 1), and 464 counties have been ordered to conduct bilingual elections as a result of 1975 amendments to the Voting Rights Act of 1965. Our major cities are beginning to publish bilingual telephone books (*New York Times,* August 26, 1975, p. 35). A number of bilingual colleges, public and private, have come into being. All in all, this is a most propitious time (and potentially a most constructive opportunity) for a study of the sociology of bilingual education to make its appearance. I humbly hope that what I will now present to the reader will rise to the occasion and that it will help the reader in turn to rise to the challenge, since what we together will do *for* and *to* bilingual education in the next few years will determine its course in the U. S. A. for a long, long time to come.

AN
INTERNATIONAL
SOCIOLOGICAL
PERSPECTIVE

BILINGUAL EDUCATION

POINT OF VIEW

PART I

Most Americans, including American intellectuals, have generally been sympathetic to the needs of "other peoples," particularly those from small and developing countries (and therefore, presumably from small and developing cultures), to learn English and, thereby, to become members of the Global Community. "It is always good to know another language (and culture)" is an old "Main street" saw in the United States, and yet, like most homegrown charitable wisdom, it has been roundly ignored in the Anglo-American heartland itself. Native (and naturalized) Anglo-Americans have long felt themselves to be "beyond that." They have felt that they were *already* members of the Global Community, indeed, that they *were* the Global Community precisely on the basis of their native control of English. Recently, however, this view has begun to change, and the movement for bilingual education is both a product of as well as a contribution to this change.

The standard American claim (or assumption) that Americans are *ipso facto* (part of) the Global Community prompts two related questions:

a) Is there a Global Community? and
b) If there is such, what does membership in it imply for membership in other communities?

The Global Community

Our answer to the first question must be in the affirmative, even though the true Global Community has an extremely small membership. If by "community" we mean a human aggregate which though largish in size, nevertheless, consensually regulates the roles and statuses of its members to an appreciable extent, whether interactionally or referentially, then it becomes clear why the Global Community is as limited in its membership as it is. With the exception of selected academicians, scientists, musicians, artists, entrepreneurs, and fadists, there is no Global Community in the societal sense, and even for the foregoing it is rarely the primary or sole community.

However, it *is* a fact of modern life that more and more humanity does indeed transcend its more primary and more essential memberships on occasion(s). Although such transcendence does not result in a Global Community, it does

BILINGUAL EDUCATION IS GOOD
FOR THE MAJORITY GROUP
Language and Culture in the Global Community

CHAPTER I

result in more global sentiments, behaviors, cognitions, and commitments than have existed before. These, then, are combined with other sentiments, behaviors, cognitions, and commitments to form the complex constellation that is "modern man." The Global Community, if it exists or can exist at all for any sizable portion of humanity, gives testimony, therefore, to man's capacity for multiple loyalties and his ability to cope with the tensions which such loyalties may engender. Mankind has previously shown its capacity to combine family and community loyalties, community and local loyalties, local and regional loyalties, and regional and national loyalties. However, the combination of national and global loyalties is not only further testimony to this combinatorial capacity but also constitutes the *only way* in which the bulk of mankind will ever be able to approach the Global Community at all. This is particularly important for Americans (and for Russians and Chinese) to grasp, for the power and size of their national community is great enough to fool them into confusing their national community with the Global Community.

Members of smaller and poorer nations already realize that they must combine narrower and broader loyalties if they are ever to attain the blessings of the Global Community. Members of larger and richer nations have yet to learn this lesson. A larger and truer Global Community will come into being only if they do.

Particularism Versus Globalism

As the above discussion has implied, the American pursuit of the Global Community has often posited a confrontation or clash between two extremes of social experience: particularism and globalism. Particularism is most commonly thought to be associated with parochialism, with intimacy but yet with isolation and exclusivity, with smallness in size and in outlook, and therefore, with the need for broadening, for cultural pluralism, in order to meet the challenges of modern life. Globalism, on the other hand, has most commonly been associated with universality, inclusivity, efficiency and effectiveness, and a putative panhuman cultural monism that requires no further pluralism precisely because it has already transcended all of its constituent parts.

The unreconstructed, self-enamoured American view of the Global Community has, in the past, attacked any defense of the smaller community and its strivings for pluralistic self-maintenance as being essentially emotional, soft-hearted and soft-headed, and romantic. Considerations of ethnic intimacy; e.g., the rights of parents and children for schooling via their language of intimacy, have been viewed like "motherhood and early spring," to be empty platitudes in the light of "higher considerations" in the real, cruel, hard world.

However, as with most other complex social-moral-ethical issues, American (and European) views of particularism vs. globalism must be considered as part of an entire cultural climate. Indeed, this very issue has been subject to rather extreme pendular swings, and once the pendulum has swung as far as it can in one direction, there is nowhere for it to go (as with women's dresses and men's hair styles) but back where it came from.

The Mid-Nineteenth-Century View

After the political consolidation of Western Europe, there developed among intellectuals there an increasing rapture for the beauty and God-given diversity of human life in the more "exotic" regions of Europe and "the East." Western Europeans discovered Greece and Poland and Finland and the "Southern Slavs," as causes and as exemplars of mankind's struggle for democracy, for honesty, for decency, for spontaneity, far before they discovered any similar beauties in Ireland, Wales, Provence, Brittany, or Valencia. Particularism was always lovelier if it was discovered in someone else's backyard, the further away the better. How nicely those people danced! How lovely their costume! How quaint their customs! How picturesque their speech! How honest their faces! How noble their traditions! God (or nature) must have intended human diversity for He (it) made so much of it! Much of modern anthropology, linguistics, comparative sociology, religion, and literature are but the later intellectualization of this "romantic" rhapsody.

The Early Twentieth Century

The constant spread of English, French, Russian, German, and American imperialism, as a result of even more obvious manifest destiny, brought with it an increasing rejection of the above point of view, particularly as "exoticisms" in one's own backyard kept refusing to disappear. The "intransigency of small communities in the grip of self-righteous self-interest" elicited the revulsion of socialist unifiers as well. "What is Poland to the Working Class?" Engels asked in all sincerity. A new specter was felt to be haunting Europe, and it was neither democracy nor Marxism but, rather, ethnic Balkanization. Ultimately this specter gained for itself the grudging acceptance or gleeful exploitation of all modern mass movements, but not before it was made the whipping boy for World War I, if not for World War II as well.

Then, as now, only the large and strong nations could disguise their self-interest as internationalism, as for the common good, as altruism, as manifest destiny. The blame for the mass calamities which they either engineered or failed to halt, hoping to benefit from them, they conveniently placed on the doorsteps of those nations that were small, poor, and problem-ridden or hung around the necks of those nationalities which aspired to nationhood without great-power permission or subvention.

The evils of Balkanization could be avoided only, it would seem, by a Global Community that would rise above petty considerations. The various Internationals—the League of Nations, the United Nations, the Pan American Union and its reincarnation: the Organization of American States, the Anglo-American Union, NATO, SEATO, The Comintern, the Organization of African Unity, the Arab Bloc—all have within them the seeds of the struggle against Balkanization. Smallness and weakness were not only no longer lovely or cute; they were not only luxuries that could no longer be afforded, they were downright evils, barriers, and stumbling blocks to be avoided at all costs.

The Late Sixties as a Watershed

Since the mass alienation fostered by the Vietnam war and by the difficulties encountered by the civil rights movement, we have been on an intimacy binge again. Once again the small community is good, the small language and the small nationality or ethnic group must be saved, the little traditions of everyday life are beautiful, the community school is precious. All the rhetoric that we were wont to lavish upon the small business we now bestow upon the small pond, the small grove, the small flower, the small people. Walt Whitman and Henry Thoreau have at least for the while triumphed over Henry Ford and Henry Kaiser! In the light of the unspeakable horrors and inhumanity perpetrated by the great and the strong bearers of mechanistic modernity, all that is "natural" once again seems sweet and good and innocent; and what could be more "natural" than the weak and small peoples of the world and of the submerged continents within the U. S. A. as a whole and on our own long-forgotten personal family trees?

Who Needs a Rhinoceros?

The climate for preserving the peoples "given in nature" and the climate for preserving the animals and plants "given in nature" have come together and have reinforced each other more than a century after the flowering of European Romanticism. A journal distributed free of charge to patrons of one of America's major motel chains is certainly "right on the ball" in the way in which it poses the basic question as seen by the man in the street:

WHO NEEDS A RHINOCEROS?*
by Lawrence Elliot

The blue whale is the largest creature ever to have lived on earth. Swimming at speeds up to twenty knots, it has few natural enemies (only parasites and smaller killer whales which sometimes gang up on it) and is at home in all the world's oceans. But there is no sanctuary for the blue whale. In little more than half a century, modern whaling fleets have slashed its population by ninety-nine per cent.

Today, down to perhaps 1,500 specimens, its chances of surviving into the twenty-first century are slim and may depend on the World Wildlife Fund (WWF), a unique international organization that worries about the state of our natural world.

However, any argument that bases itself only on the ethics and esthetics of diversity, is, in our more advanced day and age, only half an argument. If natural diversity is so central to a truly human existence, then there must be some demonstrable loss or damage when and if the balance of nature is disturbed. This is demonstrably true when the animal and plant kingdoms are tampered with. There ethics and esthetics do not end the argument but merely begin it:

---

*Imperial 400 Motel Outdoor World, 1974, 6, No. 5, pp. 6 and 44-45.

... there are other, practical considerations. Humankind clings to but one thread of the complicated and sometimes mysterious web of life on earth. We pluck on the others at our own peril. In some agricultural regions of South Africa, where the hippopotamus was considered a nuisance, the people earnestly set about exterminating it. The result: widespread epidemics of debilitating schistosomiasis; the hippo, it turned out, had been a major factor in curbing the water snail that carried the disease. In Pakistan, coastal mangrove forests were "reclaimed," and the denuded shore offered no protection from deadly floods, which then swept deep inland.

Nor are the Western nations immune from such destructive short-sightedness. In Great Britain, the filling up of breeding ponds has reduced the number of ordinary frogs, with a consequent surge in insect pests, some of them harmful to crops. In other parts of Western Europe, the lynx and wolf, natural predators of deer, have all been exterminated, and the deer population has increased to such an extent that it is doing extensive damage to commercial forests and crops. And in the oceans and our own inland waters, pollution and over-fishing threaten the loss of a vitally important source of food.

For the first time we are beginning to get a glimmer of an inexorable truth. If the world becomes an inhospitable place for wild animals, man himself might well follow them into extinction.

If WWF fails and the blue whale passes into oblivion, it will not go alone. More than one thousand species of animals and twenty thousand forms of plant life—having shared this planet for two billion years—now stand in danger of extinction. Among them are the polar bear, Bengal tiger, red wolf, tortoise, European sea eagle and California condor. All are beset by the same implacable adversary—man. All are the concern of WWF, a sort of intercontinental rescue squad and one of history's first meaningful efforts to save our dwindling wildlife resources.

Why? What would happen if one or more or all of these threatened creatures disappeared forever? After all, who needs a rhinoceros or an orangutan? Who needs the Lincoln Memorial? Or the Taj Mahal or Michelangelo's Pieta?

We all do, for they enrich our lives. We know that only a vandal would contemplate their destruction. We accept our responsibility to preserve the inspired works of man for the generations to come. But we have yet to learn that the obliteration of our wildlife is vandalism, too, and of the worst sort, for once an animal species is gone neither repentance nor all men's genius can bring it back.

In a parallel vein, the heartless, insensitive and mechanistic might well ask: "Who needs Chicanos?, Who needs Puerto Ricans?, Who needs Israelis?, Who needs Navajos?, Who needs Biharis?" And the answer would come back in very similar terms: "We all do, for they enrich our lives. We know that only a vandal would contemplate their destruction. We accept our responsibility to preserve the inspired words of man for generations to come. But we have yet to learn that the obliteration of cultural life is vandalism, too, and of the worst sort, for once a cultural species is gone neither repentance nor all man's genius can bring it back."

The focus of analogical thinking leads us to ask whether there is not also a "balance of nature" vis-à-vis cultural phenomena and whether there are not also unrecognized negative system-linkages when smaller nationality/ethnic groups and their cultures are destroyed. Indeed, that is so, the argument continues further. The very mechanization, routinization, impersonalization, meaninglessness, and valuelessness of modern American urban life is a consequence of the destruction of the intimate, small-scale ethnic roots of most of those who are caught up in it. The very ruthlessness of the big powers to each other and toward the world at large is but a cataclysm-threatening generalization of their hitherto unpunished ruthlessness toward Jews, toward American Indians, toward Armenians, toward aborigines in Brazil and Australia-New Guinea, toward little people everywhere. The latter, therefore, are not "merely" beautiful, they are also the symbiotic indicators of mankind's total ability to survive the rapaciousness of the dinosaur nations that control its future.

On the Limits of Analogy

It is high time to ask how far the putative parallel between the plant and animal worlds, on the one hand, and the human cultural world, on the other hand, holds. There are certainly a number of instructive similarities. Above and beyond those already mentioned here is the very openness of both systems to new formations. Certainly it is a misreading of human cultural history to conclude that smaller nationalities and their cultures are on the way out (just as it is a misreading of animal and plant development of the last 300 years to suspect that there can only be a decrease in the total number of species that obtain). It is a mistake, I believe, to conclude that mankind is inevitably headed toward fewer and ever larger cultural groupings. Indeed, just as newer plant and animal species are constantly coming into being, so newer cultural formations are constantly being formed, some of them larger and some of them smaller than others that came before them. The existence today of Indonesians and Israelis and Palestinians and Pakistanis (as well as Chicanos and blacks and Boricuas), none of whom were massive primary cultural groups a third of a century ago, is a tribute to the human need for meaningful and immediate groups of this kind. As certain groups disappear (coalesce, break up, assimilate), others arise to take their place, leaning upon religion, occupation, social class, and other experiential communalities in the constant formation and reformation of cultures. The Global Community, if it is ever to come, will certainly not come inevitably, by the withering away of smaller nationalities.

However, there is one *major* difference between cultural and plant or animal evolution, and that is the phenomenon of multiple-group membership. In the human mind, dogs and horses and lions and mice are all *mammals* and *quadrupeds,* but none of them ever have or ever can appreciate their communality with respect to each other. Human cultural experience is quite different. It not only exhibits but can be aware of and can value multiple-group membership. Thus, while the constant openness of the plant and animal systems militates against the final evolving of any one membership in those systems, the openness of the human cultural systems does *not.* New or old culture-group memberships do not necessarily militate against simultaneous memberships in yet newer or larger cultural formations. It is this possibility that bilingual and bicultural education can foster, particularly if it is adopted by the high and mighty cultures rather than shunted aside merely for the poorer and smaller ones.

Bilingual and Bicultural Education

It is precisely those educators and intellectuals most interested in the Global Community who must be most interested in bilingual and bicultural education *for all our children,* for it is only out of such education that the multiple-group membership can come that can foster such a community for the masses rather than for elites. Monolingual and monocultural education is artificial and false, particularly if we have One World in mind. The world is not unifiable on the basis of cultural monisms. Indeed, such monisms are more likely to destroy the world than to save it! Only bilingual and bicultural education provides for multiple memberships and for multiple loyalties in an integrative fashion and, therefore, for a training that is essentially different from that which plants or animals can be given. The small nationalities of the world have already (and have long) recognized this truism. Even when in the grips of integrationist and protectionist passions, they most readily recognize and implement their need for additional linguistic and cultural exposure for their young. Thus, it is precisely the child who is a native speaker of a language of wider communication (and first and foremost among these, the Anglo-American child) who constitutes a problem in the formation of a larger Global Community. It is this latter child who most rarely sees the human world as it is—peopled by a rich diversity of culturally creative aggregates—and who most rarely senses what it is that this human world might become: a network of interlocking and simultaneous memberships and loyalties.

Poor Little Rich Kids

In today's world it is the poor little rich kids who most desperately need bilingual and bicultural education. It is they who most lack education for world-cultural realism and for global-cultural desiderata. The biculturism and bilingualism so needed by most Anglo-American children need not be found in Paris, nor in the junior year abroad, nor in FLES programs, valuable though all of these may be. They can be found on the Anglo-American child's own doorstep, where his black, Chicano, Boricua, Indian, Jewish, and other ethnic neighbors are located. The black, Chicano, Boricua, etc. parents and their children know that *they* need bilingualism and biculturism; but unless the Anglo-American child participates in such education as well, it can only be a "sop to the poor" or a "gimmick for the disadvantaged" rather than a serious quest for a better society and a saner world. For bilingual and bicultural education to succeed in its greater cultural mission, it must be available to all, be they large or small on the world scene, be they in the grips of integrationism or self-protectionism, be they in need of broader exposure or deeper roots. All education must be bilingual and bicultural if all children are to learn to handle multiple loyalties and memberships constructively, openly, proudly, without suppression, without shame, without conflict, and without tension.

Job Insurance and World Insurance

If I were a white, middle-class, American teacher or teacher-to-be today, the best thing that I could do to guarantee my own professional security and mobility would be to make myself functionally bilingual and bicultural. The best thing that I could do to give my students job security and world security would be to make them functionally bilingual and bicultural. If I were teaching minority-group children, I would do this in such a way as not to harm their minority-group membership, but rather to strengthen it and deepen it and, then, to broaden it and enrich it by adding to it as much of the Anglo-American experience as I possibly could. If I were teaching Anglo-American children, I would add to their good fortune the additional sensitivity and perspective that come from knowing an American minority culture in real depth, nonpatronizingly and unapologetically. All American children must have American sentiments and loyalties, but they must also simultaneously have more particularistic sentiments and loyalties, as well as more global ones, if their American loyalties are to be both humane and realistic for the world round about them. Both minority and majority children need strong multiple-cultural memberships and multiple-cultural loyalties, narrower, broader and yet broader, if they are to reach their true *human* potentials and, in doing so, save the world itself.

Bilingual and bicultural education is not a favor for the poor; it is an obligation and opportunity for us all—particularly for the high and mighty—if we are to survive.

The American bicentennial celebration undoubtedly provides us with many opportunities for "stocktaking"—culturally, socially, educationally, and economically. Such opportunities should be very welcome, for they are needed in every society and particularly in one such as ours, marked as it is more by change and haste than stability and reflection. Indeed, such national stocktaking should also provide us with opportunities for gaining a better perspective on ourselves—as individuals, as citizens, and as professionals, engaged, at least part-time, in the process of building a better America. For those of us whose ages are in or near the fifties—the fact that we are "suddenly" roughly a quarter the age of our country will come as something of a shock. It's not that we didn't know that America was a young country, but we always felt it was "older than that." And it's not that we didn't know that we were getting older, but we always thought we were "younger than that." We really don't know how to explain it, but in the last few years (indeed, since the bicentennial celebration appeared on the horizon) a great injustice has transpired, namely, most of us have suddenly become an awful lot older and the country as a whole has become an awful lot younger, whereas, in all justice, it should have been the other way around.

Among other topics that should gain from "bicentennial perspective" are non-English-language maintenance, non-Anglo ethnic maintenance and, indeed, the teaching of English to speakers of other languages, all of which are every bit as old on American shores as the republic itself, if not a good bit older. Of course 200 years is a rather brief perspective for social historians, but as the man said, "That's all we've got." However, since the pattern of the American past is rather clear in connection with these topics, and since we have all of time and all of space—reaching far beyond the time and space of the U. S. A.—to give us additional perspective on the American experience, our task may not be an unreasonable one after all. I propose, therefore, to dive in, using language maintenance as my initial vantage point and ethnic maintenance as my basic concern. My goal throughout is to clarify what has happened, what is happening, and, if possible, to gingerly speculate as to what will happen on the language-maintenance and ethnic-maintenance fronts during the approaching third century of the American adventure.

BILINGUAL EDUCATION IS GOOD
FOR THE MINORITY GROUP
*The Third Century of Non-English-Language Maintenance
and Non-Anglo Ethnic Maintenance in the U.S.A.*

CHAPTER II

The Basic Pattern

The predominant pattern of non-English-language maintenance during the first two centuries of American national life—and certainly during its one century of post-Civil War industrialization—has been (a) rapid and widespread adoption of English as a second language by the immigrant first generation and (b) widespread transmission of this second language to the young as their mother tongue. Although there are exceptions to the above general pattern—and they must be commented upon separately, because only a clinical awareness of exceptions brings about a rich awareness of the real essentials in any pattern—it *is* the general pattern nonetheless, notwithstanding the largest immigration in modern world history, as well as an immigration which was substantially non-Anglo in either language, culture, or religion.

The basic pattern specified above was neither inevitable nor miraculous, neither a foregone conclusion nor manifest destiny. It is certainly not the only pattern that obtains between immigrants and hosts. Immigrants do not always adopt the languages of their hosts. For example, Anglo- and New Canadians coming to Quebec have, until recently, not even learned French as a second language, let alone passed it on as a first language to their children (Lieberson, 1970); nor have most immigrant Amharas learned Galla (Cooper *et al.*, in press); nor have immigrant Tamils learned Hindi (Das Gupta and Fishman, 1971); nor have the immigrant French in Alsace-Lorraine or in Luxembourg learned local German (Verdoodt, 1971); nor have immigrant Russians learned the languages of the various Soviet republics and autonomous regions to which they have migrated (Lewis, 1971). Indeed, as several of the above examples imply, it is not at all unheard of for *hosts* to adopt the language of a *major immigrant group*, either as a second language (L_2) alone, or subsequently also as a first language (L_1). Furthermore, where immigrants *have* adopted the languages of their hosts as second languages, it is by no means inevitable for these L_2s to then become the L_1s of the second generation. (This tends *not* to happen among the Overseas Chinese; among ultra-Orthodox Jews whether in Israel or in the Diaspora [Fishman and Fishman, 1974]; among the most recent generations of immigrant Dutch-speakers in Brussels [Lorwin, 1970]; nor among the most newly urbanized populations in Africa [Tabouret-Keller, 1971]). Indeed, as we study immigrant-host interaction throughout the world (Fishman, 1972a), we find ample evidence for two patterns that are quite rare in the annals of American history: namely, (a) where both immigrants and hosts increasingly shift to a third language which is the regional lingua franca, and (b) where populations live side by side for generations—one being historically the immigrant group and the other being historically the host group—without any widespread bilingualism developing on either side and with meager intergroup communication being channeled via bilingual middlemen. Finally, it is not even the case that immigrants speaking *smaller* languages (in regional or world perspective) constantly shift to the languages of hosts speaking *wider* languages (in the same perspective), otherwise the Roman and Greek cities of the ancient Mediterranean world (Lewis, Appendix

3, this volume) and the German cities of nineteenth-century eastern and southeastern Europe would not have been engulfed by hitherto rural vernaculars as readily as they were (Fishman, 1972b).

From the above examples alone, it is obvious that the clearly predominant outcome in the American case is not a result of immigration *per se,* nor of differential language status *per se.* Indeed, an outcome as nationwide as the one we are dealing with (and yet as unprecedented on the world scene) must have been supported by many different social processes. Yet it seems to me that one cluster of processes is predominant over all; interaction-based social mobility (Fishman, 1966).

The Basic Process

America! America! America! How many have blessed you! After living abroad for three years, and in a comparatively rapidly developing country at that, I see even more clearly than before the extent to which America represented (and still represents) the promise of a better life: a more comfortable life, a freer life, a safer life. Notwithstanding the initial years of sweat shops, discrimination, intermittent depressions, and dawn-to-dusk, seven-day-a-week labor, the industrialized greenbacking of America "paid off" quickly. Within their own lifetimes illiterate, rural-based immigrants could become "self-made men" and proud suppliers of labor-saving conveniences for their womenfolk, good educations for their children, and small inheritances for their grandchildren. However, the fountainhead of all these benefits was the Anglo-controlled economy, the Anglo-controlled government, the Anglo-controlled school, and the Anglo-dominated institutions and style of life. Those who could achieve mobility *without interacting* either with the Anglo institutions or with the highly diversified urban immigrant populations (drawn to a lingua franca that facilitated communication and mobility within the ranks of the Anglo power elite) escaped the full brunt of language shift somewhat longer. However, these were largely rural and agricultural settlers coming en masse to good public land that could be worked without major investment for equipment and irrigation. The new city dwellers—and the bulk of our immigrants came to and stayed on in the cities—neither had nor sought such an opportunity. Their mobility derived from interacting intensively with immigrants from other backgrounds rather than from interacting with their "own kind" and with the Anglo authorities. There were few sections in the country in which one non-Anglo group alone clearly predominated and controlled the means of production. Bread winners (and even teenagers were bread winners until a mere fifty years ago) eagerly brought English into their own homes and families, thus culturally dislocating them all the more, because it was through English that their own status as providers flowed, and with it they sought to open doors for their dear ones as well. It was this readiness to make virtually any accommodation needed in order to improve one's lot in life that has prompted the view that many immigrants were "Americans" even before they arrived on these shores.

However, there were two major exceptions to the story of "rapid success at any price," which interactive social mobility made possible for so many. One, those who slowly moved ahead economically on a rural basis and with far less interaction, has already been mentioned. The other consisted of those who did *not* move ahead economically (certainly not relative to the mobility of their neighbors) and who, therefore, not only became the rural and the urban poor of a fantastically rich society, but who also Anglified little, if at all. The latter, not caught up by either industrialization or interactions, were usually ignored by their betters, as if the American dream did not pertain to them and as if the dream was fully confirmed regardless of what happened to these unfortunates. We will return to them, because they did not vanish merely because they were ignored. Indeed, they very forcefully called themselves to our attention and, in doing so, changed the future of non-English-language maintenance and non-Anglo ethnic maintenance for years to come.

However, for the majority of newcomers the process would have been the same had we been dealing with diversified *indigenous* rural populations drawn to the cities. The rootlessness and powerlessness of our immigrants merely hastened the process. Traditional family practices, role relations, ethnic beliefs, and observances (even those intertwined with religion, as most were) give way under the dislocating impact of supra-ethnic and non-ethnic industrial efficiency, rationality, monetary commensurability, and blatant materialism as an end in itself. De-ethnization was not, by and large, a plot of America's Anglo populations. They, too, were swept up by the same processes whose gate-keepers they were, to such an extent that Old World English ethnicity and Old World Scotch-Irish ethnicity weathered the storm not a whit better than did traditional German, Jewish, Italian, Polish, French, or Spanish ethnicity. The difference, of course, was on the language front. The Anglo ethnics did not have to undergo language shift as well in order to acquire their share of the American dream; the non-Anglo ethnics did (Fishman, 1966). Nevertheless, the resulting de-ethnization was finally about the same, and all lost at least part of their souls in order to gain some part of this world.

In contrast to interactive social mobility the importance of other factors is pale indeed. Interactive social mobility is encompassed by such empirical indices as educational requirements of employment, ethnic diversity in district of residence, ethnic diversity in place of employment, interactive requirement of employment, etc. In comparison to the foregoing, the total size of the immigrant group, the particular culture and the particular language of origin of the immigrant group and their developmental stage vis-á-vis Anglo/English culture and language, the original motives of immigration (political, religious, or economic), and the absence or presence of successive waves of newcomers—all these and many more made little long-range difference (Fishman, 1966). Indeed, more recent newcomers have often made the transition more rapidly than did old-timers of similar backgrounds. Not only have they been helped into Anglo conformity (Gordon, 1964) by their own greater sophistication with modern urban skills and practices, but they have also been helped by their *landslayt* who preceded them here and who have often gone out of their way to show the newcomers that they (the old-timers) were no longer country bumpkins and that they too owned, used, and appreciated all the finer things or better ways of modern life.

By the time we come to imposition of racist immigration controls in the early twenties, the process described above is already so well established as to make these controls superfluous vis-à-vis the immigrant masses that had already arrived. By the time we come to the black and brown protests of the sixties and their further disruption of old ethnic urban neighborhoods throughout the United States, non-Anglo ethnic maintenance and non-English-language maintenance among ethnic participants in interactive social mobility was at a low ebb quantitatively and qualitatively. The non-English ethnic mother tongues of such groups were not only no longer functional *mother tongues*, they were not even *other tongues* for any but a small and shrinking proportion of the second and third generations. Their non-Anglo ethnicities had not only departed substantially from their original moorings, but they had become increasingly disjointed patches of original and American elements, often lacking either rationale or respect among their own practitioners (Nahirny and Fishman, 1965).

And yet, after 20, 50, 100, and even 200 years of Americanization, non-Anglo ethnicity remained an ingredient in American life of the early 1960's. Just as non-English-language maintenance never died, so non-Anglo ethnic maintenance never disappeared. Of course, both were commonly dependent upon transfusions from abroad. Of course, even 200 years is a very brief period (the life spans of no more than three or four men), and few social phenomena disappear completely that quickly. Whatever the explanation, and we will have to look for a satisfying explanation later, ethnic maintenance and language maintenance were both there, often battered and bruised, when the fitful mid-sixties arrived and gave them both a new lease on life.

The New Ethnicity

We have all lived through it so recently that we really have no perspective or objectivity about it. It is as if it were a massive projective technique, interpretable only on the basis of the emotional, intellectual, and group biases of the beholder. However, all of a sudden there "it" was: ethnic hairdos and ethnic dress and ethnic foods and ethnic music and ethnic soul and ethnic courses and ethnic studies and even a bill for an Ethnic Heritage Act (see *Congressional Record,* Vol. 118, No. 168, Tuesday, Oct. 17, 1972). Where did all this come from? Why? The first question is far easier to answer than the second.

The "new ethnicity" (called by others the "new tribalism" and the "new apartheid") had one major source and three more minor auxiliary sources. All in all, it derived from the very groups that had experienced least interaction-based social mobility and for whom a variety of standard American English had rarely become even their L_2. From these origins it spread to other non-Anglo groups who had, by and large, adopted a variety of standard American English as their L_1

and who normally had to struggle to maintain even a metaphorical grasp of their erstwhile ethnic mother tongues. It is clear testimony to the emotional compellingness of the black protest (and, in part, also of the Mexican-American, Puerto Rican, American Indian protests) that it so widely triggered corresponding reactions among Jewish-Americans, Italo-Americans, Polish-Americans, Norwegian-Americans, Franco-Americans, and others. It brought about a massive redefinition of the WASP category, to such an extent that few wanted to be included in the "soulless" mixture of material comfort, middle-class values, environmental pollutants, and Vietnamization with which it was variously identified. The black protest was initially against exclusion, against rejection, against exploitation, and against discrimination. However, like all other ethnic mass movements (Fishman, 1972b), it finally turned a corner and also became a movement "for": *for* black (and, more generally, ethnic) personality, *for* black pride, *for* black roots, *for* black dignity, *for* black culture with as much historical depth and substantive content as possible (Eissen-Udom, 1969; Greeley, 1971; Imari, 1970; Scott, 1972).

The same phenomenon repeated itself, with greater or lesser similarity to the black protest depending on local circumstances, in the cases of all other major and several other minor ethnic groups in the U. S. A. (Young Lords Party, 1971; Camejo, 1971). The full dimensions and impact of this phenomenon (to call it a "whirlwind" or "tidal wave" would be to imply a passing and destructive phenomenon) cannot yet be gauged. It still engulfs some of us and surrounds all of us. However, two new and major ingredients have been added to the American ethnic scene as a result of its onset.

Ideological Ethnicity

One need not study ethnic and linguistic diversity long as a worldwide phenomenon to realize the frequency with which it is not merely *politicized* but *ideologized* in many parts of the world. Ethnic differences are not merely instrumentally exploited by politicians at election time. They are not merely the bases upon which in-group leaderships and enterprises and organizations are built for the attainment of short-range goals. They are also related to ideologies, to *Weltanschauungen,* to philosophies of life-and-death. Until the ethnic explosion of the mid-sixties the U. S. A. was remarkably free (not entirely free but still remarkably free) of ideologized ethnicity. Whatever weak ideologies did exist were either intellectualistic/rationalistic, and therefore lacking in mass gut-appeal (here I would classify Horace Kallen's philosophy of cultural pluralism to which I personally wholeheartedly subscribe), or they were apologetic ("every dog has a tail"), and therefore lacking in righteous anger (here I would classify all of the attempts to "prove" that it is *"not bad"* to be bicultural or to know two languages, etc.). They were pseudoideologies rather than real ideologies because they were afraid to be vehemently against anything "American." "America" was the sacred cow of ethnic groups and movements. Ethnics wanted to be loved by

America as completely as they themselves loved it. To be critical might be mistaken for being antipatriotic, ungrateful, disloyal.

In the "new ethnicity," as a movement primarily of second- third- and fourth-generation Americans, this fear of criticizing America is completely gone. Indeed, the "new ethnicity" is so "at home" with America that it relishes a good scrap rather than backing away from criticizing those American traits and values that it finds wanting. One's ethnicity, no matter how far back its genuine roots may lie, is viewed as a supreme value, a supreme beauty, a supreme tenderness, a supreme authenticity, because—well, because all ethnicity is authentically beautiful and tender. It claims that if America is any good at all, any better at all than the purported "bad guys" elsewhere, then it should value ethnicity, protect ethnicity, develop ethnicity, foster ethnicity, particularly ethnicity X that has contributed so much to the poetry, music, wit, wisdom, humor, and gentleness of life in this world and the next. And, indeed, it asks, "What is America without ethnicity? " What has Anglo conformity produced, it insinuates, other than Coca Cola and Rice Krispies and color TV and oil-scarred beaches and despoiled forests and genocidal attacks on Vietnamese villages and napalm and police brutality and get-rich-quick with the devil taking the hindmost? If there is any soul left in America, it is in the Waspishly neglected and subverted medley of forgotten ethnicities. These ethnicities must be revived, restored, reborn, regrouped. They alone can provide the pure air and the pure hearts which America has so tragically lost in its wild stampede after the superficialities rather than the essences of life. The rejection and degradation of ethnicity led to a decline and fall of America. The revival and re-enthronement of ethnicity will lead to America's rise and shine! What we note here is a reevaluation of self and others on a massive scale. What we have here is revivalistic, messianistic, and powerfully moving. Ethnicity has never been that before in America, particularly not for the American-born young.

As a devotee and practitioner of a particular non-Anglo ethnicity and as a speaker and partisan of a particular non-English language, I nevertheless find the "new ethnicity" overly simple and overly brash. Others may find it downright wrong. But it is not the purpose of ideology to be right, let alone to be subtle. Its purpose is to mobilize and motivate, to clarify (even by distorting) and to activate (even by overdramatizing). The blacks and Chicanos and Indians and Ricans (Nuyoricans and Puerto Ricans) have contributed an ideological tenor to ethnic life and labor in the U. S. A. This ideological tenor has already influenced other groups as well, and it has even found acceptance among segments of the Anglo power structure. It is a new element to be reckoned with. It will not easily go away or quickly fade away. Ideologies are exceptionally self-sustaining (even when they are not successful), extremely more so than are traditional behavior systems, once they have reached the white-heat stage. We have witnessed a decade of tragic disappointment with America, particularly among many of the young. In many cases ethnicity has been associated with this conscious disappointment and has transmuted itself and the disappointment in the process. More than ever before, therefore, ethnicity is here to stay, as an ideologized and, therefore, as a long-term, social-issue-related part of the American scene (Greeley, 1971). Ethnicity never had anything to fight for but itself before. Now it is fighting for justice, honesty, decency, and beauty—for itself and for all of America!

Publicly Subsidized Pluralism

Another novel aspect of non-English-language maintenance and non-Anglo ethnic maintenance efforts in the sixties was the extent to which they aimed at public support. The "new ethnics" have viewed themselves not only as *tearing down* American Anglo conformity but as *building up* a new society that would diversify, enrich, and ennoble American life (Scott, 1972). As such they expected that the courses, programs, pageants, publications, organizations, and communities that they demanded and fostered be supported from the general till, since they were intended to serve the general good. It is not surprising, perhaps, that in the age of the welfare state such demands should have been made. It *is*, perhaps, somewhat surprising to note the ultimate identification with America that such demands imply. They amount to a demand that the much maligned "system" pay for its own compulsory modification; but they also amount to an attempt to remain with and within the system, rather than entirely outside of it. Finally, most surprising of all is the extent to which the demands have been met.

Only a bare decade ago nearly the entire world of American non-English-language maintenance and non-Anglo ethnic maintenance was dependent on meager within-group resources for its financial wherewithal. This amounted to a double penalty, for the ethnics were primarily those already a notch or two below the economic level of their de-ethnicized peers. The hope for public subsidy never disappeared (see e.g., Fishman, 1959) and, indeed, was restated again by an impartial observer just before the "new ethnicity" appeared on the scene (Glazer, 1966). However, it was clearly definitely the furor of the black protest (and, secondarily, that of its brown and red counterparts) that broke through the traditional Anglo silence and foot dragging on this score. The stance taken could not be morally denied, once its major premise was granted: that the U. S. A. is a multiethnic society and that each of its strands, functioning for the cultural enrichment of the whole, deserves the recognition and support of the whole. However, it was not entirely the rationality or morality of the case that ultimately won the day, but the combined pressure: political, economic, and even physical.*

---

*There is a tendency to overemphasize the role of force in the attainment of ethnic goals in the U. S. A. There is also a tendency to overly fear that the "new ethnicity" will lead to and prolong interethnic hostility in the U. S. A. I believe there is enough opportunity in our social and economic system to obviate both of these dangers. However, if I am wrong on either count, the result will be a strengthening rather than a weakening of ethnicity.

The combination has paid off most dramatically in the recent burgeoning of ethnic studies, a field that I consider simultaneously the greatest asset as well as the greatest debit of the "new ethnicity." It is a debit because it easily shades into ethnic "interest" of a merely intellectual sort rather than remaining fully in the area of ethnic maintenance *per se.* You don't have to be black (Jewish, Scandinavian) to take black (Jewish, Scandinavian) studies. However, it is without doubt an asset as an institutionalized avenue of keeping ethnicity young, relevant, and in interaction with the best of general American culture. While it is true that ethnic-studies-at-general-expense have flowered far too quickly, and too widely, to make it likely or even possible for that growth to be characterized by "proper qualitative standards," it is also true that the pursuit of "proper standards" can be an interminable delaying factor. No such subjective delaying tactics were permitted to hold back the growth of American academic expansion in other areas, particularly during the early sixties, when federal, state, and local governments were willing and able to pay the bill. "Standards" ultimately caught up with supply and demand, and this will probably be the case also in connection with many of those ethnic studies programs that began not quite at the level at which their critics would like to see them. Indeed, "standards" always have come after rather than before growth in the history of American education and in the history of every other aspect of general American life. Thus, it appears to me that the real question that we must examine is not the one of instant standards (a question to which neither TESOL nor sociology nor any other field gave satisfactory answers for several years after their appearance in American universities) but, rather, since standards always take time, whether the "new ethnicity" forces can keep the pressure on, to a sufficient degree, so that their courses and programs will continue to be maintained until their qualitative standard is improved (Davis and Satterwhite, 1972; Valentine, 1972). This query, in turn, brings us full circle again, for it again prompts the question: Is ethnicity necessary? Perhaps it will just vanish after a while from the American scene, and the programs so massively "pushed through" can be quietly shelved and Anglo conformity quietly returned to, as in the good old days.

Question: Is Ethnicity Necessary?

Just as language shift occurs, so does ethnicity shift. Throughout human history populations have been re-ethnicized into different cultural systems from those that their ancestors once observed (Fishman, 1972b). Beginning with nineteenth-century Europe this process of re-ethnification reached many millions of hitherto ethnically unmobilized city (and later rural) denizens via mass nationalist movements. For those made conscious of and fiercely loyal to their ethnicity via such movements, no further rapid de-ethnization and re-ethnization were possible (without catastrophic defeats and dislocations). Finns no longer became Swedified; Czechs no longer became Germanized; Poles no longer became Russianized; Ukranians no longer became Polonized. Only the passage of a generation or more of postnationalistic calm and concentration on other issues would again make ethnic shift and language shift possible for their progeny. However, most of those countless millions who crossed the Atlantic, the Rio Grande, or the Caribbean Sea into what was or became the continental U. S. A., had not yet been ethnically mobilized one way or the other. Their ethnicity was largely of the little tradition variety; i.e., it was neither fierce nor conscious, although it was eminently integrated and satisfying for all that.*

Their confrontation with the American dream was the major mobilizing experience for our immigrants and their children. This confrontation not only de-ethnicized them to a large extent by piercing and crumbling the folk ethnicities that most immigrants had brought with them, but it bid mightily to re-ethnicize them in the image of the conscious General American, a by-product of the unhyphenated State-Nationality culture that the American dream was rapidly fashioning. Once so re-ethnicized and mobilized it would be difficult, if at all possible, for the original ethnicities, or reasonable facsimiles thereof, to be reconstituted. "Americanism" was well on the way to becoming the secular unifying religion of our theologically diverse and permissive society.

However, like most messianic dreams of the past 100 years the American dream had two faults built into it: (a) it did not pay off as widely or as all-inclusively as promised (thus leaving and ignoring huge pockets of dissatisfied nonparticipants), and (b) it did not recognize the "local color" needs that modernization (for all its massification and mechanization) *elicits* rather than *eradicates.* As a result of these two chinks in the armor of Americanization, non-Anglo ethnicity not only was not crushed among those who never had a chance to fully savor the creature comforts and patriotic poetry of Americanism, but it did not really fully die out among many, many of those who *had* the benefit of both. Ethnicity remains, and, indeed, it even becomes modern "everyman's" personal link with socially patterned unique intimacy and intimate uniqueness. As such it is always available to soothe, to comfort, to provide tenderness and rootedness, even when it is not needed as a launching pad for social action. As such it is a great loss to those who have lost it and who do not know where or how to recover it.

As a result of both *inner* need for ethnicity, as well as the disappointment generated by the *outer,* "nonethnic" American world, non-Anglo ethnic mainten- ance remained, transformed and weakened to be sure, far beyond the staying power of non-English-language maintenance (Fishman, 1966). It remained in the very structure of daily American life, with its ethnic humor, clubs, politics, foods, and celebrations—even among the Scandinavian-Americans, even among the Irish-Americans, even among the old Sephardic- and German-Jewish families—i.e., even among those whose Americanization and social mobility was greatest.

---

*Even among Germans and Jews, the two immigrant groups coming with the proportion- ately largest urban and intellectual contingents, conscious and integrated nationalist (rather than localist) commitment was rather restricted and ephemeral.

Non-Anglo ethnicity was always a quiet, hidden, lost continent, a veritable Atlantis. American life, for millions of Americans, was always bicultural. Below the public surface, with its cultura franca and lingua franca of General American life, there was the private depth, the color and individuality of non-Anglo ethnicity.

What has happened in the past ten years is that this lost or invisible continent has come into view and that many Americans have come to feel, believe, and say that it should be so. Will it sink from view again, perhaps to be fully and finally disintegrated? Perhaps, but probably not. It will probably settle a bit and be less noticeable than it was from 1968-1972, and, indeed, it has already begun to do so. However, mobilized ethnicities that have developed their own ideological systems (as has the "new ethnicity" in the U. S. A.), and their own publicly legitimated structural supports (as has the "new ethnicity" in the U. S. A.) disappear very slowly, if at all. Remember also that they have become part and parcel of the generational self-definition of many of our young people. For them it is related to a view of the world, to a view of themselves, to a view of what America is all about and must yet become. Ethnicity has become a base for tackling social problems, and as such, it will be infinitely more capable of self-regeneration and innovation than in former days. It no longer tries to be a pale copy of "long ago" in "the old country." It is a happily evolving, open-ended, creative process with both strictly American and old country nuances, but with a resultant force and flavor of its own.* It still has intimacy, but it also seeks relevance and quality, a trinity that is hard to beat.

My prediction, therefore, as we approach the third century of American life, is that non-Anglo ethnic maintenance will continue to bear fruit on our fair shores; and that for some of its adherents, it will include and will foster various degrees of non-English-language maintenance as well. Indeed, I am convinced that there will be all degrees and all combinations of both non-Anglo ethnic maintenance and non-English language maintenance. Both will be somewhat quieter, perhaps, than they have been of late (provided our overall political and social scenes also quiet down and ease up with respect to the reward systems under their control), but, basically, they will both be sufficiently multifaceted to appeal not only to blacks, Chicanos, Indians and "Ricans," but also to the fancy Protestants, fancy Catholics, and fancy Jews from whose ranks so many TESOL teachers come. All in all, this will be not only good for TESOL but for all language teaching in the U. S. A. (Grittner, 1971; Pacheco, 1971; Morain, 1971). In sum my prediction is that when your great-grandchildren and mine celebrate the 300th anniversary of the U. S. A., there will still be non-Anglo ethnic maintenance and non-English language maintenance. They will find them changed. They will find them enriched. They will find them creative. They will find them stimulating. They will find them self-critical and critical of others. They will find them wonderful. They

---

*Note, e.g., the "Scandinavian," "Slavic" and Jewish ethnicities exist in the U. S. A. without any corresponding "old country" equivalents at all.

will find them part and parcel of America, just as they have always been. And they will find America richer because of them, more exciting because of them, and matured because of them, just as it has always been. Via bilingual education your great-grandchildren and mine can partake of this richness, this excitement, and this maturity. I pray that they will.

With the Bilingual Education Act (signed into law by Lyndon B. Johnson on January 2, 1968), America found itself with a new panacea for "whatever it is" that ails a segment of our economically disadvantaged. The segment that this act (ultimately Title VII of the Elementary and Secondary Education Act of 1965, as amended in 1967, or Public Law 90-247) recognized for special assistance consisted of those "who came from environments where the dominant language is other than English." Although the act does not restrict itself either to the poor or to the Hispanic and Indian populations of the U. S. A., President Johnson did make this restriction when signing the bill into law, and the "Draft Guidelines to the Bilingual Education Act" prepared by USOE for implementing the act did so quite explicitly. Thus, while any hopes (or fears) that the U. S. A. would support bilingual education more generally (see the *Proceedings* of the Spring 1967 *Hearings on S428*) were quickly dissipated, the act as such has slowly but surely supported (or, together with state and local authorities co-supported) a steadily growing number of programs.

At this writing, some 220 bilingual education programs are receiving at least partial support under this act, and a like number of others—some that received support in former years and others that have been stimulated by the act indirectly—function entirely on nonfederal funds. Indeed, while five years *before* passage of the act few envisaged any such possibility, now only five years after its passage, half of our states and very many local education authorities have instituted bilingual education codes or programs of their own (among them California, Illinois, New York, Texas, Maryland, Massachusetts), and bilingual education has become an established part of the programs of all major language teachers' associations. In the spring of 1973 new bilingual education bills were introduced in conjunction with congressional plans to revise the Elementary and Secondary Education Act of 1965. These resulted in a substantial budgetary increase for Title VII at a time when many other educational budgets were cut. Bilingual education has also enjoyed a modicum of publicity in struggles for control of local school boards or as state and local education budget reviews have come to realize that it "costs money" to prepare and obtain the personnel, curricula, and materials that bilingual education requires. It is at such junctures

BILINGUAL EDUCATION IS GOOD
FOR EDUCATION
Bilingual Education, What and Why?

CHAPTER III

that the questions have begun to be raised—as they must inevitably be raised, for all promising educational solutions to social problems—"does it work and is it worth it?"

What Is Bilingual Education?

In very general terms, bilingual education implies some use of two (or more) languages of instruction in connection with teaching courses other than language *per se.* Thus, neither the smattering of foreign-language instruction that FLES (Foreign Language in Elementary Schools) programs have long been providing to many grade schoolers in the U. S. A. nor the smatterings more normally offered subsequently in most American secondary schools, in the course of foreign-language instruction, qualify as bilingual education. However, wherever courses such as mathematics or history or science (or Bible or Talmud) are taught via a language other than English, while other courses (such as mathematics or history or . . .) are taught via English, then bilingual education may be said to obtain. However, within this broad definition, it is obvious that vastly different types of programs and program goals can be and are being pursued.

Four Broad Categories of Bilingual Education Programs

It may be instructive to propose (as I have in the past; Fishman and Lovas, 1970) a tentative sociolinguistic typology of bilingual education programs based on four differing kinds of community and school objectives. Each of these types will be briefly illustrated by an existing or proposed bilingual education program for some Spanish-speaking community.* In presenting this typology of bilingual education programs, I would like to distinguish clearly between them and English-as-a-second-language programs. The latter are programs which include no instruction in the student's mother tongue as part of the program.

Another point about this typology is that it is not based on student and schedule characteristics such as proportion of students speaking a certain language and proportion of time devoted to each language. Rather it looks to the kinds of sociolinguistic development implied in the program objectives and suggests that various kinds of programs assume and lead to particular societal rules for the language taught.

Type I: Transitional Bilingualism. In such a program Spanish is used in the early grades to the extent necessary to allow pupils to "adjust to school" and/or to "master subject matter" until their skill in English is developed to the point that it alone can be used as the medium of instruction. Such programs do not strive toward goals of fluency and literacy in both languages with opportunity throughout the curriculum for the continuing improvement toward mastery of

---

*Many examples of other than Spanish-related bilingual education at the elementary level are provided in John and Horner, 1971; and in Andersson and Boyer, 1970. An appreciably different (and much more detailed) typography of bilingual education is available in Mackey, 1970.

each. Rather, they state goals such as "increasing overall achievement of Spanish-speaking students by using both Spanish and English as media of instruction in the primary grades." Such programs (consciously or unconsciously) correspond to the societal objective of language shift and give no consideration to long-range institutional development and support of the mother tongue. An example of such a program can be found in the grant proposal of the Las Cruces (N. M.) School District No. 2 for support of their Sustained Primary Program for Bilingual Students. Perhaps the best way to characterize this program would be to cite the three primary objectives against which the program is to be evaluated:

1. To increase the achievement level of Spanish-speaking youngsters through the use of a sustained K-3 program.
2. To determine whether Spanish-speaking youngsters achieve more in a program that utilizes instruction in both Spanish and English or in a program that is taught in Spanish only.
3. To involve the parents of Spanish-speaking students in the educational program as advisers and learners, thus enriching the home environment of the child.

The entire proposal makes no mention of measuring performance in Spanish or continuing Spanish in the curriculum past grade 3—or of making any survey of the language situation in the community. Such programs (and there are many of this kind) are basically interested only in transitional bilingualism, i.e., in arriving at the state of English monolingual educational normality just as soon as is feasible without injuring the pupil or arousing the community.

Type II: Monoliterate Bilingualism. Programs of this type indicate goals of development in both languages for aural-oral skills but do not concern themselves with literacy skills in the non-English mother tongue. Thus, such programs emphasize developing fluency in Spanish as a link between home and school, with the school providing recognition and support for the language in the domains of home and neighborhood; but they are not concerned with the development of literacy skills in the non-English mother tongue which would facilitate the child's use of the language in conjunction with work, government, religion or book-culture more generally. This type of program is intermediate in orientation between language shift and language maintenance. The likely societal effect of such a program might be one of language maintenance in the short run, but, given the exposure of students to American urban society which stresses and rewards literacy, it might well lead to shift. One example of such a program can be found in Christine McDonald's proposal for the El Rancho United School District in Pico Rivera, California. The program is designed for preschool children, and the parents' and children's home language is used throughout its entire course. However, the focus of the program would be on ultimately developing literacy in English with no reference to similar development in Spanish. Bilingual programs for American Indians frequently fall into this category because, in many instances, there is no body of written literature for the child to learn in his mother tongue. Obviously the intellectual imbalance between English literacy and mother-tongue illiteracy poses a difficult situation for any language-maintenance-oriented community, particularly if it is exposed to occupational mobility through English.

Type III: Biliterate Bilingualism, Partial. This kind of program seeks fluency and literacy in both languages, but literacy in the mother tongue is restricted to certain subject matter, most generally that related to the ethnic group and its cultural heritage. In such a program, reading and writing skills in the mother tongue are commonly developed in relation to the social sciences, literature, and the arts, but not in science and mathematics. This kind of program is clearly one of language maintenance coupled with a certain effort at culture maintenance (perhaps even cultural development should the program result in the production of journalism, poetry, and other literary art forms). In general, the program in the Dade County (Florida) Public Schools (as described in the administrative guideline) exemplifies this type of bilingual education. (See also Rojas, 1966.) The program provides special instruction in English in all skills for all Spanish-speaking students who need it. Additionally, the program provides formal instruction in reading and writing Spanish with emphasis on Spanish literature and civilization as subject matter. Other areas of the curriculum do not utilize Spanish as a medium of instruction. Other programs of this type are conducted by numerous American ethnic groups in their own supplementary or parochial schools.* Such programs imply that while non-English mother tongues are serious vehicles of modern literate thought, they are not related to control of the technological and economic spheres. The latter are considered to be the preserve of the majority whose language must be mastered if these spheres are to be entered. Nationalist protest movements since the mid-nineteenth century have consistently rejected any such limiting implication.

Type IV: Biliterate Bilingualism, Full. In this kind of program, students are to develop all skills in both languages in all domains. Typically, both languages are used as media of instruction for all subjects (except in teaching the languages themselves). Clearly this program is directed at language maintenance and development of the minority language. From the viewpoint of much of the linguistically and psychologically oriented literature this is the ideal type of program, since, in the words of one specialist, it results in "balanced, coordinate bilinguals—children capable of thinking and feeling in either of two languages independently."

Programs such as these enable us to ponder the difference between developing balanced competency in individuals and producing a balanced bilingual society. Though highly bilingual societies might find individuals with highly developed competency in all skills and domains very useful in a variety of roles (teachers, translators, business representatives), a fully balanced bilingual speech community seems to be a theoretical impossibility. Balanced competence implies languages

---

*Over a thousand such programs under other than Jewish auspices are reviewed in Fishman, 1966, Chapter 5: "The Ethnic Group School and Mother Tongue Maintenance" (pp. 92-126).

that are functionally equivalent, and no society can be motivated to maintain two languages if they are really functionally redundant. Thus, this type of program does not seem to have a clearly articulated goal with respect to societal reality.

Several examples of this type of program exist, but all of them are small pilot or experimental programs. The Coral Way Elementary School (Dade County, Florida) and the Laredo Unified Consolidated Independent School District (Texas) are two frequently cited instances which exemplify this kind of program (Gaarder, 1967; Michel, 1967; Andersson, 1968), not to mention much more recent experiments by Lambert. In the Coral Way School, students take all subjects in both languages, English in the morning from one teacher, Spanish in the afternoon from another teacher. At Laredo Unified, students receive all instruction from the same teacher who uses English half the day and Spanish the other half. The evidence so far suggests that these programs are quite successful, but looking at them from the view of the functional needs of the community, there is serious reservation in my mind whether they should serve as ideal models for large-scale American programs.

Clearly, few American educators or laymen have pondered the four alternatives presented above, let alone their societal implications and requirements. In part this is due to the fact that most American bilingual education programs are of Types I and III above and, therefore, are minimalist insofar as their non-English-language/culture components are concerned. In part this is because Americans tend to view bilingual education as if it were a strictly American sin or virtue; i.e., without any historical or cultural perspective whatsoever.

Why Bilingual Education?

It may be possible to examine at least some of the worldwide and timewide span of bilingual education while reviewing the rationales advanced for it and the evidence pertaining thereto. Clearly, most American bilingual education programs are viewed as academically *compensatory* to begin with, and, hopefully, therefore also as socioeconomically compensatory for the disadvantaged *minority-group child* from non-English-speaking environments (Gaarder, 1970).

Compensatory Programs. This constriction of bilingual education to overcoming "diseases of the poor," distasteful though it may be, has its well-established precedents in other climes and in other centuries, but most particularly in Europe since the Reformation, wherever the expansion of educational opportunity (or obligation) was stymied by the fact that the official language of education was not always the mother tongue of students new to the educational system. In such circumstances, whether in early-modern France or Germany, in turn-of-the-century or in recent-day Yucatan, Manila, or Moncton, the same claim has been advanced: start the learner off in the language he knows best. The more rapid progress made as a result, insofar as developing learning confidence and satisfaction is concerned, will then pay off in terms of much more rapid progress when the majority language is turned to (and, as some would have it, when more serious educational work is begun). Thus, this approach, when transferred to the

American context, typically claims that "learning English" and "getting educated" are not one and the same and that it is worth pursuing the latter via the mother tongue until the former can be tackled and, indeed, that the one will facilitate the other.

A serious evaluation of the above claim is still to come, if by "serious" we mean an opportunity to disentangle the mother tongue effect *per se* from the social, cultural, economic, linguistic, and educational contexts in which it is necessarily embedded. What little research there has been in connection with this claim indicates that there are certainly circumstances under which it is supported,* but that, on the whole, bilingual education is too frail a device, in and of itself, to significantly alter the learning experiences of the minority-mother-tongue-poor in general or their majority-language-learning-success in particular. It is of course true that foisting a language other than their own upon such children is equivalent to imposing an extra burden upon those least capable of carrying it. However, precisely because there are so many other pervasive reasons why such children achieve poorly the goals of majority-oriented and -dominated schools (and societies), removing this extra burden above—and leaving all else as it was—does not usually do the trick, particularly when the teachers, curricula, and materials for bilingual education are as nonoptimal as they currently usually are. My own feeling is that just as there is no simple school-based solution to the learning problems of the alienated-in-general, we cannot and should not expect bilingual education to provide such a solution for the non-English-mother-tongue-alienated-poor in particular. If there is a sufficient rationale for bilingual education, and I believe there is, it must be found on other than compensatory grounds, particularly inasmuch as most compensatory programs are merely transitional or monoliterate and, therefore, hardly constitute bilingual education in a context in which it is most likely to succeed. Who among us would care to defend the contribution of (or the prospects for) science education or social studies education on the basis of its effectiveness with alienated and dislocated populations such as those receiving compensatory bilingual education?

Enrichment Programs. When we turn our gaze from the poor to the middle class and above, we find bilingual education typically far more intensive and justified not on the grounds of compensation but of enrichment "To them that hath shall be given." Those who are relatively secure in their social, economic, and political power can afford and, indeed, often seek an additional educational and cultural exposure to that afforded them by their own mother tongue and immediate milieu. Thus, rather than merely being a palliative for the poor,

---

*Among the supportive evidence cited by John and Horner is that contained in reports by Modiano (1968), Osterberg (1961), Pryor (1967), Richardson (1968), pertaining to Mexican Indians, Swedes, Mexican-Americans, and Cuban-Americans, respectively. In Osterberg's project young speakers of Pitean (a nonstandard Swedish dialect) learning to read in their dialect fared better than Pitean-speaking children learning to read the literary dialect. Indirect support is also available from other programs that employ a nonstandard dialect for transitional or monoliterate purposes.

bilingual education has been long and widely viewed by advantaged groups as "an elitist thing." Whether we are interested in the classical world (E. Glyn Lewis, Appendix 3, this volume) or in the modern, in the West or in the East, bilingual education has been savored by the fortunate few and, apparently, found to be very good indeed.*

There have been several attempts to expand such efforts in recent decades so that the enrichment formerly reserved for the patrician might be made more widely available. Most of these have not been exposed to research evaluations, but the impressions of serious and sophisticated observers are positive regarding the bilingual schools of Singapore (largely in Chinese and English), or of LWC schools in the Soviet Union (Lewis, 1972), of areas in Wales, and of the Yeshiva movement in the U. S. A.** It is felt that the intellective and nonintellective results obtained are generally as good as or better than those in monolingual schools for students of comparable backgrounds. However, the one serious study of truly widespread compulsory bilingual education, the one conducted in Ireland (Macnamara, 1966), disclosed negative findings as well. Because of the time and effort invested in teaching Irish *per se,* as well as in teaching via Irish, to children who neither knew it nor used it out of school, elementary school graduates were on the average a year behind students of comparable backgrounds in England with regard to tested achievement in English and in mathematical problem solving—at the same time that their active grasp of Irish remained rather marginal at best. Once again, it is not possible to say, on the basis of one such study, whether it is the overextension of bilingual education *per se* that exacted this toll or whether it was exacted by the particular context of widespread disinterest in and perceived uselessness of Irish in present-day Ireland. On the whole, I would tend to favor the latter interpretation of the Irish findings (primarily because it agrees with my own preliminary findings based on international data) and to believe that well-disposed and supported schools, serving well-disposed and reasonably comfortable clienteles, can carry on bilingual education as successfully as most others carry on monolingual education and that the resulting educational product may be deemed well worth the additional cost and effort that may be entailed.

Group-Maintenance Programs. No matter how successful enrichment-oriented bilingual education for the relatively comfortable and secure may be, it still does not come to grips with the problems of self-perceived minorities, poor or otherwise. What spokesmen for some of the latter have been emphasizing (and, once more, throughout the world and across time) is neither "compensation" nor "enrichment" but rather the preservation and enhancement of the group as such.

---

*Two recent and well-done evaluative case studies of such programs, both with general positive findings, are to be found in Mackey, 1972 and in Lambert and Tucker, 1972.

**The bilingual nature of traditional Jewish education does not properly fit into our discussion here because, on the one hand, it was not rationalized on the grounds of enrichment, and on the other, it was a reflection of *within-group* bilingualism (Yiddish and Loshen Koydesh) rather than of between-group bilingualism such as that best characterizing all the other examples cited in this paper.

However, bilingual education rationalized in group-maintenance and culture-maintenance terms is also considered to help the individual learner. A minority student who is confident of and recognized in his more intimate primary-group membership relates more positively both to school and to society (both of which are majority-dominated) and, as a result, profits more from schooling. There is hardly any research evidence pertaining to such claims in conjunction with bilingual education, although the view itself is a long- and well-established one, particularly in the context of cultural pluralism and minority rights. In this context, however, it is primarily an article of faith, a moral and ethical position, a basic social right, and as such, not likely to benefit seriously from, or to be much subjected to, objective and empirical research.

The common argument *against* group-maintenance-oriented bilingual education is that it is conducive to sociopolitical tensions, at the very least, and to sociopolitical ruptures, at worst. This may well be so, in certain minority-majority contexts at particular times and in particular places and, therefore, would seem to merit more or less consideration as local circumstances dictate. Certainly the demand for group-maintenance-oriented bilingual education has been advanced by both groups and individuals who have had only sociocultural goals rather than sociopolitical ones. As a result of such demands the growth of mother-tongue instruction for minority-group children, at least during the early elementary school years, has been truly phenomenal during the past quarter century and may become worldwide before this century is out (Chapter V, this volume). The result of this movement has been a corresponding increase in partial bilingual education, if the entire period of school attendance is considered. Very few, if any, secessionist movements have been spawned thereby or related thereto, and it would seem to me to be more wicked than wise to raise any such bugaboo in conjunction with discussions of bilingual education in the U. S. A. today. The right of large concentrations of parents to have their children educated in their own mother tongue at public expense; the right of individuals to defend and protect the primary groups to which they belong most intimately, at the same time that they hold and cultivate multiple loyalties to more inclusive groups; the right of much smaller groups to coexist within the larger groups with which they have symbiotic ties—all these must not be philosophically beclouded by possibly baseless innuendos. When coterritorial groups move toward separatism, it is almost never because of conflicts over bilingual education.

Like much else that has transpired in American education during the past decade, bilingual education has come about as a result of the confluence of organized pressures and innovative initiatives. Like much else that is promising in American education today, bilingual education suffers from four serious lacks: a lack of funds (Title VII has been pitifully starved), a lack of trained personnel, a lack of evaluated experience (with respect to curricula, materials, and methods) and a lack of sociohistorical perspective. It is not and cannot be a cure-all for the myriad disadvantages faced by the millions of poor non-English-mother-tongue children in our society. It could possibly be a powerful enrichment for the many other millions of more affluent American children, but such is our current blindness with respect to it that we largely insist on seeing it merely as "something for the poor." Nevertheless, it is in this latter *general* enrichment manifestation, as well as in the context of the self-maintenance efforts of our various non-Anglo cultural groups, that its true contribution to American education and society will ultimately be made.

An Exciting Field

I have been a "language teaching watcher" for many years, and my impression is that this is an exciting field. During the past third of a century, there has been as much innovative theory, curricular and methodological rethinking, and sophisticated debunking in the language teaching field as in the much stressed mathematics-sciences field. This says a great deal about the intellectual vitality of the field of language teaching, and it clearly distinguishes it (as well as math-sciences) from the social sciences and the humanities, which regrettably have remained comparatively quiescent in terms of revisions in instructional theory or methodology. Indeed, the *growing* relationship between the language field and the math-science field on the one hand (in terms of the forces that shape American life and American education) and the shrinking relationship between the language field and the humanities-social sciences field on the other hand is related both to the *heights* and to the *depths* that American language teaching has experienced since the beginning of World War II.

Extrasocietal and External Societal Influences

During and immediately after World War II—war needs themselves being among the most dramatic influences that American language teaching has *ever* experienced—the most influential ideas shaping American language teaching methods were derived from linguistics and from psychology. I refer to these as *extrasocietal* influences since neither the view that gave primacy to syntax and phonology over lexicon and use, nor the view that gave primacy to listening comprehension and to speech over reading and writing, had any societal image, purpose, or function explicitly in mind. They did not attempt to cope with the question: "What should be the role of subsequent languages in the life of the learner and in the life of society?" There was absolutely no conscious "language-in-society" model underlying either of these powerful methodological approaches, both of which are still very much with us today.

Although the same extrasocietal designation is *not* true with respect to the *second most powerful force* influencing American language teaching during the past third of a century—here I refer to the post-sputnik panic and the realization

BILINGUAL EDUCATION IS GOOD
FOR LANGUAGE LEARNING AND LANGUAGE TEACHING
Bilingual Education and the Future
of Language Teaching and Language Learning in the U.S.A.
(with Robert L. Cooper)

CHAPTER IV

that language expertise was vital for defense-related purposes—that force was an *external* societal factor rather than an internal one. The threat of Soviet technological modernization imposed itself upon us from outside our own boundaries, and even when language instruction responded to that threat with all the "nondeliberate" speed at its command, it never (well, "hardly ever") linked up its contribution to national defense with the indigenous language resources internal to American society. The "Language Resources Project" that I headed from 1960-1963, and that resulted in my *Language Loyalty in the United States,* tried to provide such an internal societal link, but it was an idea whose time had not quite yet come. The common American approach to language learning (and, indeed, the common approach of the language teacher *per se* to the commodity he was "pushing") was that additional languages are useful or crucial for our national well-being *particularly* if such languages are (a) learned in school rather than in the context of home and community, (b) learned as a mature adult (in college and graduate school), (c) learned as a target, in itself, rather than as a process for the mastery of other material, and are (d) exotic to the American content in terms of easy access to the learner.

The Ascendancy of Societal Concerns

Let us quickly skip over all that the concentration on external threat enabled foreign-language teaching to accomplish. The rapid expansion (indeed duplication) of programs, increase in positions, and mushrooming of student incentive funds has been recounted many times. Let us turn immediately to the realization that during the past decade (1965-1975) most of the impetus for change in language teaching and language learning has had strong indigenous societal roots, although external considerations still play their part. In this past decade language teaching in the United States has had to respond, as never before, to internal social issues and social needs such as the urban disadvantaged, the alienation of youth, the ethnic minorities, the rebirth of ethnicity among some whose parents fancied that they had escaped from it, and, most recently, the fiscal crunch. Many of these societal needs and reemerging lost continents have hit language instruction *directly,* in that the high priorities given to them have left proportionately fewer taxpayer and foundation dollars for other needs. In addition, the educational establishment's reaction to those needs and pressures have often hit language instruction *indirectly,* by permitting greater latitude in student choice of subjects to be studied, greater opportunity for "alternative" forms and contents of education, and, correspondingly, lesser insistence on language learning as new subjects and as new populations enter our high schools, colleges, and universities.

For one reason or another, language enrollments have generally been dropping, language requirements have been fading, the attack on language learning has been mounting, and—as in all times of strife and disappointment—the time and mood are ripe for a new panacea, a good bet, a stimulating idea, a rallying cause, or, at the very least, a straw to clutch at. It is at this point that bilingual education enters the picture to save Little Red Riding Hood from the Big Bad Wolf.

Bilingual Education and Compensatory Education

There is growing recognition in language teaching circles—as in education circles more generally—that a sizable proportion of the disadvantaged lack facility in English—not to mention standard school English—and that if their educational progress is not to be appreciably delayed and diluted, they had best be taught most subjects in their non-English mother tongues, at least until ESL gets through to them. The recent *Lau* decision of the Supreme Court may soon foster a nationwide approach along these lines, and yet, with all of its welcome relief for all children whose English is really insufficient for the burden of educational effort, I doubt that it will do much for language instruction. Bilingual education that is merely compensatory, merely transitional, is merely a desperate attempt to fight fire with fire. If a non-English mother tongue is conceptualized as a disease of the poor, then in true vaccine style this disease is to be attacked by the disease baccilus itself. A little bit of deadened mother tongue, introduced in slow stages in the classroom environment, will ultimately enable the patient to throw off the mother tongue entirely and to embrace all-American vim, vigor, and vitality.

My own evaluation is that compensatory bilingual education is not a good long-term bet, neither for language teaching nor for bilingual education *per se.* The multiproblem populations on whose behalf it is espoused—underprivileged, unappreciated, alienated—cannot be aided in more than an initial palliative sense by so slender a reed as compensatory bilingual education. Populations that would present almost insuperable problems to our schools and to all of our establishment institutions, even if they were *monolingual* English speakers, will not cease being such problems merely because they are offered a year or two of introductory education primarily in their non-English mother tongues. Their problems and our hangups are not that simple to overcome.

Bilingual education "sold" as a compensatory promissory note will disappoint us all—teachers and citizens alike. It will not solve the basic societal problems of the non-English-speaking poor, and, therefore, will not solve their basic educational problems. It will soon be just another educational gimmick gone sour, and language teaching as well as bilingual education as a whole will both suffer needlessly as a result of having made yet another bad bet.

Bilingual Education and Ethnic Legitimacy

There is another rationale for bilingual education, and it might well be of somewhat greater interest to language teachers and to American society at large. Thanks to our recent sensitivity to ethnicity, the non-English mother tongues and cultures in our midst are recognized as things of beauty, to be maintained and treasured forever and ever. These languages and cultures are recognized not for manipulative, compensatory, and transitional purposes, but as basic ingredients of a healthy *individual* self-concept and of sound *group* functioning. Groups that are deprived of their languages and cultures are dislocated groups. Such groups have no alternative but to dump dislocated and alienated students on the doorstep of the school and of all other institutions of the larger society. Greater *self-*

acceptance among non-English-mother-tongue children (including acceptance of their parents and their traditions and their immediate societies) and greater mutual acceptance between such children and the American mainstream will also foster greater genuine school progress. Bilingual education under this rationale is *group-maintenance*-oriented, and, as a result, not merely a compensatory, transitional "quickie."

Note, however, that therein lies an unstated assumption, namely, that bilingual education is needed only for the "unmeltable ethnics." Such a view is still patronizing—although "patronizing once removed"—in that it assumes that nonethnics are above or beyond bilingual education and "all that." Language and ethnicity are still assigned to the "outer fringe," beyond the propriety of White Anglo-Saxon Protestantdom. Enlightened patronization would not be a propitious approach to strengthening the impact of mathematics or history in American education or in American life, and I predict that, welcome though it may be among the Navajos, it will do little or nothing for the place of language learning in our schools and in our society more generally.

Bilingual Education for Enrichment

In various parts of Canada (and not only in French Canada) economically comfortable English-speaking parents are voluntarily sending their eager youngsters to primarily-but-not-entirely French schools. Such "immersion schools" for societally favored youngsters also exist in France, Germany, Latin America, the Soviet Union, the Arab World, Italy, Belgium, not to mention many, many parts of Africa and Asia. They bring together two languages of wider communication—rather than one pitifully small language and one gargantuanly large one. They involve the populations most able to pay for a good education and most likely to succeed educationally and societally—rather than those least favored in these respects. They require the most advantaged to *stretch further* educationally and, thus, are really an enrichment for the rich. They continue, albeit at a somewhat more accessible level, the bilingual education tradition practiced by most elites from the days of the ancient Egyptians, Greeks, and Romans on. They are eminently successful and therefore attract the best students, teachers, and administrators. Regrettably, such schools are almost unknown in the public sector of American education.

Of course, bilingual education for enrichment also involves some unspoken assumptions. It assumes that it is particularly the well off who not only stand to gain by an additional cultural exposure but that, indeed, they are the very ones for whom such an exposure is an acceptable and even a powerful motivating argument. My own view is that enrichment (or immersion) bilingual education is the best way of demonstrating the *academic* and *societal* advantages of bilingual education. I am sure that it is *this* kind of bilingual education that could become the most reliable prop for language teaching in the United States, just as it has become such in some of the countries I have mentioned. Such a prop would be more than a fad, more than a nostrum, if it were ever to catch on. It represents bilingual education not only at its best but at its broadest. However, I am not sure that "middle America," in whose image most of our secondary and higher educational institutions are shaped, is ready for it, or ever will be.

Bilingual Education in Sociolinguistic Perspective

If there is anything that bilingual education has to contribute to language teaching more generally, it is its maximization of *language learning for the communication of messages that are highly significant* for senders and receivers alike, both in their individual as well as in their actual and potential societal capacities. There is simply no way in which language teaching which focuses on language as a *target of instruction* can fully capture the total impact upon the learner which is available to language teaching which also capitalizes upon language as the *process of instruction*. Because bilingual education does just that—particularly in its enrichment guise, but also in its compensatory and group-maintenance guises which definitely have a validity of their own (although of a more temporally or demographically restricted nature)—it provides a powerful and worldwide boost to language teaching. However, like every potential solution, it poses potential problems as well.

Is the American public mature enough for enrichment-oriented bilingual education? Are we and our colleagues in the language teaching profession mature enough to move toward it rather than to reject it because of our personal inadequacies and societal biases? My own tendency is to view the future in optimistic terms. I see the future of language teaching and language learning in the United States as including a greater variety of rationales, goals, and methods than has hitherto been the case. I see bilingual education as part of this variety, and I see more language teachers able to engage in it than previously, whether for compensatory, group-maintenance, or enrichment purposes. Indeed, I see American bilingual educators being able to engage in *various kinds* of bilingual education, rather than merely in one kind or another, depending on the students and communities to which they are addressing themselves. Finally, I see more second-language teachers also able to engage in bilingual education and more bilingual educators being able to engage in second-language instruction, rather than two quite distinct groups of language practitioners, as is most often the case in the U. S. A. today.

As for bilingual education itself, it is *but one* opportunity to revitalize language teaching among many. It is itself *internally diversified* into compensatory, group-maintenance, and enrichment streams and must not be viewed as one undifferentiated blob. It has its own problems of training and funding. It can no more *remake society, education,* or even *language teaching* than can any other partial solution to all-encompassing and multifaceted problems. It should not be underrated, but it should not be *oversold* on false premises. It has functions that go above and beyond language teaching. However, I know that it is *here to stay* as a *worldwide phenomenon* today, with outcroppings in over 100 countries, and I trust that America too will profit from it and contribute to it in the days to come.

The Sociology of Second-Language Learning and Teaching*

The decisions which a second-language teacher must make about teaching can be divided into two major categories. First, he must make decisions about *what* to teach. For example, should he assign greater importance to spoken or to written skills as goals of instruction? Should he assign greater importance to goals dealing with syntax or to those dealing with the lexicon? Should he teach irregular forms which occur with great frequency before he teaches regular forms which are more productive but less frequent? Which phonological contrasts, syntactic structures, and lexical items ought he to emphasize? For what language-usage contexts should he prepare his students: for understanding university lectures, for casual conversation among peers, for talking to street vendors, for reading scholarly material, or for reading a newspaper?

The second set of decisions a language teacher must make concerns *how* to teach. For example, what types of pattern-practice drills, if any, should he employ, and for what types of structure? What types of materials and texts should he select or construct? How often should students be asked to repeat an item? Should students be permitted to make mistakes or should their utterances be so carefully programmed that only grammatically correct utterances are produced? Should the student's mother tongue be used as a medium of instruction in the second language? Should the teacher provide vocabulary definitions in the mother tongue of his students? Should the teacher provide explicit statements of grammatical rules?

Teachers rely on several sources for help in answering such questions about what and how to teach. First, they rely on their personal experience, both as language teachers and as language learners. Second, they consult experienced colleagues. Third, they rely on the advice offered in the lectures and writings of experts in language pedagogy. Finally, they apply principles learned from courses or readings in linguistics, psycholinguistics, sociolinguistics, the sociology of language, and other language-related sciences.

Many language teachers find the descriptions and the insights provided by linguistics useful in answering questions about *what* to teach. The descriptions provided by contrastive analysis, for example, are often helpful in predicting what items will be difficult for speakers of a given language and thus in suggesting what items ought to be given special attention (see, for example, Levenston, 1970). Although it is doubtful that linguistic grammars can be used directly as pedagogic devices, it is plausible that knowledge of the former can assist in the preparation of the latter.

The principles discovered by psycholinguistics are perhaps harder to apply to problems in teaching than are those of linguistics. However, those psycholinguistic principles which *are* relevant apply primarily to the set of questions dealing with *how* to teach. Findings, for example, about the relative effectiveness of audiolingual versus grammar-translation procedures with respect to specific goals

---

*Robert L. Cooper co-authored the material in this chapter beginning at this point.

of instruction and at specific levels of proficiency are clearly relevant to this set of questions (see, for example, Scherer and Wertheimer, 1964).

In contrast to linguistics and psycholinguistics, sociolinguistics and the sociology of language are relevant to both sets of questions—what and how to teach. It is the purpose of the next two subsections to indicate the relevance of sociolinguistic principles to second-language teaching.

Societally Patterned Linguistic Alternation

Sociolinguistic research and theory are concerned with the discovery and description of systematic covariation between linguistic and social facts. There are few if any single-style speakers. It is the task of sociolinguistics and the sociology of language to discover the societal norms which constrain a speaker's alternation among the verbal resources at his disposal.

We speak differently in different situations, and this variation is systematic. We may speak differently to a child than to an adult, to a subordinate than to a superior, to a member of the same sex than to a member of the opposite sex, and to a coreligionist than to a person we consider a nonbeliever. We may speak differently when telling a joke than when giving a university lecture, when present at a liturgical ceremony than when present at a football game, when talking about a topic in which we are professionally engaged than when talking about current events. Some of these differences in ways of speaking are seen in the content of what is said. We say different things to different people on different occasions. Other differences in ways of speaking are structural. Our pronunciation may vary, the lexical items we choose may vary, and the syntax we employ may vary from one context to another. Not only may our pronunciation, vocabulary and syntax vary, but the very language we choose may vary as well, inasmuch as we may regularly employ one language for one set of purposes and another language for another set.

Speech communities may differ with respect to the social occasions for variation in ways of speaking. Thus, for example, among the Subanun, drinking encounters require an elaborate linguistic etiquette (Frake, 1964). Among traditional Amhara, ritual purity commands deferential verbal behavior (Hoben, in press). Among some groups of Jews in the Diaspora, synagogue services are the scene of systematic switching between Yiddish, Hebrew, and the local vernacular. Among the Arabs, classical and vernacular Arabic each has its allocation of functions, with speakers systematically switching from one to the other, for purposes of within-group communication, according to clearly defined societal norms (Ferguson, 1959). The point is not only that people systematically vary in the way they talk but also that societies differ with respect to the social features which covary with language use.

What to Teach

The existence of societally patterned linguistic alternation within speech communities has two important implications for the decisions which a language teacher must make about what to teach. First, the teacher ought to specify the contexts in which the student plans to use the target language. Second, the teacher must attend to rules of speaking as well as to rules of grammar.

It is sometimes convenient to assert that a given language is spoken in the same way by all speakers at all times. Such a view ignores variation associated with social stratification, regional diversity, and social context. Sociolinguistic research, to say nothing of common experience, belies this view. It is clear, for example, that the English of an educated New Yorker differs from that of an educated Londoner, that the speech of each differs from that of uneducated speakers, and that the speech of each is not the same on formal occasions as it is on relaxed ones. Thus, even if the language teacher aims to teach the speech of a single standard language variety (usually his own, if he is a native speaker of the target language), he is still faced with the problem of teaching a target which changes according to the situation in which it is used. Similarly, in the case of Hebrew, the kind of speech which might be appropriate among football players in the locker room after a game would probably be inappropriate for use with a clerk at a government agency or for use in a university seminar, and all three would be viewed as peculiar if used with a three-month-old infant.

It is the rare student who will need to use the target language in all the social contexts in which he participates. Usually his requirements are far more modest. He needs the language for a restricted range of functions. He might, for example, require only a reading knowledge of the language, and, moreover, the contexts in which he needs to read it may be confined to his professional specialty. Another student may need the language for purposes of diplomatic representation. A third may be a person who needs the language primarily for routine transactions in shops, banks, and post offices. Sometimes it may not be immediately clear what purposes the students have in mind. One teacher of English to a class of Ethiopian women, for example, found after some time that the chief reason her students wanted to learn English was to enable them to consult physicians, inasmuch as most doctors in the country were expatriates. While each of the students in the examples cited will need to learn some things in common, there are many things which each must learn that the others need not. By specifying the contexts and purposes for which the student is going to use the target language, the teacher can concentrate on what it is the students will most need to know.

Specifying the particular contexts or functions for which the target language is to be used and then concentrating on them has several advantages over an approach which attempts to impart global knowledge of a language in all possible skills and for all possible functions. First of all, the latter goal is unattainable not only by students but also by native speakers. No one knows how to speak a language appropriately in all the contexts in which it is used, because no one has access to all the societal roles in which the language is used and which constrain language usage. For example, while many of us are both students and teachers and know the ways of speaking appropriate to both roles, few of us are both priest and parishioner, judge and petitioner, physician and patient, and no one is simultaneously male and female or child and adult. If access to such roles is restricted and if role differentiation and speech differentiation are associated with one another, then the verbal resources available to a community as a whole will not be equally available to each member of the community. No one will have equal knowledge (or equal need) of all ways of talking.

A second advantage is that one can teach a person what he needs to know more efficiently by concentrating on the contexts in which he will need to use the language than by using an unfocused, shotgun approach. Thus, for example, it would be efficient to use technical journals in the target language as a primary source of teaching materials for the student who wishes to use the language only for professional reading. It would also be efficient to use prepared dialogues between customer and clerk as a primary teaching device for the student who wants to learn the language mainly for routine marketing transactions. But it would not seem efficient to use both types of material with both types of student.

A third advantage is that an approach that focuses attention on the particular contexts or functions in which the student will need to learn the language is likely to sustain his interest and motivation better than an approach which is unfocused with respect to the student's needs.

Just as it is unrealistic and counter-productive to deny the existence of variation in the target language, it is also unrealistic and counter-productive to deny the existence of functional bilingualism as a goal of instruction. Most students will neither want nor need to use the target language in all domains of everyday life. They will continue to use their mother tongue, as well as second languages in *addition* to the target language, for some and perhaps most purposes. To deny the usefulness of the languages which the student brings with him is not only depressing to the student but discourages the maintenance of language skills which are useful to the society as a whole. Thus, a fourth advantage of contextualizing second-language teaching is the support it gives to the maintenance of skills in languages other than the target language.

A corollary of contextualization of instruction is concern with rules of speaking. Linguistic competence, the ability in principle to produce any and all the sentences in the target language, is an insufficient goal of instruction. As Hymes (1972) has observed, anyone who speaks any of the sentences of the language without regard to where he is or to whom he is speaking would quickly be institutionalized. We must learn when to speak and when to remain silent, and what to say to whom and when. We need, in short, what Hymes has called communicative competence. Thus, communicative competence must be the goal of second-language teaching if the target language is to be more than of rudimentary use to the student. Since the student usually needs the target language in a more restricted set of contexts than does the native speaker, the task of imparting communicative competence in a second language is not so formidable as it might otherwise seem.

In some cases, existing sociolinguistic description can help the teacher specify explicitly the rules of speaking which the student must learn for a given set of contexts. For example, studies of rules of address in American English (Brown and Ford, 1961; Ervin-Tripp, 1969) can help the teacher prepare material designed to teach the student of (American) English when it is appropriate to address an interlocutor by the first name alone. It is more usual, however, that the rules of speaking which the student needs to learn have not been explicitly described. Clearly, sociolinguists have been less successful in identifying and describing communicative competence than have linguists in describing linguistic competence, partly because the former competence includes the latter. However, if the language teacher has specified the language-usage contexts on which he will concentrate his attention, and if his material is drawn from these contexts, the student will have appropriate models from which to infer for himself the rules of speaking which he must learn, even if neither he nor his teacher is able to describe them explicitly or fully.

How to Teach

What implications result from the teacher's identification of the specific contexts and functions for which the student will use the target language and from the teacher's recognition of communicative competence as the goal of instruction? The chief implication is that the teacher should attempt to replicate in the classroom the target contexts, as far as this is possible. Thus, for example, in the case of students who wish to learn a language in order to use it with expatriate physicians, the teacher could construct dialogues between physician and patient or between physician and patient's mother in which the students could take on the appropriate roles. Memorization of dialogues could be followed by structured role playing in which the students were given not only specific symptoms to discuss but also the lexical items and syntactic structures necessary to discuss them (but without providing the exact sentences to be used). Finally, freer role playing could take place with the teacher providing only the scenario—the symptoms and the history of their onset—and with the student expressing her part of the dialogue in her own words. Another device which the teacher could use would be tape-recorded, realistic (but acted or role-played) conversations between patients and physicians. Students could be asked to imitate the speakers' roles in such dialogues. They could also be asked to specify their manifest content (what was said) as well as to interpret their latent content (what was meant). While the usefulness of context-specific material seems obvious, it must be stressed that its preparation is not an easy task. In order to prepare valid and realistic material for the example cited, for instance, the teacher would probably have to consult physicians and patients and to observe physician-patient interactions.

The student need not be at an advanced level before such realistically contextualized material is used. Indeed such material can be used from the beginning, although the level of discourse would be much simplified at the early stages of instruction. Thus, while no one would argue that the simple past in standard English varies as a function of context (although its phonological representation may vary with context for speakers of some varieties of English), one could still introduce the simple past in appropriate context-specific material.

The use of contextualized material in the classroom is one implication of a sociolinguistic approach to second-language teaching. Another implication is that the teacher should place increased reliance on partially structured procedures (i.e., procedures which emphasize communicative intent and which allow the student relative freedom of expression) and less reliance on the carefully controlled elicitation procedures of the classical audiolingual method. This follows from a recurrent theme of sociolinguistic research, the frequency of societal bilingualism.

Speech communities in which all or most members are bilingual are commonplace. Although it would be difficult to make an accurate estimate of the number of bilinguals in the world, it is probably safe to say that bilingualism is as common a phenomenon as monolingualism, historically as well as at present. The importance of this to the language teacher is not so much the *incidence* of bilingualism as the fact that a substantial proportion, if not the majority, of bilinguals acquire their second language *outside the school.* Thus, for example, in sample surveys of Galla-speaking areas in Ethiopia, it was found that only half of the Gallas who claimed proficiency in Amharic, the official language and the only medium of instruction in government primary schools, had ever gone to school (Cooper *et al.,* in press). In any of the surveyed communities the best predictor of the proportion of Gallas who claimed proficiency in Amharic was the proportion of Amharas in that community. The greater the proportion of Amharas, the greater the proportion of Gallas who claimed Amharic. Clearly, Gallas who had not been to school "picked up" Amharic from interactions with Amharic-mother-tongue-speakers outside the school. The greater the percentage of Amharas in the community, the greater the opportunity and incentive for the Gallas to learn Amharic.

That millions of people become successfully bilingual without formal instruction does not imply that we can dismiss classrooms as a means for creating bilinguals. But it does imply that we should attempt to adapt to classroom use the contexts outside the classroom which successfully create bilingualism. The circumstances whereby second languages are acquired outside the classroom have been little studied. But two things seem clear. First, learners have an opportunity to hear and to practice the language in contexts in which nonverbal cues can help the learner decipher the meaning of verbal ones. Second, the verbal interactions in which the learner participates serve a communicative function. The learner speaks (and listens) in interactions in which it is necessary to communicate. If the teacher can create realistic communicative situations in which supporting nonverbal cues exist and in which emphasis is placed on the communicative function or purpose of the interaction, he will have gone far toward simulating the conditions under which successful language learning takes place outside the classroom. The use of partially structured procedures is more likely to simulate such conditions than highly structured conventional audiolingual techniques, inasmuch as the latter are usually entirely verbal (without supporting nonverbal cues) and are usually devoid of any communicative intent.

Summary

This chapter has attempted to demonstrate the usefulness of a soci‹
perspective on second-language teaching with respect to both what an‹
teach. It was argued that language learners in the classroom would bene,
the contextualization of second-language teaching and from the adaptation, for
classroom use, of naturally occurring language-learning situations. Bilingual
education in which the languages taught are related to real, live communities, on
the one hand, and are utilized as media of instruction and real, live communication, on the other hand, is understandably a truly natural way to teach and learn
languages effectively.

INTERNATIONAL FINDINGS

PART II

The year 2000! The year 2000! The younger one is, the more the number has a mystical and utopian quality about it, one that inspires the altruistic and millennial inclinations that we all harbor. The older one is, the more it merely implies another illusion, another impossible dream, another sad and dreary letdown of the kind we have all experienced. In reality, of course, the year 2000 is neither the one nor the other. It is what we will make it—neither more, nor less. Given the inevitable inaccuracy in postdating the birth of Christ, the year 2000 will not even really be the year 2000. So much for revealing my own psychological age and UQ (utopianism quotient)!

The question posed by the title of this chapter is not even meant to be taken seriously. If it were, we could merely answer yes and let it go at that. What is really of interest is not whether mankind will continue to speak and teach a huge array of *mother tongues* for interaction with kith and kin and other intimates, and whether it will continue to speak and teach a rather small number of *other tongues* for interaction with those who are physically and psychologically more removed, but rather *whom* it will define as being in the one category or the other (and when), and *which* other tongues will be involved.

Yes, I do assume that most vernacular mother tongues are here to stay. Those that are protected by their own political establishments certainly are, and most of the others, that have no political power to back them, have learned or are learning to utilize modern social institutions and media on behalf of the sentimental, ideological, moral, esthetic, religious, or purely customary power with which they are associated. Of course, among the vernaculars without political power, some will wax and others will wane, and still others will vanish, particularly the ones that are most exposed to participatory social change guided by power structures related to other vernaculars. However, new vernaculars are also being born out of pidgins round the world. All in all, therefore, I foresee only a small possible diminution in the total number of mother tongues by the year 2000 or by other foreseeable dates. Frisian- and Catalan- and Breton- and Basque- and Yiddish-speaking mothers are likely to continue to feel and believe that their mother tongues are as good and as beautiful and as inimitable—at least for everyday use with their children, husbands, and grandmothers—as do mothers who speak

WILL FOREIGN LANGUAGES STILL BE TAUGHT IN THE YEAR 2000?

CHAPTER V

Albanian, Afrikaans, or Hebrew. And the latter are likely to continue to believe that their mother tongues, for these same functions of intimacy, are every bit as good as French and English and Russian.

Thus far, we have made three dichotomous distinctions: mother tongues vs. *other* tongues, nonpolitical vs. *political* power, and intimacy functions vs. *status/distance* functions. However, in reality, more refined distinctions need to be made and additional dimensions need to be considered if the language situation of the world in the year 2000 is to be fully appreciated and if the language teaching consequences thereof are to be accurately gauged. Nevertheless, let us hang on to our three dimensions as long as we can. They still have heuristic value, even if they are not exhaustively productive.

Just as speakers of politically unprotected languages (not to mention speakers of politically threatened ones) must come to a *modus vivendi* with the political establishment that surrounds them, so must smaller political establishments recognize larger ones. Such recognition needs arise in connection with education, work, commerce, travel, military experience, and intergroup contact of whatever kind, whether free or forced. There are, of course, societies whose bilingualism is fully indigenized and internalized—and these should be a lesson and a light to us all—but, by and large, second-language learning, whether societal or individual, involves a we-they distinction. The first question, therefore, is whose language is to be dominant in we-they interactions; and the second and more interesting one, into which, if any, internal function should "their" language be admitted if *it* turns out to be the dominant one for intergroup purposes? In this latter connection I foresee a long-term trend toward greater mutual toleration than would have seemed likely in 1900, when many nationlist movements were still at the white heat stage.

More and more politically unestablished and unprotected vernaculars are being admitted into at least primary (or early primary) school function in the Western world, and I would expect that tendency to continue there and also to become more common, within the limits of feasibility, in other parts of the world with modernizing and consolidating minorities. The better-known cases of Landsmoal (Nynorsk), Frisian, Irish, Catalan, Lappish, Valdostian, and Romansh have their less well-known but equally numerous and revealing counterparts in Southern and Eastern Europe, Canada, the U. S. A., Latin America, and elsewhere. Indeed, I do not expect that the pressures for similar recognition for Basque, Breton, Occitan, and the like to disappear by the year 2000. Rather, I expect them to be increasingly admitted into the elementary school of one type or another, in one form or another, very much as is and will be the case with vernacular forms of Arabic and of the sizable sedentary and concentrated African and Asian populations without political establishments that are primarily their own. Often such recognition carries with it a modicum of further momentum into local governmental institutions and local mass media. However, it is really quite instructive to note the extent to which the latter half of the twentieth century has witnessed the tapering off of secessionist movements and their satisfaction, instead, with a modicum of localized cultural autonomy. Of course, different parts of the world are at different stages in this accommodation process. While one part has cooled off, others are still boiling and steaming. Nevertheless, all in all, I would expect *more* vernaculars to be used/taught in the early elementary grades in the year 2000 than is the case today. Even Israel—a by-product of very recent efforts on behalf of cultural consolidation—is already timidly experimenting in this direction with its varied Jewish populations. Can France and other mono-myth-makers be far behind? The result, however, will be that speakers of non-state languages will more often be taught two languages at school rather than one—the language of their intimacy and the language of their functional polity.

Shifting Sun

Oddly enough, the same will also be true for almost all speakers of mother tongues that correspond to small and intermediate polities. These speakers are learning languages of more powerful regional and/or international intergroup contact (and will continue to do so increasingly). Indeed, for some reason this is a more conflicted process than it is for them to permit their own minorities a modicum of self-dignity. The latter they can write off as petty nonsense (conveniently forgetting that they themselves once struggled for the same privilege). The former is a blow to their *amour propre*. Some have themselves only recently established their political and cultural autonomy. It is hard for them to admit that *another* language—however useful—should be made part and parcel of everyone's postprimary education when their own language has only so recently been admitted to academic respectability. For others, who recently basked in the sunlight of regional or international splendor, it is hard to admit that the fickle sun has shifted to others now and that they themselves must now do what they formerly glibly advised others to do: learn a language of wider currency and functional generality. Nevertheless, hard though it may be, I expect this trend to continue. France may be among the last to submit, for the pill is hardest to swallow in her case. Nevertheless, she will do it, as have Germany, Spain, Italy, and Japan, and find her self-image untarnished in the end, for true culture will (in France) still and always be only French.

Will I really come to an end without mentioning English, the linguistic *éminence grise,* at all? Will it continue to spread as a second language the world over, as a benevolent bonus or creeping cancer of modernity? Perhaps, particularly since Russians and Chinese and Arabs (even "Francophone" Arabs) are increasingly inclined toward it, rather than toward each other's regionally dominant languages. Perhaps, because it is not dependent on either overt political or cultural control for its spread, but rather on less threatening commercial and technological expertise and efficiency. Nevertheless, *sic transit gloria mundi.* The mid-nineteenth century could not foresee the end of French dominance as the international language of culture and diplomacy, but it came with the political and economic downgrading of certain centers and the upgrading of others during the past century. English may enjoy a longer or shorter period of basking in the international sun. The fact that we cannot now foresee the end of its sway does not mean that it is greater or stronger or nobler than any of the other imperial languages of the past. Indeed, among sedentary populations other tongues have displaced each other much more rapidly than have mother tongues; and when they have receded, far fewer tears have been shed.

In the meantime, during its heyday, the major negative impact of "English only" is on the Anglos themselves. Unlike linguistically less-favored populations, they have little need to learn other languages or to learn them well. They are even too thick-skinned to be embarrassed by the ridicule of Francophones. They simply go elsewhere for their vacations! Surely they are paying a high price for the linguistic dominance that they have in the world of know-how and consumerism. The non-state peoples are grateful for minimal recognition of their mother tongues, but they often (and increasingly) learn both a national/regional language and an international one as well. The small state, intermediate state, and even large state peoples often (and increasingly) learn a wider regional or international language as well as their own. Indeed, all in all, there is more language teaching today (i.e., *more languages being taught more widely)—and* there will be even more in the year 2000—than ever before in world history. Even corners of the Anglo world have had to swallow their pride (e.g., in Canada, in the Philippines, in South Africa, in Puerto Rico). But the Anglo heartland continues to speak only to God, and, as is well known in the U. S. A. and Great Britain, God has always spoken English when He is serious. However, if God were to become fickle and begin to speak Russian or Chinese in His more efficient undertakings, Anglos too might begin to discover the broadening impact of bilingualism.

Fate of Fraternity

And, finally, we come to consider the fraternity of mankind: the real question of questions and, certainly, the one underlying the title of this chapter. Are we not all becoming more alike? Do we not realize more fully with each passing decade the danger and folly of ethnocentrism? Do not both capitalist pragmatism and communist ideology require and lead to one language for us all? Perhaps, but not by the year 2000 and, if ever, not as a mother tongue and, therefore, not as the vehicle of our deepest feelings, our most sensitive creativity, our most human humanity. The unity of mankind is a unity of fate and not a unity of face; it is a unity of ultimate interdependence, not of ultimate identity. It is true that modern technology and modern ideology lead everywhere in similar directions with respect to behavior and life-styles. However, modernity is just one stripe in the cloak of many colors that every society wears. Other stripes are of treasured traditional, regional, local, and even class-derived vintage, and, as a result, societal multilingualism will not merely linger on in backward corners of the globe, but it will defend and advance itself via modern methods and media (rather than merely giving in to such) and will do so within the very heartland of modernity *per se.*

The new ethnicity movements in the U. S. A. and similar movements already in existence (and others yet to come) in Great Britain, France, Spain, Germany,

Italy, and the Soviet Union will help to clarify the need of modern man for unique societal intimacy and intimate societal uniqueness: in his food and dress, in his music and poetry, in his art and artifacts, in his celebrating and mourning, in his dying and giving birth. Thus, by the year 2000, with the continued cooling off of embattled, exclusivistic, and ideologized ethnicity (nationalism) in most parts of the globe, it may become clearer even to the intellectuals (who are always the last to understand reality since they are so convinced that it is merely their task to create it) that the fraternity of mankind requires a recognition and acceptance of mankind's diversity and of the creative use thereof. Thus, it is the dialectic between uniformation and diversification which must be seen not only as the true foundation for sharply increased foreign-language teaching by the year 2000 but additionally as the true foundation for much of what is most challenging and creative in modern society (local, regional, and international) the world over.

Overall, therefore, the cut-and-dried "yes" that we originally gave as an answer to the question in the title of this chapter is, in reality, a very resounding "yes." Isn't the world getting smaller all the time? Exactly; and that is the chief reason that more, rather than less, foreign-language teaching will be done in the year 2000. Almost regardless of the size and power of mother-tongue speech communities, these are being admitted into elementary instruction. Again, almost regardless of the power and size of mother-tongue speech communities, one or more larger and more powerful languages are being required in upper elementary, secondary, and tertiary education. Both of these trends taken *together* lead to more rather than less foreign-language teaching. Both of these trends together also indicate that diversifications and uniformation in language and culture are concomitant tendencies in modern times. The smaller world, the brave new world, will be neither entirely the one nor the other. It will, indeed, require foreign-language teaching in order to be one world, and even in order to exist to and beyond the year 2000!

The problem of modern man is not that he does not love, but that he must integrate a larger number of loves than ever before: love for himself, love for his family, love for his neighbor nearby, and love for neighbors at successive distances. Most of these loves bring with them an additional language. Ultimately modern man will be sufficiently mature to fully demonstrate the parable that to know another is to love him, to love him is to know him, and nothing is more centrally identified with us or with others than the languages we speak best and most. The language teacher's potential contribution to the future of mankind is a fateful one indeed. Would that we were all equal to the task ahead, or, failing that, that we not permit our personal failings to color our societal goals and perspectives.

One hundred ten countries will be briefly reviewed in this chapter, in alphabetical order, with respect to bilingual *secondary* education within their borders. The purpose of this review is to give educators everywhere, but particularly those in the U. S. A., an idea of the worldwide scope of bilingual education in general and of the current and coming growth in bilingual *secondary* education in particular. In the process of obtaining the information recorded in this chapter, some 1,200 bilingual secondary schools or programs were contacted throughout the world (during 1972-73). Doubtless, the total number of such programs or schools in existence is many times greater. Furthermore, with political democratization and economic development, the number of such programs is destined to increase, since its current absence or scarcity in many parts of the world is more a result of lack of opportunity than lack of interest. Bilingual secondary education is undoubtedly a widespread and growing international phenomenon.

Afghanistan

Before the adoption of the 1964 constitution only the Afghan Institute of Technology, which conducts most of its coursework in English, offered bilingual education. Since then regular secondary education not only devotes considerable attention to the teaching of Persian and other foreign languages, as well as some attention to Arabic, but, theoretically, also to instruction via Dari and Pashto, the two official languages. Nevertheless, the lack of trained teachers and of adequate texts for these languages still leaves most bilingual education in the planning rather than in the implementation stage, except for those schools also serving foreign colony children (e.g., the Nedjat Technical High School in Kabul).

Albania

The small Greek minority in the south of the country attends secondary schools in which Greek is the major language of instruction through the completion of the eighth year. No similar schools seem to be available for Macedonian speakers, nor is there as yet any evidence of bilingual education for mainstream Albanian high school students.

**WORLDWIDE PERSPECTIVE
ON BILINGUAL EDUCATION**

CHAPTER VI

Algeria

Since the early 1960's, secondary education has been "Algerianized," leading to the use of Arabic as the language of instruction in literature, history, geography, and philosophy in all secondary schools. Other courses are taught in French, particularly in the *lycées classiques et modernes* and *lycées techniques.* Bilingual education is firmly established in that both Arabic and French are widely available and desired. The alternation between local Algerian and classicized Arabic also tends to add to the bilingual nature of education, particularly since both varieties may be presented separately for the baccalaureate examination. Thus far, however, little attention has been paid to the Berbers, insofar as utilization of their language is concerned at the secondary level.

Argentina

Bilingual secondary education is normally available only for "foreign colony" or minority-group children, either of short-term (e.g., American, French) or long-term (e.g., Jewish, German) residence in the country. A tiny proportion of mainstream Argentinian children also attend these schools as well as a small number of secondary schools specializing in languages.

Australia

Although there are a few privately maintained bilingual secondary schools associated with post-World War II immigrant groups, no such schooling is provided for youngsters receiving publicly supported education. Although still essentially Anglo-Saxon and monolingual, the climate of opinion toward language learning in general and toward bilingual education in particular is improving, as demonstrated by the growing number of studies, conferences, and publications dealing with these and related topics.

Austria

Although the majority of Austrian high school students have no access to bilingual secondary education (other than through foreign colony schools), such education *is* available for the Croatian and Slovene minorities in the southeastern section of the country. No information concerning similar opportunities for the smaller numbers of Czech or Hungarian students is available.

Bangladesh

The renewed and redoubled stress on Bengali may hasten a long-term trend to deemphasize English. Meanwhile, the latter is currently still prominent in secondary education, thus making bilingual education a quite common experience.

Belgium

The two major language groups (Dutch, French) teach each other's languages (and, increasingly, also English) in their high schools but do not engage in bilingual education *per se.* A modicum of bilingual education *is* available (in German and French) to the German minority in East Belgium, through the two European Schools (in Brussels and in Mol) and through a small number of schools serving religious minorities and recent immigrant groups, and, on occasion, in Brussels more generally.

Bolivia

A number of foreign colony bilingual secondary schools and a smaller number of schools for the resident German and Mennonite minorities in the country reach a tiny proportion of mainstream Bolivian youngsters. No bilingual secondary education is as yet legally available to the indigenous Indians (some 60% of the population), although bilingual-bicultural communities abound. Compensatory bilingual elementary education is currently again receiving attention after having been discouraged by a former regime.

Botswana

Although most students are either bilingual (Setswana and English) or trilingual (e.g., Herero, Setswana, and English), all secondary instruction is in English (except when Setswana itself is being taught). Nevertheless, governmental use of Setswana is growing, and its use as a colanguage of instruction in the not too distant future seems very likely.

Brazil

A number of American, German, and Jewish bilingual secondary schools exist, but these hardly reach the mainstream Brazilian student. Nor is bilingual education available for the extremely diverse indigenous Indian population, although the need for such is great (if education for Indians is really to become the rule rather than the exception), and awareness thereof is growing.

Bulgaria

Russian is widely and intensively taught, and, in addition, there is a separate stream of secondary education receiving almost all of its instruction via Russian. There are also a few secondary bilingual schools with French, German, or English as their major language of instruction as well as a number for the Turkish and Armenian minorities. No such schools seem to exist for the unrecognized Macedonian or the recognized Romanian minorities.

Burma

Although English is widely taught, it is not generally used as a language of instruction except in private secondary schools. Bilingual education for minority nationalities is prohibited as is mother-tongue education for those populations.

Burundi

Although elementary education commonly employs Kirundi during the first two or three years, only French is used thereafter through the end of the secondary school program. More extended use of Kirundi (Rundi) as a comedium in the future is likely as the number of schools grows and the shortage of trained personnel in that language is overcome.

Cambodia (Khmer Republic)

Both French and Khmer are widely used as languages in instruction at the secondary level with exclusive use of the latter growing as texts and teachers become available. Nevertheless, French is strongly coestablished in both public and private secondary education, and its rapid or widespread displacement is unlikely.

Cameroon

This is one of the few (and perhaps the only) West African countries where bilingual secondary schools (French and English) are part and parcel of the public school system. Experimentation with bilingual elementary education has also begun. Where monolingual education is pursued, it is usually in French. Thus far, the indigenous mother tongues have been ignored as media of secondary education, and as a result bilingual education has very shallow roots in indigenous life, even in the north, where French-Arabic bilingual education is available at the lycées in Garua and Marua and where some use of Fulfude has recently elicited interest. All in all, a trilingual educational system may yet develop in which fewer Western languages and more local languages are utilized as media, with the exact languages so recognized varying in different parts of the country.

Canada

The earlier voluntary experimentation with French-immersion schools at the elementary level, to help Anglo-Canadians really learn French, has recently spread to the secondary level as well, both in Montreal as well as elsewhere. English-immersion schools for Francophones are also being considered but are rare except in the private sector. For the immediate future, growth in bilingual education will be due to voluntary as well as mandatory increases in instruction via French for Anglo-Canadians and for "New Canadians" (Italians, Jews, etc.) who would not previously have been exposed to it. Successful results have been demonstrated (usually with highly motivated and academically superior students). Note that there are also many schools (particularly in New Brunswick, Newfoundland, and Nova Scotia but also in Quebec) that have two separate monolingual programs. These are not to be confused with bilingual education.

Central African Republic

In recent years Sango has been introduced as a comedium in elementary education, together with French. In future years it may be recognized at the secondary level as well.

Chad

The major exception to the completely French system of education, primary and secondary, in language and in culture, is the Collège Franco-Arabe with its bilingual and bicultural curriculum.

Chile

Neither the small number of foreign colony secondary schools nor the somewhat larger number of resident German secondary schools reach more than a tiny proportion of the mainstream student body. Bilingual education is also nonexistent for the roughly quarter million indigenous Indians.

China

Government efforts to promote the use of *p'u-t'ung-hua* (a speech form based on the grammar and lexicon of the North China dialects and the phonology of the Pekingese) have also resulted in its increased use as the language of instruction at the secondary level in southern and western areas of the country. Nevertheless, local languages are still utilized considerably, and bilingual education may, therefore, still be said to be the rule outside of North China. (The written form is, of course, the same everywhere, regardless of what spoken form is used.) Bilingual education involving foreign languages is still rare, except at specialized institutes of higher education.

Colombia

A modest number of English-Spanish and German-Spanish secondary schools exist, both for foreign colony and resident minority students. Neither the mainstream student nor a third of a million Indians is reached by either of these school types.

Costa Rica

Except for a small number of American- and German-sponsored schools, no bilingual secondary education is available. Even the foregoing do not reach the mainstream student.

Curaçao

Papamiento has already been admitted as a medium alongside Dutch in elementary education. It may yet displace Dutch entirely, here as well as elsewhere in the Netherlands Antilles; this is particularly likely if and when political independence is desired. At that time a Papamiento-Spanish or Papamiento-English bilingual educational system is quite likely, instead of the current administratively sponsored artificial stress on behalf of Dutch.

Cyprus

Bilingual secondary education is not unusual, both for foreign residents and for the Greek Cypriot majority. Turkish Cypriots alone generally receive their secondary education only in their mother tongue, although even among them English or French is beginning to be used instructionally.

Czechoslovakia

The two major population segments of the country tend to receive secondary education only in their respecitve mother tongue. However, Slovak students must take the Czech language quite seriously since it constitutes a required part of the written and oral high school leaving examination. More fully bilingual education (elementary and secondary) is available for the Hungarian, Ukranian, and Polish minorities.

Denmark

With very rare exceptions, the secondary schools for students of German ethnic background in Northern Schleswig are entirely in German (although the primary schools of the region are more frequently bilingual). Bilingual secondary education *is* provided in the Faroe Islands as well as in private foreign colony schools in Denmark proper. Greenland is listed separately below.

Dominican Republic

Some of the foreign colony secondary schools also provide elective instruction in Spanish (e.g., in "History of the Dominican Republic") for the benefit of those students who plan to attend a local university after graduation from high school.

Ecuador

Although a third of the population is Indian (largely Quechua speakers), no secondary bilingual education exists other than that provided by a small number of private schools for children of American, German, or other foreign colony extraction. Political changes may lead to recognition of the need for elementary bilingual education, probably with compensatory emphases.

Egypt

With the nationalization of ex-mission schools and other formerly French or English schools, some 25,000 students attend French-Arabic, English-Arabic, German-Arabic or Italian-Arabic secondary schools. The English-Arabic stream continues to increase and may ultimately become the model for academic and technical secondary education in the country generally. Finally, the alternation between local Egyptian and classicized Arabic adds to the bilingual climate of secondary education, both in the public schools as well as in the Koranic (religious) schools.

Ethiopia

English is the major language of instruction in most secondary schools, with Amharic language and literature being taught in Amharic. In addition, there are foreign colony schools (e.g., for students of French, Italian, German, or American origin), which also offer instruction via their home-country language, primarily to expatriate children but also to a small number of Ethiopian nationals. Indigenous religious schools use vernaculars as media in teaching Arabic and Geez. Recent political changes may result in long-sought recognition for Tigrinya, Gallinya, and perhaps other minority tongues.

Finland

Although sizable Swedish and Lappish minorities exist, no secondary bilingual education is available (notwithstanding the fact that there are many fine Swedish secondary schools). However, interest in bilingual education is quite marked in bilingual communities, particularly among those of Swedish ethnic affiliation. The youth organization of the Swedish People's Party has recommended that bilingual schools be established at least on an experimental basis.

France

Long the leading exponent of a hard-line policy vis-à-vis indigenous minorities (some 1,000,000 Bretons; 90,000 Basques; 250,000 Catalans; roughly 1,000,000 German-speaking Alsace-Lorrainers; 200,000 Netherlanders; millions of Occitans, and a quarter million Corsicans), France nevertheless has established several dozen French-German bilingual secondary school classes as a result of a cultural relations agreement with West Germany. Still struggling to overcome the memory of their "recognition" in education and broadcasting under the Nazi regime, the submerged regional languages may now be taught for a few hours/weeks as "extra" electives. There are, in addition, many foreign colony private secondary schools and even one (Ecole Active Bilingue) for French children *per se*, as well as another (Lycée Internationale-St. Germain-en-Laye) that is government-sponsored, albeit attended by both French and foreign colony children. There is, of course, strong governmental interest in bilingual education abroad in which French is employed as a medium. In this case charity begins and ends abroad.

Francophone Africa

Those parts of Francophone Africa that are not separately enumerated in this chapter are those with even fewer bilingual education opportunities currently and even smaller prospects for such in the near future. Nevertheless, almost every one of these countries has a language spoken by a quarter or more of the population (e.g., Congo Brazzaville: Kongo; Dahomey: Fon-Ewe; Gabon: Fang; Ivory Coast: Akan; Niger: Hausa; Togo-Ewe; Upper Volta: Mossi; Zaïre: Kongo). As the French educational and cultural heritage loosens up, with economic and social progress, it is likely that an increasing number of these and other major vernaculars will receive educational recognition as may Western languages of wider communication other than French.

Gambia

Almost all education is in English and is likely to remain so until a considerable expansion in educational opportunity becomes possible.

German (Federal Republic)

In addition to the expected foreign colony secondary schools (some of which, like the noted J. F. Kennedy School in West Berlin, have appreciable German enrollments), there is also one European School as well as nearly two dozen German-French bilingual secondary schools established in accord with a special cultural relations agreement with France. The Danish minority attends secondary schools that are entirely in Danish, and the North Frisians may *study* their mother tongue at the secondary level but have neither schools all-their-own nor real bilingual education. There is also a governmental agency supporting and monitoring schools abroad in which German is a comedium (see Appendix 2).

Germany (People's Republic)

The Sorbs enjoy two kinds of bilingual education, one in which both Sorbian and German are about equally employed as instructional media and the other in which Sorbian is utilized only for teaching Sorbian language and literature.

Ghana

Although primary education is usually bilingual in practice, and is to be so officially in the future (in English and in a local language; e.g., Akan, Ewe, Ga, Kasem, etc.), secondary education is almost everywhere exclusively in English. The only exception, as elsewhere in West Africa, is a Muslim Arabic boarding school (The Ahmadiyya Secondary School in Kumasi).

Great Britain: England

Until very recently (when experimentation with French-English "sections bilingues" was begun) England had almost no bilingual secondary education at all, except for those few schools maintained in the private sector by religious and foreign colony groups. Wales (Great Britain: Wales) and Ireland are listed separately in this chapter. There is little to report for Scotland at this time, although support for Scottish nationalism and separatism is growing and, along with it, interest in Gaelic. The latter has survived as a language of home, school, and community life only in the Hebrides and in a few isolated mainland points but may again come to receive wider attention of one kind or another.

Great Britain: Wales

The number of bilingual secondary schools is growing and their quality is improving, even though (or perhaps because) the most recent activity has been in the larger cities and towns that became Anglified a generation or more ago. Welsh teaching materials and teachers are now available for all subjects while achievement in and through English has not suffered in the least.

Greece

Until very recently secondary education was bilingual (actually: diglossic) by necessity, if only because students and teachers alike speak modern Greek whereas instruction was in a classicized variety thereof (Katharevusa). Currently "vernacularization" alone is in political favor. There are, in addition, foreign colony schools which are quite popular among local students (e.g., American, German, and French schools) as well as special bilingual schools for the Turkish minority in western Thrace. No bilingual secondary schools seem to exist for Albanians or for Romanians.

Greenland

Both Greenlandic and Danish are now used as media throughout the public educational system at both the elementary and secondary levels.

Guam

Although no bilingual secondary education exists, there is bilingual elementary education involving English and Chamorro. If interest in Chamorro-in-school continues to grow, bilingual secondary education is only a few years off.

Guatemala

Although over half of the population is Indian (involving four or five major languages), bilingual education is just getting under way, first at the elementary and at the teacher-training levels. However, bilingual secondary education is *not* uncommon in upper-class high schools in the capital city, with English, French, and German schools to pick from.

Guinea

French and a local language (most frequently Malinke) are already comedia at the elementary and secondary levels, and an intensification of this approach may be expected in the future.

Haiti

Foreign colony schools provide the only bilingual education at either the primary or the secondary level.

Honduras

Foreign colony schools provide the only bilingual education at either the elementary or the secondary level.

Hong Kong

There are literally dozens of Chinese-English bilingual secondary schools which provide the bulk of the secondary education on this island. The Chinese schools tend to place considerable emphasis on English, and the English schools tend to teach Chinese and Chinese history in Chinese (usually Cantonese, though Mandarin is also used as a medium).

India

Bilingual secondary education is rarer than one might expect in this highly multilingual country, since most high schools are either entirely in English or, increasingly, in one or another of the major vernaculars (even though Hindi or another vernacular will also be taught). There are, however, some 110 fully bilingual Central Schools, conducted by the central government for the children of its civil servants. These secondary schools teach the social sciences and humanities in Hindi and other sciences in English, regardless of what part of the country they may be in. While there are a small number of other bilingual secondary schools, there are a large number of schools which house two separate monolingual programs (e.g., one in Gujarati and one in Marathi). The latter are not to be confused with bilingual education.

Iran

Some foreign secondary schools, particularly those serving resident communities, also offer some instruction via Persian in addition to offering the bulk of their program through their "home" language (English, German, etc.). Bilingual secondary education has not been provided for the varied indigenous populations of the country.

Iraq

The common Arab-bloc alternation between vernacular and classicized Arabic obtains, as does a growing attention to English, particularly in conjunction with the sciences. No special bilingual secondary education is provided for the considerable and alienated Kurdish minority.

Ireland

Secondary schools in which some subjects are taught in Irish and others in English are still somewhat rare, since the language revival movement long concentrated (without noteworthy success) on all-Irish schools. A recent government policy may lead to converting many of the all-Irish secondary schools—established during an earlier and more nationalistic period—to bilingual schools. If the all-English secondary streams are also guided toward bilingual education, then the resulting more modest expectations (relative to the original one of making Irish the first language of the country) may be more fully met. On the other hand, both of the above changes may have only "ceremonial Irish" in mind and could lead to the final abandonment of any serious role for Irish in education.

Israel

Three types of bilingual secondary education exist as exceptions to the monolingual rule which governs almost all of Jewish and Arab education in the country. For Arab youngsters there are a small number of secondary schools in which Hebrew literature and a few other subjects are taught in Hebrew. For recently arrived Jewish youngsters, there are a few special high schools offering partial instruction via the mother tongues of the newcomers. For ultra-Orthodox Jewish youngsters, there are secondary schools (tolerated rather than officially recognized or supported) that are conducted primarily in Yiddish (rather than in Hebrew). In addition to the foregoing, there are a few foreign colony schools that also offer some instruction via Hebrew in addition to instruction via their home-country vernacular (English, French, etc.), as well as a few village schools for Circassians who received permission in 1973 to utilize their vernacular as a comedium in their schools. Thus, bilingual education is still largely unknown in Israel, except as a memory of the past. It may come again, to begin with because of Anglo-Jewish and Arabic considerations.

Italy

Two of the northern border areas offer bilingual secondary education, namely, Valdoste (French and Italian) and the Bolzanei areas (German, Italian, and Ladino). Other areas offer only non-Italian monolingual education, either in German (Sudtirol) or in Slovenian (Venezia Giulia). There is also a European School (in Varese) and an International School (in Milan), but neither bilingual nor mother-tongue education is available for the one and a half million Sardinians, the 260,000 Albanians (not to mention the 800,000 Friulans and the 200,000 Corsicans, most of whom have come to view themselves as speakers of a nonstandard regional variety of Italian, rather than as speakers of separate languages). All in all, although there are also a number of foreign colony and religious-minority bilingual secondary schools, the mainstream of Italian youngsters cannot share in the benefits of bilingual education.

Japan

Except for foreign colony and mission schools, many of which serve indigenous students as well (or even primarily), there is no bilingual secondary education in Japan (except for study of the Chinese classics in the upper secondary schools, made possible by the shared writing system). In recent years interest in such education, particularly in connection with a Western language, has become evident.

Jordan

Many public secondary schools are bilingual, in Arabic and in English. Private schools, on the other hand, are required to teach Arabic and history and civics in Arabic. Both types of schools prepare pupils for the General Certificate of Education (England). The alternation between classicized and local vernacular Arabic, common in other Arab countries, is also found in Jordan.

Kenya

English is clearly the dominant language of instruction at the secondary level, but the amount of attention given to Swahili is increasing. Swahili is often used as the language of instruction in courses dealing with Swahili literature, and this use is expected to increase further.

Kuwait

Bilingual secondary education involving both vernacular and classicized Arabic, on the one hand, and English on the other hand is growing rapidly, with this same pattern being extended into higher education as well.

Laos

Some thirty secondary schools, a large proportion of all secondary schools in the country, are bilingual (Lao and French). As the number of Lao textbooks and teachers increases, the French component in secondary education is expected to decrease, but it will probably be maintained to some extent in many secondary schools. Thus the six newly established Fa Ngm Comprehensive High Schools are primarily Lao-medium schools with either English or French as a second working language.

Lebanon

Secondary education is typically bilingual, certain subjects being taught in Arabic (e.g., religion, civics, philosophy, Arabic, history) and others being taught in French (or, less frequently, in English). In addition, a large number of foreign colony and mission schools serve local students as well and function partially in Arabic and partially in the vernacular of their mother country (English, French, German, Armenian, Italian).

Lesotho

Thus far, English is the only official and normal language of secondary instruction. There are signs that interest in Lesotho is increasing rapidly (it is already used at the primary level wherever it is the vernacular) and may reach the secondary level before long.

Liberia

Although only 40% of the population speaks English natively, the latter is the only language recognized for educational purposes. Mande would seem to have the best prospects of recognition as a comedium, it being the mother tongue of 44% of the indigenous population.

Libya

The strong postwar emphasis on English alongside of Arabic has more recently been revised in favor of an all-Arabic approach. Such an approach has traditionally been followed in the Koranic schools. Both Koranic and public schools reveal alternation between classicized and vernacular Arabic. As elsewhere in North Africa, there is no recognition of Berber in secondary education.

Luxembourg

A European School exists in Luxembourg, as do a few foreign colony schools. Otherwise, the majority of the local youngsters speak Litzembergish, pray in German, and receive their education entirely in French.

Malagasy

Malagach is currently utilized only in early elementary education, but there is growing interest in its utilization in higher grades as well. Currently it is only available as an elective (rather than as a medium of instruction) at the secondary level.

Malawi

Bilingual education in Malawi at the elementary level involves Nyanga (Chinjanja), the mother tongue of some 60% of the population, in addition to English. Its extension to the secondary level is predicted.

Malaysia

Although the official tendency is to stress Malay and Malay only in all public education, there is still substantial bilingual education involving English, Chinese, and (more rarely) Tamil as well. Ultimately, a program in Malay and English is the one most likely to obtain official support.

Mali

In previous years both French and Arabic were media of elementary and secondary education. In recent years Arabic has been deemphasized. The future growth of bilingual education may well involve Bambara, the mother tongue of a third of the population.

Malta

Both English and Maltese are employed as media of secondary education, with English still being dominant because of its greater association with literacy, and with pride in Maltese and its educational-literary use still growing.

Mauritania

With Arabic as its national language, with a school program modeled after the French, and with increased contacts desired with Anglophone Africa, all three indicated languages are recognized as languages of instruction at the secondary level. In practical terms most instruction is in French. A few Koranic schools function entirely in Arabic.

Mexico

Foreign colony and resident-minority secondary schools abound in the larger cities and serve a small proportion of the local student body as well. Nevertheless, no bilingual secondary education is available for the vast majority of Mexican youngsters, nor for any of the four and a quarter million Indians who constitute nearly ten percent of the total population. For the latter, a small proportion of whom know no Spanish, transitional and compensatory elementary bilingual education is once again receiving limited experimental attention, after over a century of on-again, off-again policy changes in this connection. Most Mexican youngsters inevitably learn a good bit of English (largely informally, from tourists and mass media), but no instructional use is made of this language due to historical and political sensitivities.

Micronesia

Bilingual education at the elementary level has just begun in Palau, Ponape, and Rota, and its spread to other areas is anticipated. The possibility of its use at the secondary level still seems remote but may yet materialize.

Morocco

French is the dominant language in Moroccan lycées. However, Arabic is the language of instruction in specifically Arabic subjects such as Islamic religion, Arabic language and literature, and history. Many Moroccan public secondary schools engage in Arabic-only instruction (*enseignement originel*), as do a few private lycées. There are a few foreign schools (particularly in Tangier and Casablanca) offering instruction in Spanish, Italian, French, or English, but few, if any, of these are bilingual schools. There has been no recognition of Berber in secondary education.

Nepal

Nepali is the compulsory medium of instruction as well as of examination for the School Leaving Certificate, but English is also used as a medium in much of secondary education. There are also Sanskrit schools which are not rigidly graded and in which much time is devoted to the study of Sanskrit religious writings. No bilingual education is available specifically recognizing minority languages.

Netherlands

There are a European School, an International School, various foreign colony and religious-minority schools, but, on the whole, no bilingual secondary education, neither for the mainstream child nor for the half million Frisians. The latter have recently succeeded in obtaining permission to use Frisian in elementary education, and demands for its use in secondary education in the future are to be expected.

Nicaragua

A few foreign colony schools (American, German) exhaust the current opportunities for bilingual secondary education in this country.

Nigeria

Vernacular languages are used instructionally in the early primary grades but have not yet been officially admitted for more advanced purposes. Ultimately, only Hausa, Yoruba, and Ibo are likely to be acknowledged regionally for secondary education, alongside English. Koranic schools in the northern region utilize Arabic and some Hausa.

Norway

Whether conducted in Bokmål or in Nynorsk, primary and secondary schools teach "the other Norwegian" as well. Nevertheless, the 15% or so whose education is predominantly Nynorsk tend to learn quite a bit of Bokmål, while the 85% whose main language is Bokmål tend to find their exposure to Nynorsk to be less productive. No secondary school gives instruction in Lappish, either as a medium or as a subject, and at the elementary level it is used for "transitional" purposes only.

Pakistan

The current stress on Urdu and English is likely to witness accommodation to one or more regional languages in the future, as has been the case in India. Whether or not this accommodation will lead to a lesser stress on English remains to be seen.

Papua-New Guinea

At the moment all secondary instruction is in English, whether the schools are under public or mission control. However, with independence, the teaching of Pidgin and of local vernaculars has been officially included in the syllabi for primary education, and their use and/or instruction at the high school level is to be expected.

Paraguay

Although 90% or more of the population speaks Guaraní, only Spanish currently is recognized for secondary school instructional purposes. Nevertheless, interest in Guaraní is widespread, and this is likely to be recognized as democratization and modernization become stronger forces in the country as a whole. For the time being, a few resident German schools and an even smaller number of foreign colony schools represent the entire secondary bilingual education picture in one of the most bilingual countries of the world.

Peru

Notwithstanding the fact that some 40% of the population is Indian and that Quechua has theoretically been made an obligatory subject at all levels, bilingual education of any kind is still all too rare. At the elementary level, programs and personnel providing such education for Quechua and Aymara speakers are currently being expanded. At the secondary level, it is still restricted almost entirely to schools for resident European minorities (Germans, Jews) and for foreign colony populations of a more fluctuating nature (largely American).

Philippines

Since 1975 Pilipino, the national language, has replaced English as a medium of instruction for civics, work education, health education, and Pilipino language and literature in all public elementary schools, with secondary schools scheduled to follow suit within a few years. English is to remain the medium of instruction for mathematics, science, and English language and literature in all grades, elementary and secondary, with local vernaculars permitted only transitional use in the first and second grades. Arabic alone may enjoy further recognition beyond that accorded the local vernaculars, due to its symbolic significance to the militant Muslim minority (none of whom speak it natively).

Poland

Public bilingual secondary schools exist for youngsters of some of the more numerous minorities (and bilingual elementary schools for youngsters of several smaller minorities as well). No such schools exist for mainstream Polish youngsters, although Russian is given considerable attention as a required additional language.

Portugal

It remains to be seen whether the new more liberal regime will encourage bilingual education for mainstream Portuguese youngsters. In the meantime, only foreign colony youngsters or resident-minority youngsters (the latter being primarily German) have the benefit of bilingual education. Portugal has exported to the rest of the former Luso-world a lack of appreciation for bilingual education which the erstwhile colonies may overcome sooner than the mother country itself.

Portuguese Africa

Until the recent liberation, vernacular education was available only at the early elementary level and even then only for pupils characterized as "lacking knowledge of the Portuguese language and further indispensable conditions for entering standard education." Now, with new educational policies being planned, new opportunities for bilingual education are present at all levels.

Rhodesia

All secondary education is still in English, but the need for transitional use of African vernaculars is recognized at the elementary level. If the political system is democratized the need for vernacular or bilingual education at the secondary level will be tackled.

Romania

Secondary bilingual education is available for larger minority groups (primarily Hungarians, Germans), although elementary bilingual education is available for many smaller groups as well (Serbs, Bulgarians, Croatians, Ukranians, Czechs, Slovaks, etc.). Hungarians, as the largest minority, also have an opportunity for bilingual higher technical and professional education, as do, to a lesser extent, German speakers. Mainstream Romanian youngsters receive a heavy dose of Russian but no bilingual education as such.

Rwanda

Kinyarwanda is utilized instructionally in the premier cycle (first four years of the six-year elementary school course) and may yet be officially admitted alongside French for use in more advanced instruction. Some future role for Swahili is also not out of the question. All such developments depend on prior social and economic change.

Saudi Arabia

Both English and Arabic are widely utilized as media of instruction with a classicized variety of the latter being held to more consistently than in most parts of the Arab world.

Senegal

Wolof has already been admitted into elementary instruction alongside French and seems destined for more advanced instructional use as well.

Sierra Leone

English has not yet been dislodged from its exclusive position in secondary education, but increased consideration is being given to Krio and to other indigenous languages (e.g., Mande) at the elementary level.

Singapore

All public secondary schools are bilingual, utilizing various combinations of English, Chinese, Malay, and Tamil. The English-Chinese and English-Malay combinations predominate, and the instructional time allocated to the second language (whatever that may be) is now 40%. "Singapore's only natural resource is its people and the government is eager that they be able to communicate effectively with each other and with the outside world."

Somalia

Until recently most secondary education used Arabic (except for foreign colony students) and English. Now that Somali has been proclaimed the national language, it may be expected that before long both it and Arabic will be utilized in secondary education, with or without English.

South Africa

Despite the fact that (a) nearly 80% of the white population speaks both English and Afrikaans, and (b) 43% of school pupils speak both English and Afrikaans at home, the policy of the National Party which came into power in 1948 has been progressively to assign English and Afrikaans mother-tongue children to separate schools, even when they live in the same community. Today, only some 2% of white children receive bilingual education, whereas 21% received such education in the 1930's. Only "Bantus" living outside of the "homelands" may receive bilingual education combining both of the above languages in approximately equal proportions (with English somewhat predominant). "Bantus" living in the "homelands" are taught almost exclusively in English, although all have received at least the first four years of their primary education through one of the Bantu languages (e.g., Zulu, Xhosa, Tswana, Tsonga, etc.).

South West Africa

The language pattern established for "Bantus" in South Africa is reversed with greater stress on Afrikaans and a marked tendency to make even less use of African vernaculars.

Spain

Except for foreign colony schools (American, French, British) and schools serving resident foreigners (Germans), no bilingual secondary education is permitted. The chief losers thereby are not so much the seven million Catalans, the 600,000 Basques or the nearly three million Gallegos (Galicians) but the millions of mainstream Spaniards. Some attention to Catalan at the elementary level was recently legalized; permission to experiment with Basque has been granted in one or two instances; and private elementary schools concerned with either are now tolerated. Future liberalizations of the regime may be expected to permit and even to support bilingual secondary education as well.

Sri Lanka (Ceylon)

Most secondary education is in the mother tongue (either Sinhalese or Tamil) with science courses, mathematics, and foreign languages continuing to be taught in English, at least as long as suitable vernacular texts and teachers are in short supply. Sinhalese-Tamil bilingual education does not yet seem to be in the offing.

Sudan

The language of primary education has been Arabic, while that of secondary education has been English. With the recent Arabization of Sudanese official and cultural life, secondary education may well become bilingual, although the partial displacement of English (except in the southern region) is also a possibility, at least to some extent, as is the partial introduction of minority vernaculars as media at some future date. Koranic schools employ Arabic alone.

Swaziland

Elementary education is still primarily in English or in Swazi, with Afrikaans available as a subject in either case. Secondary education is normally in English with both Afrikaans and Zulu available as subjects. Additional use of Zulu as a medium is expected, but the displacement of English is unlikely.

Sweden

In addition to foreign colony (American, French) and international schools, there are also a few foreign-resident secondary schools (e.g., for Estonians, Germans, etc.) and a few Swedish-Finnish and Swedish-Lappish secondary schools.

Switzerland

Although renowned for its multilingual central government organization and for its multilingual schools for foreign students, the vast majority of the Swiss receive their education (elementary or secondary) entirely in their own mother tongue ("German," French, or Italian). Some recent minor exceptions for Italian and Romansh students, if continued, would represent a significant departure from the sensitive balance that is Switzerland, as would incipient efforts to teach reading and writing of Swiss-German.

Syria

In addition to vernacular and classicized Arabic, there is also frequent use of French and, more recently, of English in secondary education. Total Arabization in the future is, nevertheless, a possibility.

Taiwan

When political democratization arrives, Taiwanese will need to be seriously considered for a role in elementary education and, possibly alongside some form(s) of Chinese, in connection with secondary education.

Tanzania

English and Swahili are joint languages of instruction with the goal of using Swahili as a medium for as many subjects as possible and as soon as possible. Physical education, citizenship, history, and the first year of high school math tend to be taught in Swahili, whereas the remainder of the science curriculum is taught in English. English may yet be displaced further as a medium once a full assortment of Swahili texts and teachers are available, but even then English would remain the medium for instruction in English literature in addition to English *per se.*

Thailand

With the exception of foreign colony or international schools, and the rare mission school for which special arrangements are in effect (e.g., Assumption College, Bangkok), only Thai is permitted as a medium of instruction. The resultant academic isolation has just begun to be counteracted by the establishment of an English-medium M.A. program in economics at Thammasat University. The experience gained in this connection may lead to experimentation with bilingual (Thai-English) education also at the secondary level. Public bilingual secondary education for Chinese speakers (in the Bangkok area) and for Malay speakers (in the southern region) may become possible if the political situation of these two large minorities continues to improve. A modicum of such education under Chinese auspices already exists but has long been regarded with suspicion. Other minorities receive even scantier attention insofar as bilingual education is concerned.

Tonga

This tiny island republic has established bilingual secondary education as the norm (English and Tonga) for its public high schools. The problem of texts and teachers in Tonga is as yet unsolved.

Tunisia

The secondary school system is bilingual, with Arabic, history, religious and civic education, and Islamic thought being taught in Arabic and all other subjects being taught in French. The alternation between classicized and vernacular Arabic is considerable, as might be expected. The attachment to French is still strong but has, of late, come under increased questioning.

Turkey

Except for international, foreign colony and resident-foreigner schools, the only bilingual secondary education in Turkey is that accorded the students of Galatasaray School (Turkish-French) and the Istanbul Erkek Lisesi (Turkish-German). All private secondary schools for minorities (Greeks, Armenians) have been closed since 1971, and with them, the bulk of bilingual education in Turkey has vanished. No such education was ever made available for Kurds.

Uganda

Although the Swahilization of education is still more a goal than a reality, an ultimate balance is likely which will involve far less English domination of the curriculum than is the case today.

Union of Soviet Socialist Republics

In the Russian Republic, bilingual secondary education takes the shape of foreign-language-medium schools for elitist youngsters. Elsewhere, for larger non-Russian populations, it takes the form of Russian and mother-tongue secondary schools as an alternative to the Russian-only schools that are most widely available. Only in unusual cases (e.g., highly mixed populations, very small minorities, or minorities exposed to special punitive policies) has education in Russian displaced the mother tongues from general use. Thus, bilingual secondary education for the eighteen largest non-Russian populations has tended to make Russian everyone's "additional" language (particularly in technical domains) alongside the mother tongues that are also used as media (particularly in ethnic domains). In some areas, as for example the Baltic states, this has necessitated the extension of the curriculum for an additional year, but this has been considered an acceptable price to pay for the advantage of mother-tongue retention plus Russian language mastery.

United States of America

Although there are hardly as many such programs as there should be, particularly if mainstream Anglo-American youngsters are considered, there are far more than most people expect. The ISBSE—the research forerunner of the present volume—located 370 programs under public and private auspices in 1972-73 alone, and the number is still growing. The major support for public programs is the Bilingual Education Act (Title VII), but it has thus far also restricted bilingual education, unfairly and unwisely, to the poor and to English-deficient groups. Similarly disadvantageous to bilingual education is the restriction on English as a medium in Puerto Rico. The golden mean obviously requires successive approximations.

Uruguay

Foreign colony and resident-foreigner schools represent the entire secondary bilingual education picture in Uruguay. Even this limited opportunity is headed for difficulties in view of the increased governmental supervision in order to enforce official opposition to the use of languages other than Spanish.

Venezuela

The only bilingual secondary education offered is that available in foreign colony and resident-foreigner schools.

Vietnam

North Vietnam quickly displaced French entirely from the school program, elementary and secondary. South Vietnam did so more slowly, but with similar results, except in higher education where traces of French instruction may still be found. While the impact of English in South Vietnam was culturally far greater than that of either Chinese or Russian in North Vietnam, the recent unification of the country under Northern hegemony can be expected to result in many years of monolingual Vietnamization of education.

West Indies

Although the former Federation of the West Indies exists no longer—Barbados, Jamaica, Trinidad, and Guyana having each gone its own way politically—the common problems continue. Among them is the problem of nonstandard varieties of English and of their schoolworthiness alongside English itself. Certainly these varieties are often heard in the schools, informally and unofficially, and their recognition cannot be long delayed, whether or not a form of bilingual education is thereby said to be in effect.

Yugoslavia

Bilingual secondary education tends to be not uncommon in Slovenia and Macedonia but quite unusual in Serbia, Croatia, Bosnia-Herzegovina and Montenegro where Serbo-Croatian alone (unofficially a single amalgam) is used as a medium. Larger minorities also enjoy the benefits of secondary bilingual education, particularly Hungarians, Romanians, and Albanians.

Zambia

Although several vernaculars are employed in early elementary education, English alone, thus far, is the only medium of secondary instruction.

It is clear from the foregoing sketches that, although bilingual secondary education may only be one twentieth as frequent as bilingual elementary education, it is nevertheless far more available than has commonly been imagined and, indeed, is becoming more so. If the International Study of Bilingual Secondary Education was able to locate some 1,200 such units, even though it was generally unable to receive responses on specific units either from Arab-bloc or Soviet-bloc countries, and even though replies from Third World countries were often beset by postal service problems, then there might easily be twice that number of secondary bilingual education units throughout the world at the present time. Given the relative infrequency of secondary education *per se* in most countries, even in this day and age, a defensible conclusion would be that if there are some 2,500 bilingual secondary education units the world over today, then there may well be some 50,000 *elementary* bilingual education units! All in all, therefore, bilingual education is a major worldwide phenomenon, and its far from insignificant secondary education component is certainly growing, both in quantitative and in qualitative terms.

However, it is equally clear, and particularly so from the foregoing country-by-country sketches, that bilingual education as a whole and bilingual secondary education in particular are not evenly distributed throughout the world. There are countries in which it is exceedingly rare and others in which it is the general practice. Indeed, there are countries that represent almost every degree of prevalence of bilingual education imaginable between these two extremes. Thus, a grouping or clustering of countries would seem to be called for, in order to clarify, at least somewhat, the current circumstances that tend to be related to the absence or presence of bilingual (secondary) education. Such a grouping is attempted in Table 6.1 below. Readers are urged to attempt their own hypothetical groupings and to seek explanatory dimensions pertaining to them by referring to the descriptive data presented in Chapter VII and in other cross-polity compendia.

Bilingual education is least prevalent in Category I countries and most prevalent in Category V countries. What are some of the differences between the countries of these two clusters? Certainly cultural homogeneity itself does not seem to be a strong differentiating factor between them. There are highly diversified countries in both clusters (e.g., Burma and Sierra Leone in Cluster I and Cameroon and Malaysia in Cluster V). There are also countries of great cultural homogeneity in both clusters (e.g., Australia in Cluster I and Greece in Cluster V). Neither degree of industrialization and urbanization nor modernization more generally seem to well characterize or differentiate between the countries in one cluster vs. those in another. Indeed, it would seem that a rather

Table 6.1: The Relative Prevalence of Bilingual Education in 117 Countries*

Cluster I	Cluster II	Cluster III	Cluster IV	Cluster V
Australia	Bolivia	Argentina	Afghanistan	Algeria
Burma	Botswana	Brazil	Albania	Cambodia
Chad+	Burundi+	Chile	Austria	Cameroon
Gambia	Curaçao	Colombia	Bangladesh	Egypt
Ghana	Ecuador	Costa Rica	−Belgium	Gr. Brit.: Wales
Liberia	Finland	Dom. Rep.	Bulgaria	Greece
Libya+	Guam	Gr. Brit.: Eng.	Canada	Greenland
Rhodesia	Guatemala	Haiti	Cent. Afr. Rep.	Hong Kong
Sierra Leone	Kenya	Honduras	China	Iraq
Taiwan	Lesotho	Iran	Cyprus	Jordan
Vietnam (PR)	Malagasy	Japan	Czech.	Kuwait
West Indies	Mali	Luxembourg	Denmark	Laos
Zambia	Micronesia	Mexico	Ethiopia	Lebanon
	Nigeria	Netherlands	−France	Malaysia
	Papua-NG	Nicaragua	−Germany (FR)	Malta
	Paraguay	Peru	Germany (PR)	Morocco
	Port. Africa	Portugal	Guinea	Philippines
	Rwanda	Spain	−India	Saudi Arabia
	Senegal	Switzerland	Ireland	Singapore
	S.W. Africa	Thailand	−Israel	Sri Lanka
	Sudan	Turkey	−Italy	Syria
	Swaziland	−Uruguay	Malawi	Tanzania
	Uganda	−USA	−Mauritania	Tonga
		Venezuela	Nepal	Tunisia
			Norway	
			Pakistan	
			−Poland	
			Romania	
			Somalia	
			Rep. of S. Africa	
			Sweden	
			USSR	
			Yugoslavia	
n = 13	n = 23	n = 24	n = 33	n = 24

*Pluses and minuses are used to indicate rather more or less bilingual education than in most other countries in the same category. Clusters, such as "Francophone Africa" and "Portuguese Africa," are not listed in this table although they *are* annotated in the body of the present chapter.

complex set of considerations must be referred to, many of them dealing with current and recent historical and political considerations rather than with socioeconomic factors alone. Several of the countries in Cluster V are marked by rather well-established diglossia relationships, i.e., by widespread and stable within-group bilingualism. The reasons for such societal bilingualism vary from the continuing impact of classical traditions through to the recent (and even continuing) political presence of a great power. Not only are both of these factors more attenuated in Cluster I, but, where present, internal political considerations have also kept them from coming to the fore. There is also a degree of peripherality to many of the countries in Cluster I. They more often than not tend to be at the outskirts of spheres of interest rather than at their center or at their intersection. Perhaps, as such, it has been easier to impose a monoethnic stance upon them without internal repercussions.

Certainly the artificiality of seeming cultural homogeneity is also evident with respect to the countries in Clusters II and III. Both of these clusters are marked by countries with neglected minority mother tongues. In Cluster II there are currently faint rumblings of recognition for these languages, particularly at the elementary level of education.

In Cluster III such rumblings are far fainter if present at all; nevertheless, the latter cluster reveals far more bilingual education of the foreign colony and language of wider communication types. Thus, the countries of Cluster II may yet achieve bilingual education within a decade or so, whereas many of those in Cluster III may vacillate between decreasing it (as their foreign colonies shrink by assimilation or expulsion) and increasing it (as neglected indigenous minorities gain recognition).

Cluster IV countries are also marked by a great deal of heterogeneity in most obvious respects. In comparison to Cluster III it contains no Latin American representation. In comparison to Category V it includes far fewer members of the Arab bloc and far more of the Soviet bloc. Cluster IV, on the whole, consists of countries that have already recognized minority mother tongues for educational purposes, even in the absence of long-established diglossia. Nevertheless, most of these countries have quite a distance to go before bilingual education, particularly at the secondary level, is as common as its adherents would like it to be. The fact that many of these countries are considerably industrialized should not be overlooked and may figure in their further progress toward more widespread bilingual education for majority-group children as well as those hailing from minority backgrounds.

All in all, the relative prevalence of bilingual education within a particular country's educational system is not an easily predictable phenomenon. Many factors tend to contribute partially and not completely to this phenomenon. Traditional diglossia, the leverage available to organized minorities during periods of more rapid change, and the operation of influential communication patterns or historical ties associated with languages of wider communication all seem to be important positive forces in fostering bilingual education. Oddly enough, more and more of the world would seem to be characterizable in the above terms, and, as a result, one would expect more and more countries to be characterized by a greater prevalence of bilingual education, particularly those currently in Categories II and III. At times, bilingual education will be espoused by "liberation movements," and at times it will be abandoned by them, depending on the degree to which erstwhile "oppressor languages" can be redefined as desirable languages of wider communication and as valuable resources. In the long run bilingual education combines and serves both vernacular and other-than-vernacular functions, and as such it has appeal to a wide spectrum of political, social, and cultural movements rather than only to those of a particular coloration.

For some educational systems (and, more and more, educational systems and national boundaries are coterminous) bilingual education is an alternative option equivalent to vernacularization or self-recognition, an educational trend which began with the modern period of history and which has not yet run its course.

For other educational systems, bilingual education is an alternative option equivalent to internationalization or other-recognition, an educational trend which began in the earliest forms of elitist education. Since both of these trends and needs tend to characterize almost all segments of mankind today, it is not possible to neatly categorize or classify countries and regions in connection with them. Even so seemingly obvious a claim as the one that identifies bilingual education with bicultural education has its limitations (e.g., in the traditional Arabic diglossia case or in the more modern imposition of two equally foreign Western languages on many African and Asian students). We must not be surprised at the diversity of bilingual education or at the multiplicity of settings in which it is encountered and of purposes that it serves. Indeed, if the sociology of bilingual education teaches us anything, it teaches us precisely this: because of its basic multifacetedness, bilingual education has something to contribute to each and every country and group in the world.

The charts in this chapter are reproduced
from *World Data Handbook,*
Washington, D.C.: U.S. Government Printing Office, 1972.

THE NATIONS OF THE WORLD:
SOME SOCIAL AND ECONOMIC CHARACTERISTICS

CHAPTER VII

COUNTRY	LAND			PEOPLE									
	Total sq mi (000)	Agricultural[1]		Population				Labor Force			Infant deaths per 1,000 live births	Life expectancy (yrs)	Average daily caloric intake
		Percent of total	Acres per capita	1970 (mill)	Growth rate (%)	Density per sq mi	Urban (%)	In agr (%)	In ind (%)	Literacy (%)			
North America													
United States	3,600	46	5.0	205	1.1	57	74	4	65	98	21	70	3,200
Canada	3,800	6	5.0	22	1.8	6	74	7	60	97	19.3	70	3,200
Latin America													
Argentina	1,072	64	18.0	24.1	1.4	23	79	19	32	91	58	67	2,920
Barbados	0.2	70	0.3	.26	1.3	1,290	45	na	na	91		65	na
Bolivia	424	13	8.0	4.7	2.4	11	36	48	na	40	108	50	1,980
Brazil	3,286	16	3.7	91.9	2.7	28	54	52	13	61 (over 14 yrs)	92	57	2,690
British Honduras	9	3	1.3	.12	2.5	14	51	26	21	89	54	60	na
Chile	292	19	3.9	9.3	1.9	33	74	27	24	84	100	61	2,900
Colombia	440	17	2.3	21.1	3.2	48	55	47	19	73 (over 15 yrs)	80	60	2,200
Costa Rica	20	30	2.2	1.7	3.2	89	34	49	18	84	87	65	2,610
Cuba	44	55	na	8.4	2.0	195	60	34	23	60	na	na	na
Dominican Republic	19	40	1.2	4.1	3.0	230	37	61	11	65 (over 15 yrs)	80	58	1,900
Ecuador	109	17	1.9	6.1	34	56	46	53	18	68	87	52	2,020
El Salvador	83	59	0.9	3.4	3.4	410	38	60	17	50 (over 10 yrs)	59	58	1,840
Guatemala	42	23	1.2	5.3	2.9	130	34	65	14	38	94	49	2,220
Guyana	83	15	10	.76	3.0	9	30	30	20	80	43	61	2,180
Haiti	11	31	0.4	4.9	2.0	490	17	83	6	10	na	48	1,780E
Honduras	43	38	3.9	2.7	3.4	63	28	67	10	45 (over 15 yrs)	48	49	2,010
Jamaica	4	42	0.6	2.0	1.9	470	36	36	22	82	33	65	2,280
Mexico	762	52	5.0	50.1	3.3	66	60	46	9	76	66	61	2,570
Nicaragua	50	14	2.3	1.9	3.2	38	45	60	15	50 (over 15 yrs)	55	50	2,350
Panama	29	18	2.4	1.4	3.0	50	50	40	10	78 (over 10 yrs)	56	66	2,500
Paraguay	157	27	11.0	2.4	3.1	15	36	54	6	74	84	58	2,520E
Peru	496	23	5.0	13.6	3.1	27	49	45	18	61	62	54	2,340
Surinam	63	1	0.3	0.40	3.5	6	38	25	12	80	48	65	2,350
Trinidad & Tobago	2	28	0.4	1.0	1.2	530	53	21	20	89	36	66	2,450E
Uruguay	72	84	13.0	2.9	1.3	40	80	21	na	91	50	69	3,170
Venezuela	352	24	5.0	10.4	3.5	30	72	32	na	76	46	66	2,490

[1]Consists of (a) arable land under permanent crops and (b) permanent meadows and pastures.

[2]GNP data in constant 1969 prices, unadjusted for inequalities in purchasing power between countries.
Growth rates: average annual growth rate, 1960-70, except as noted.

Primary language of central govt.	Ethno-Cultural Heterogeneity above 15%	ECONOMY									COUNTRY
		Gross National Product[2]				Imports		Exports			
		1970 ($ bill)	Growth rate (%)	1970 per capita ($)	Per capita growth (%)	1969 ($ mill)	Percent from U.S. 1970	1969 ($ mill)	1967-69 primary (%)	Percent to U.S. 1970	
											North America
Eng		977	4.8	4,754	3.7	59,300	0	63,600	varied	0	United States
Eng, Fr	+	81	5.0	3,770	2.0	13,308	71	16,400	varied	65.3	Canada
											Latin America
Span		21.0	3.8	871	2.3	1,576	25	1,612	26 meat 22 grain	9.0	Argentina
Eng		0.13 (1969)	na	523 (1969)	na	114	18	40	41 sugar 12 petrol	22.0	Barbados
Span	+	0.9	5.1	201	2.8	167	33	182	52 tin 13 petrol	15.0	Bolivia
Port		33.7	5.5	366	2.8	2,265	32	2,311	39 coffee 7 cotton	25.0	Brazil
Eng		.05E (1969)	na	410E (1969)	na	30	33 (1969)	17	40 sugar 19 citrus	36.0 (1969)	British Honduras
Span		6.3	4.1	682	2.2	902	33	1,069	76 copper	14.0	Chile
Span		6.6	5.1	313	1.9	723	48	672	61 coffee 9 petrol	35.0	Colombia
Span		0.9	6.3	509	3.0	245	35	190	33 coffee 26 bann	42.0	Costa Rica
Span		3.5	1.7 (1965-70)	409	na	1,095 (1968)	..	650 (1968)	85 sugar	..	Cuba
Span		1.3	3.7	332	0.7	243	52	184	54 sugar 11 coffee	84.0	Dominican Republic
Span	+	1.8	5.1	294	1.7	262	33	183	52 bann 17 coffee	44.0	Ecuador
Span		1.0	5.8	288	2.4	209	30	202	45 coffee	21.0	El Salvador
Span	+	1.7	5.1	326	2.0	250	35	262	33 coffee 16 cotton	28.0	Guatemala
Eng		.23 (1969)	na	317	na	118	21 (1969)	121	44 bauxite 32 sugar	26.0 (1969)	Guyana
Fr		.42 (1968)	na	91 (1968)	na	40	53	37	39 coffee 13 bauxite	65.0	Haiti
Span		0.7	4.6	249	1.2	184	41	167	46 bann 11 coffee	52.0	Honduras
Eng		1.1	4.6	556	2.5	443	43	289	51 bauxite 18 sugar	51.0	Jamaica
Span		31.6	7.1	630	3.8	2,078	64	1,430	13 cotton	60.0	Mexico
Span		0.7	6.2	390	3.1	177	36	155	35 cotton 14 coffee	31.0	Nicaragua
Span	+	1.0	8.0	693	5.0	294	38	116	56 bann	64.0	Panama
Span	+	0.6	4.7	245	1.6	82	23	51	29 meat 19 lumber	14.0	Paraguay
Span	+	5.4	4.7	396	1.6	597	32	864	28 copper 26 fish	33.0	Peru
Dutch		.24 (1969)	na	617	na	110	39 (1969)	120	88 bauxite & alum	46.0 (1969)	Surinam
Eng	+	.77 (1969)	4.5 (1965-70)	751 (1969)	na	483	16	473	77 petrol & prod	48.0	Trinidad & Tobago
Span		2.0	1.1	705	2.7	197	13	200	42 wool 30 meat	9.0	Uruguay
Span		10.1	5.9	974	2.4	1,817	48	2,523	92 petrol	45.0	Venezuela

Nations of the World   79

COUNTRY	LAND			PEOPLE								
	Total sq mi (000)	Agricultural[1]		Population			Labor Force			Infant deaths per 1,000 live births[1]	Life expect-ancy (yrs)	Average daily caloric intake (1969-70)
		Percent of total	Acres per capita	1970 (mill)	Growth rate (%)[1]	Density per sq mi 1969	Urban (%)	In agr (%)[1]	Literacy (%)			
WESTERN EUROPE												
EEC												
Belgium	12	53	0.4	9.7	0.3	822	69	5	97	22	74	3,150
France	211	56	1.6	50.8	0.9	239	67	15	97	16	75	3,270
Germany, West (FRG)	96	56	0.5	61.7	1.2	636	81	10	99	23	74	2,940
Italy	116	68	0.9	54.5	0.6	460	53	22	94	30	73	2,950
Luxembourg	1	52	1.0	0.3	0.6	341	67	12	98	17	73	3,150
Netherlands	16	56	0.4	13.0	1.2	819	71	8	98	13	76	3,030
EFTA												
Austria	32	47	1.3	7.4	0.2	229	54	19	98	25	73	2,950
Denmark	17	72	1.5	4.9	0.6	296	80	12	99	15	75	3,140
Finland[3]	130	8	1.6	4.7	-0.4	36	61	25	99	14	73	2,960
Iceland	40	22	27.5	0.2	1.0	5	72	19	99	12	76	2,900
Norway	125	5	0.6	3.9	0.7	31	53	15	99	14	77	2,900
Portugal	36	54	1.3	9.6	1.2	270	37	32	65	57	69	2,730
Sweden	174	9	1.1	8.1	1.1	47	80	9	99	13	76	2,750
Switzerland	16	52	0.9	6.3	0.7	393	58	8	98	15	75	2,990
United Kingdom	94	80	0.9	55.7	0.3	593	81	3	99	19	74	3,180
OTHER												
Cyprus	4	57	2.0	0.6	1.6	177	44	38	82	26	66	2,460
Greece	51	67	2.4	8.9	0.7	174	49	50	82	32	74	2,900
Ireland	27	68	4.0	2.9	0.8	109	47	28	99	21	72	3,450
Malta	0.12	60	0.1	0.3	0.9	2,657	68	7	83	24	70	2,680
Spain	195	68	2.7	33.3	1.1	169	61	31	90	30	72	2,750
Turkey	301	68	3.7	35.2	2.5	114	35	72	55	³153	55	2,760
EASTERN EUROPE												
COMECON												
Bulgaria	43	52		8.5	0.8	198	51	38	95	31	73	3,070
Czechoslovakia	49	56		14.5	0.4	294	52	18	99	22	74	3,030
East Germany (DRG)	42	58		17.1	0.0	411	81	13	99	19	74	3,040
Hungary	36	74		10.3	0.3	289	43	26	97	36	72	3,050
Poland	121	63		32.5	0.9	270	53	38	98	33	74	3,140
Romania	92	63		20.3	1.1	218	42	57	99	50	70	3,010
USSR	8,649	26	314	242.8	0.9	29	57	32	99	25	70	3,180
OTHER												
Albania	11	43		2.1	2.7	187	38	61	70	87	66	2,370
Yugoslavia	99	57	1.8	20.5	0.9	208	37	50	80	55	69	3,130

[1] 1969 and 1970.

Primary language of central govt.	Ethno-Cultural Heterogeneity above 15%	ECONOMY										COUNTRY
		Gross National Product				Imports		Exports		Transportation[1]		
		1970 ($ bill)	Growth rate (1960-70 avg %)	1970 per capita ($)	Per capita growth avg % (1960-70)	1970 ($ mill)	Per-cent from U.S. 1970	1970 ($ mill)	Per-cent to U.S. 1970	Roads (miles)	Rails (miles)	
												WESTERN EUROPE EEC
Fr, Dutch, Ger	+	25	4.8	2,595	4.2	11,400	9	11,600	6	57,000	2,873	Belgium
Fr		146	5.8	2,874	4.7	19,100	10	17,900	5	487,600	24,679	France
Ger		186	4.7	3,007'	3.7	30,400	11	34,800	9	249,200	21,095	W. Germany (FRG)
Ital		92	5.6	1,684	4.8	14,900	10	13,200	10	126,500	12,890	Italy
Ger, Fr		1	3.3	2,847	2.5	(Included in Belgium)				3,070	203	Luxembourg
Dutch		31	5.0	2,402	3.7	13,400	10	11,800	4	46,000	1,956	Netherlands
												EFTA
Ger		14	4.5	1,861	4.0	3,550	3	2,860	4	20,356	4,073	Austria
Danish		16	4.7	3,197	3.9	4,400	8	3,300	8	38,275	2,399	Denmark
Finn, Swed	+	10	4.8	2,166	4.2	2,640	5	2,300	5	44,200	3,720	Finland [2]
Iceland		0.5	4.4	2,319	2.9	160	8	150	30	7,400	none	Iceland
Norweg		11	4.9	2,879	4.1	3,700	7	2,500	6	44,180	2,711	Norway
Port		6	6.3	659	5.4	1,560	7	950	9	18,500	2,230	Portugal
Swed		31	4.6	3,896	3.9	7,000	9	6,800	6	60,925	7,767	Sweden
Ger, Fr, Ital	+	21	4.5	3,266	2.9	6,470	9	5,140	9	31,300	3,040	Switzerland
Eng		117	2.7	2,092	2.1	21,700	13	19,400	12	200,000	12,876	United Kingdom
												OTHER
Gr, Turk	+	0.5	6.4	844	5.4	238	7	109	1	5,050	none	Cyprus
Gr		9	7.4	1,035	6.7	1,960	6	640	8	22,200	1,620	Greece
Eng, Gaelic		4	3.6	1,314	3.2	1,570	7	1,030	10	53,700	1,332	Ireland
Eng, Malt		0.2	4.8	694	4.8	161	4	39	4	743	none	Malta
Span	+	32	7.6	974	6.7	4,750	19	2,390	14	83,080	10,763	Spain
Turk	+	9	5.5	247	3.0	900	19	600	10	35,730	5,286	Turkey
												EASTERN EUROPE COMECON
Bulgar	+	12	6.7	1,375	5.9	1,831	1	2,004	neg	20,700	2,650	Bulgaria
Czech, Slovak	+	33	2.6	2,240	2.0	3,700	neg	3,792	neg	45,500	8,269	Czechoslovakia
Ger		40	3.8	2,320	3.8	4,847	0.7	4,581	neg	54,055	9,109	East Germany (DRG)
Hungarian		16	3.7	1,530	3.4	2,506	1	2,317	neg	18,300	5,948	Hungary
Polish		46	4.7	1,420	3.8	3,608	2	3,548	3	190,095	16,469	Poland
Romanian	+	24	6.0	1,200	4.9	1,960	3	1,851	neg	48,000	9,700	Romania
[4] Russian		486	5.3	2,095	4.0	11,739	1.0	12,800	0.6	934,000	83,263	USSR
												OTHER
Albania		1	na	570	na	143 (1969)	neg	80 (1969)	neg	3,100	127	Albania
[4] Serbo-Croatian	+	19	na	900	na	2,874	5.6	1,679	5.3	56,565	6,640	Yugoslavia

[2] Associate member of EFTA.

[3] Represents 1967.

[4] Plus major important ethnic languages.

Nations of the World

COUNTRY	LAND Total sq mi (000)	Agricultural[1] Percent of total	Agricultural[1] Acres per capita	Population 1970 (000)	Population Growth rate (%)	Population Density per sq mi	Population Urban (%)	Labor Force In agr (%)	Labor Force In ind (%)	Literacy (%)	Infant deaths per 1,000 live births	Life expectancy (yrs)	Average daily caloric intake
I. ISLAMIC–ARAB													
Algeria	920	19	8	13.8	3.2	15	43	66	8	25	103	51	1,950
Bahrain	.23	na	na	.215	3.1	927	75	9	17	25	146	na	- -
Egypt	387	3	0.2	34.2	2.5	88	43	57	11	30	120	53	2,960
Iraq	168	27	3.0	9.8	3.4	58	47	48	14	20	104	na	2,050
Jordan	38	14	1.4	2.4	3.3	64	44	35	21	35-40	115	52	2,400
Kuwait	6	8	0.4	.77	3.3	125	80	1	29	47	41	na	na
Lebanon	4	31	0.3	2.9	24	736	41	55	na	86	na	na	2,360
Libya	679	2	4.6	1.9	3.7	3	27	36	18	27	na	37	2,340
Morocco	172	35	2.5	15.8	3.2	92	35	61	10	14	145	55	2,180
Oman	82	na	na	.66	3.1	8	5	na	na	very low	na	na	na
Qatar	8	na	na	.79	3.1	9	68	na	na	very low	na	na	na
Saudi Arabia	830	40	38	5.5	2.8	7	25	72	- -	10-15	157	30-40	2,080
Sudan	967	12	4.9	15.8	2.9	16	10	86	6	10-15	121	50	1,940
Syria	71	61	4.4	6.3	3.4	88	44	62	12	35	98	30-40	2,450
Tunisia	63	50	3.9	5.2	2.8	78	44	46	21	30	120	52	2,190
United Arab Emirates	32	na	na	193	3.1	6	55	na	na	very low	na	na	na
Yemen (San'a)	75	na	0.2	5.9	2.9	78	6	89	neg	10	160	30-40	1,910
Yemen (Aden)	111	32	17.5	1.3	2.9	12	33	78	- -	10	160	na	2,080
II. ISLAMIC–NON-ARAB													
Iran	636	11	1.5	29.5	3.0	46	41	42	24	35	160	na	2,030
Turkey	301	69	3.7	36.1	2.5	120	35	72	10	47	119	54	2,760
III. NON-ISLAMIC													
Cyprus	4	57	2.0	.65	1.5	182	44	40	25	76	25	66	2,460
Greece	51	67	2.4	9.0	0.8	176	49	54	19	82	32	69	2,900
Israel	8	59	1.0	3.0	2.4	370	80	10	34	88	19	71	2,930

[1]Consists of (a) arable land under permanent crops and (b) permanent meadows and pastures.

[2]GNP data in constant 1969 prices, unadjusted for inequalities in purchasing power between countries. Growth rates: average annual growth rate, 1960-70, except as noted.

Primary language of central govt.	Ethno-Cultural Heterogeneity above 15%	ECONOMY									COUNTRY
		Gross National Product[2]				Imports		Exports			
		1970 ($ bill)	Growth rate (%)	1970 per capita ($)	Per capita growth (%)	1969 ($ mill)	Percent from U.S. 1970	1969 ($ mill)	1967-69 primary (%)	Percent to U.S. 1970	
											I. ISLAMIC–ARAB
Arabic	+	3.7	9	275	6	998	8	916	65 crude petrol 12 wine	1	Algeria
Arabic		na	na	420	4.7E	206	5	230	petrol	5	Bahrain
Arabic		6.1	na	188	1.2E	636	9	745	45 cotton 14 rice	2	Egypt
Arabic	+	2.7	na	288	3.0E	1,528	4	2,099	93 petrol	2	Iraq
Arabic		.6 (1967)	na	286	4.7E	190	11	41	41 fruits/ veg 33 phosph	2	Jordan
Arabic		2.4 (1969)	na	3,360	4.3E	646	10	1,476	97 petrol	1	Kuwait
Arabic		1.4 (1969)	na	511	2.1E	576	11	172	21 fruits/ veg	4	Lebanon
Arabic		3.0 (1969)	21.8	1,601	18.1	676	17	2,167	99 petrol	2	Libya
Arabic	+	3.1 (1969)	4.1	203	1.0	562	11	485	17 foods 24 phosph	2	Morocco
Arabic		na	15.4	210E (1969)	12.2E	108 (1968)	- -	512 (1968)	petrol	- -	Oman
Arabic		.05 (1966)	1.8	1,550	-0.9E	72 (1968)	- -	242 (1968)	petrol	- -	Qatar
Arabic		2.8 (1969)	na	592	7.1E	734	18	2,001	96 petrol	1	Saudi Arabia
Arabic	+	1.7 (1969)	na	113	na	266	3	248	58 cotton	4	Sudan
Arabic	+	1.6 (1969)	na	273	4.7E	368	3	207	40 cotton	1	Syria
Arabic		1.2 (1969)	3.7	242	1.3	256	17	166	26 phosph 18 petrol	1	Tunisia
Arabic		na	na	1,590E (1969)	28.3E	114 (1968)	- -	192 (1968)	petrol pearls	- -	United Arab Emirates
Arabic		0.4 (1969)	na	80	2.3E	60 (1968)	- -	10 (1968)	90 cotton/ coffee	- -	Yemen (San'a)
Arabic		0.13 (1969)	na	110	-4.6E	218	1	144	70 petrol prod	- -	Yemen (Aden)
											II. ISLAMIC–NON-ARAB
Farsi	+	9.9	7.9	345	5.0	1,528	20	2,007	90 petrol	3	Iran
Turkish	+	8.2	5.5	232	3.0	754	19	537	24 cotton 19 tobacco	10	Turkey
											III. NON-ISLAMIC
Greek Turkish	+	.53	6.4	828	5.4	206	7	96	28 copper pyrites 20 citrus	1	Cyprus
Greek		9.0	7.4	1,011	6.7	1,404	6	553	22 tobacco 15 fruits & nuts	8	Greece
Hebrew Arabic	+	5.1	8.9	1,751	5.7	1,331	22	729	35 dmnd 18 fruits	19	Israel

COUNTRY	LAND			PEOPLE									
		Agricultural[1]		Population				Labor Force					
	Total sq mi (000)	Percent of total	Acres per capita	1970 (mill)	Growth rate (%)	Density per sq mi	Urban (%)	In agr (%)	In ind (%)	Literacy (%)	Infant deaths per 1,000 live births	Life expect-ancy (yrs)	Average daily caloric intake
Angola	481	24	13.4	5.7	1.3	11	14	82	na	10-15	230	35	1,870
Botswana	232	69	152	.62	3.0	3	22	91	3	20	175	na	na
Burundi	11	64	1.1	3.6	2.0	330	3	95	na	10	161	39	2,020
Cameroon	183	35	5.3	5.8	2.1	32	20	84	na	10-15	110	49	2,130
Central African Republic	241	10	10	1.5	2.2	6	26	90	na	5-10	160-170	35 (1960)	2,120
Chad	496	40	35.9	3.7	1.6	7	8	92	na	5-10	179	35	2,180
Comoro Islands	.84	49	na	.27	3.9	na	na	na	na	na	na	na	na
Congo (Brazzaville)	132	44	39	.94	1.9	7	39	64	na	20	148	37	2,120
Dahomey	43	18	2	2.5	2.1	58	17	84	na	20	149	38	2,170
Equatorial Guinea	11	12	2.8	.28	1.7	27	15	na	na	20E	na	na	na
Ethiopia	472	67	8	25.3	2.3	54	8	90	na	5	162	35	2,050
Fr. Terr. of Afars & Issas	9	11	na	.13	na	na	na	na	na	10	na	na	na
Gabon	103	20	27	.49	1.2	5	21	84	na	12	184	39	2,200
Gambia	4	53	4.1	.36	2.0	83	10	87	na	10	125	43	2,320
Ghana	92	12	0.8	9.0	2.7	96	31	58	14	25	122	45	2,130
Guinea	95	na	na	3.9	3.0	43	11	85	na	5-10	na	43	2,060
Ivory Coast	125	52	9.9	4.2	2.8	34	21	86	7	20	154	39	2,440
Kenya	225	10	1.2	11.2	3.4	50	10	88	na	20-25	126	47	2,240
Lesotho	12	94	7.3	1.0	2.8	82	2	na	na	na	137	48	na
Liberia	43	37	7.0	1.5	3.0	28	26	81	9	22	143	41	2,260
Malagasy Republic	227	63	12.5	7.3	2.2	32	13	84	15	39	161	40	2,360
Malawi	45	30	2.0	4.4	2.5	98	5	81	13	15	119	47	2,110
Mali	479	34	20	5.1	2.4	11	12	90	..	5	190	50	2,130
Mauritania	398	38	84	1.2	2.2	3	2	89	..	1-5	137	40	1,980

See footnotes at end of table.

Primary language of central govt.	Ethno-Cultural Heterogeneity above 15%	ECONOMY									COUNTRY
		Gross National Product[2]				Imports		Exports			
		1970 ($ bill)	Growth rate (%)	1970 per capita ($)	Per capita growth (%)	1969 ($ mill)	Percent from U.S. 1970	1969 ($ mill)	1967-69 primary (%)	Percent to U.S. 1970	
Port		1.1 (1969)	na	210	1.4	323	13	327	43 coffee 18 dmnd	16	Angola
Eng		.054 (1969)	na	94	0.8	29	na	11	96 animals & prod	na	Botswana
Kirundi Fr		.207E	na	60	0.0	22	5	12	80 coffee	68	Burundi
Eng Fr	+	.85 (1969)	na	150	na	205	6	226	24 cocoa 24 coffee 8 alum	6	Cameroon
Fr	+	na	na	130	0.0	38	5	36	49 dmnd 24 cotton 16 coffee	9	Central African Republic
Fr	+	.24 (1968)	5.7	70 (1968)	2.2	54	5	31	77 cotton	*	Chad
Fr		na	na	na	na	na	na	na	van copra	na	Comoro Islands
Fr	+	.2	4	220	2.5	83	7	44	52 wood 27 dmnd	2	Congo (Brazzaville)
Fr	+	182 (1968)	5	70 (1968)	1.1	55	4	26	42 palm prod	18	Dahomey
Span		na	na	290	4.7	15.3	- -	32.5	60 cocoa	- -	Equatorial Guinea
Amharic	+	1.69	4.8	67	2.8	155	11	119	57 coffee 10 hides	42	Ethiopia
Fr		na	na	na	na	29.6	na	4.5	na	na	Fr. Terr. of Afars & Issas
Fr	+	.16	8.8 (1965-66)	325	0.7	78	11	142	33 oil 28 wood 32 mang	11	Gabon
Eng		.032 (1969)	na	100	-0.1	19	5	16	75 peanuts	1	Gambia
Eng	+	2.32	2.4	262	-0.3	347	18	387	55 cocoa	12	Ghana
Fr	+	.397 (1969)	na	104	na	53E	23	57E	63 alum	10	Guinea
Fr	+	1.26 (1969)	7 (1960-69)	308	4.8	331	8	456	30 coffee 27 wood 20 cocoa	14	Ivory Coast
Eng Swahili		1.54	8.0 (1965-70)	137	4.6 (1965-70)	360	7	272	24 coffee 15 tea 9 oil	5	Kenya
Sesotho Eng		.09 (1969)	na	100	1.2	(³)	(³)	(³)	44 wool 25 lvstk	(³)	Lesotho
Eng	+	.289 (1969)	na	196	na	115	34	195	68 iron ore 16 rubber	28	Liberia
Malagasy Fr		.755 (1969)	na	106	na	178	6	113	31 coffee 9 van	24	Malagasy Republic
Eng Chichewe		.285	4.7 (1965-70)	64	2.2 (1965-70)	84	4	53	25 tobacco 23 tea	6	Malawi
Fr	+	.447 (1969)	na	90	na	39	3	17	26 lvstk 26 cotton	**	Mali
Fr Arabic	+	.170	9 (1962-66)	140	4.6	39	16	77	86 iron	1	Mauritania

COUNTRY	LAND			PEOPLE									
	Total sq mi (000)	Agricultural[1]		Population				Labor Force		Literacy (%)	Infant deaths per 1,000 live births	Life expect-ancy (yrs)	Average daily caloric intake
		Percent of total	Acres per capita	1970 (mill)	Growth rate (%)	Density per sq mi	Urban (%)	In agr (%)	In ind (%)				
Mauritius	0.72	70	.3	.84	1.8	1,166	48	38	25	61	70	64	2,300
Mozambique	302	60	15.4	7.7	1.6	25	5	69	..	7	92	45	2,050
Namibia (South-West Africa)	318	65	212	0.75	1.7	2	34	55	13	15E	111	na	na
Niger	489	11	9.7	3.8	2.9	8	3	96	..	5	148-159	37	2,170
Nigeria	357	52	2.1	55.1	2.8	158	23	80	15	25	157	39	2,170
Portuguese Guinea	14	na	na	.55	0.2	39	na	na	na	5	na	na	na
Reunion	1	33	0.5	.46	2.3	464	40	43	na	52	59	57	na
Rhodesia, Southern	150	17	3.2	5.3	3.3	35	22	73	25	25-30	65	56	2,510
Rwanda	10	71	1.3	3.6	3.0	354	0	95	..	10	120-130	46	1,900
Senegal	76	58	7.1	3.9	2.4	52	26	74	..	5-10	156	45	2,300
Seychelles	0.16	54	na	.05	2.0	na	na	28	na	50	49	na	na
Sierra Leone	28	82	5.5	2.6	2.1	95	14	75	..	10	136	na	2,120
Somali Republic	246	34	19	2.8	2.2	11	26	89	..	5	na	na	1,770
South Africa[6] [7]	471	84	12.6	21.5	2.3	43	48	30	15	Whites 100; Bantu 35	138	51	2,870
Spanish Sahara	103	na	na	0.06	na	na	na	na	na	na	na	na	na
Swaziland	7	88	8.9	.42	2.9	63	4	31	11	36	169	48	na
Tanzania	363	60	10.5	13.3	2.7	37	7	95	..	15-20	165	45	2,140
Togo	22	42	3.1	1.9	2.6	86	16	79	..	5-10	163	40	2,220
Uganda	91	42	2.5	9.8	2.5	107	6	89	..	20-40	124	46	2,160
Upper Volta	106	85	11.3	5.1	1.8	48	5	87	..	5-10	181	36	2,040
Zaire (Congo-Kinshasa)	906	31	10	17.8	2.4	20	16	63	21	35-40	115	45	1,920
Zambia	291	51	22.1	4.2	3.1	15	22	81	10	28	159	44	2,290

[1] Consists of (a) arable land under permanent crops and (b) permanent meadows and pastures.

[2] GNP in constant 1969 prices; unadjusted for inequalities in purchasing power between countries. Growth rates: average annual growth rate, 1960-70, except as noted. Gross Domestic Product (GDP) figures used whenever GNP figures unavailable.

Primary language of central govt.	Ethno-Cultural Heterogeneity above 15%	ECONOMY									COUNTRY
		Gross National Product³				Imports		Exports			
		1970 ($ bill)	Growth rate (%)	1970 per capita ($)	Per capita growth (%)	1969 ($ mill)	Percent from U.S. 1970	1969 ($ mill)	1967-69 primary (%)	Percent to U.S. 1970	
Eng		.158 (1969)	na	230	-0.4	68	2	68	91 sugar	5	Mauritius
Port		1.2	na	158	3.3	261	7	142	17 cotton 12 cashew 11 sugar	10	Mozambique
Afrikaans Eng		.4 (GDP)	na	600 (GDP) (1968)	na	(³)	(³)	(³)	(³)	(³)	Namibia (South-West Africa)
Fr	+	.321 (1969)	na	90	na	49	5	24	66 nuts 9 lvstk	1	Niger
Eng	+	4.83 (1969)	2.6 (1969-70)	90	-0.3	691	12	904	32 oil 20 cocoa 17 nut	12	Nigeria
Port		.10	na	200	na	23.3	na	3.6	66 nuts	na	Portuguese Guinea
Fr		na	na	610	na	126	1 (1968)	46.2	84 sugar	2 (1968)	Reunion
Eng		1.30 (1969)	3.7	255	0.5	313	2	318	33 tobacco	5	Rhodesia, Southern
Kinyarwanda Fr		.15 (1969)	na	40	1.5	24	7	14	51 coffee 28 tin	1	Rwanda
Fr	+	.71 (1969)	2 (1969)	186	na	198	6	123	68 nuts	*	Senegal
Eng		na	na	na	na	6.3	na	3.0	50 cin/van 40 copra	na	Seychelles
Eng	+	.43 (1969)	na	164	na	112	5	106	63 dmnd 9 iron	2	Sierra Leone
Somali		.175 (1969)	na	63	na	52	10	32	54 lvstk 29 bann	2	Somali Republic
Afrikaans Eng	+	16.83	6.2	740	3.8	3,291	17	2,199	⁶ 35 gold	7	South Africa⁴ ⁵
Span		na	na	na	na	1.4 (1968)	na	.45 (1968)	fish skins	na	Spanish Sahara
Eng SiSwati		na	na	180	3.2	(³)	(³)	(³)	24 sugar 23 iron	(⁵)	Swaziland
Swahili	+	1.27 (1969)	5.7 (1965-70)	98	3.0 (1965-70)	240	5	251	16 cotton 15 coffee	7	Tanzania
Fr	+	.225 (1969)	na	124	na	56	5	44	33 phosph 30 cocoa	*	Togo
Eng	+	1.13	5.4	116	3.2	175	3	225	54 coffee	21	Uganda
Fr	+	.25 (1969)	na	50	na	50	4	21	45 lvstk 22 cotton	*	Upper Volta
6 langs	+	1.80	5.2 (1965-70)	101	2.8 (1965-70)	400E	17	600E	68 copper	7	Zaire (Congo-Kinshasa)
Eng		1.67 (1969)	7.9	398	4.9	493	10	1,073	94 copper	1	Zambia

³ Included in data for South Africa.

⁴ In 1966, the United Nations terminated the rights of the Republic of South Africa over the former mandated territory of South-West Africa and placed this international territory under the direct responsibility of the U.N. General Assembly; South Africa, however, remains the *de facto* administrator of the territory.

⁵ Includes South-West Africa.

*Less than ½ unit.

Nations of the World 87

COUNTRY	LAND			PEOPLE									
	Total sq mi (000)	Agricultural[1]		Population				Labor Force		Literacy (%)	Infant deaths per 1,000 live births	Life expectancy (yrs)	Average daily caloric intake
		Percent of total	Acres per capita	1970 (mill)	Growth rate (%)	Density per sq mi	Urban (%)	In agr (%)	In ind (%)				
China, People's Rep of	3,700	11	0.34	800	2.2	215	15	85	na	40-50	na	50	2,000
China, Rep of	14	25	0.2	14.6	2.4	1,045	64	44	16	85	28	68	2,650
Hong Kong	.4	13	0.01	3.9	2.4	9,850	92	5	na	71	21	70	2,370
Japan	143	18	.2	103.5	1.2	724	72	17	34	99	14	72	2,300
Korea, North	47	17	na	14.5	2.8	286	34	80	54	90E	na	na	na
Korea, South	38	24	0.2	31.8	2.2	837	38	49	17	71	53	58	2,430
Mongolian Rep	604	0.5	0.9	1.3	3.4	2	na	65	na	80	na	64	2,540

[1] Consists of (a) arable land under permanent crops and (b) permanent meadows and pastures.

[2] GNP data in constant 1969 prices; unadjusted for inequalities in purchasing power between countries. Growth rates: average annual growth rate, 1960-70, except as noted.

COUNTRY	LAND			PEOPLE									
	Total sq mi (000)	Agricultural[1]		Population				Labor Force		Literacy (%)	Infant deaths per 1,000 live births	Life expectancy (yrs)	Average daily caloric intake
		Percent of total	Acres per capita	1970 (000)	Growth rate (%)	Density per sq mi	Urban (%)	In agr (%)	In ind (%)				
Afghanistan	250	22	2.0	17.4	2.7	70	8	87	neg	8	190	na	2,060
Bangladesh	55.1	64	0.3	74	2.7	1,340	5	85	na	22	135E	47	2,350E
Bhutan	18	15	na	0.87	2.5	48	na	na	na	under 5	na	na	na
Ceylon (Sri Lanka)	25.3	37	0.5	12.8	2.4	505	20	49	12	70-80	50	62	2,210
India	1,262	55	.8	547,000	2.6	448	21	73	11	28	118	50	1,940
Maldives	.12	na	na	0.11	1.9	na	na	50E	na	low	na	na	na
Nepal	54	30	0.9	11.3	2.2	208	5	92	2	5-10	162	25-40	2,540
Pakistan	310.4	24	0.8	60	2.7	190	22	59	--	16	135E	51	2,350E

[1] Consists of (a) arable land under permanent crops and (b) permanent meadows and pastures.

[2] GNP data in constant 1969 prices; unadjusted for inequalities in purchasing power between countries. Growth rates: average annual growth rate, 1960-70, except as noted.

Primary language of central govt.	Ethno-Cultural Heterogeneity above 15%	ECONOMY Gross National Product² 1970 ($ bill)	Growth rate (%)	1970 per capita ($)	Per capita growth (%)	Imports 1969 ($ mill)	Percent from U.S. 1970	Exports 1969 ($ mill)	1967-69 primary (%)	Percent to U.S. 1970	COUNTRY
Man Chin	+	120	4.6E (1965-70)	145	na	2,100	- -	2,150	agr prod/ text/light mfg (% na)	- -	China, People's Rep of
Man Chin		6.2	10.0	410	7.0	1,213	30	1,049	19 text 11 metals	37	China, Rep of
Eng		3.4	9.0 (1968-70)	820	na	2,500	13	³2,200	32 clothing 14 text	20	Hong Kong
Japanese		196.0	11.1	1,898	10.0	15,000	28	16,000	44 mach 13 iron/ steel 12 text	32	Japan
Korean		2.9 (1967)	na	230 (1967)	na	300	- -	400	min/ chem/ metals (% na)	- -	Korea, North
Korean		7.8	9.3	245	6.7	1,800	30	600	13 woods 6 fish	50	Korea, South
Khalkha Mongol		.75	0 (1965-70)	577	na	300	- -	117	wool, hides (% na)	na	Mongolian Rep

³ Includes $442 million reexports.

Primary language of central govt.	Ethno-Cultural Heterogeneity above 15%	ECONOMY Gross National Product² 1970 ($ bill)	Growth rate (%)	1970 per capita ($)	Per capita growth (%)	Imports 1969 ($ mill)	Percent from U.S. 1970	Exports 1969 ($ mill)	1967-69 primary (%)	Percent to U.S. 1970	COUNTRY
Pushtu Dari	+	1.4 (1969)	na	85	0.3E	125	8	82	37 fruits/ nuts 17 karakal	4	Afghanistan
Bengali		7.6	4.5E	105	na	732 (1970)	31	545 (1970)	jute	21	Bangladesh
Dzongkha		na	na	100-	na	1.4	- -	1	rice/ dolomite	- -	Bhutan
Sinhala	+ .	2.0	4.7	165	2.3	427	6	322	61 tea 19 rubber 13 coconut	7	Ceylon (Sri Lanka)
Hindi Eng	+	53.0	3.8	96	1.3	2,090	29	1884	23 jute 12 tea 7 iron	14	India
Divehi		.01	na	80E	na	2.5 (1967)	na	2.5 (1967)	90 fish	na	Maldives
Nepali	+	0.9	na	80	na	45E	na	40E	70-80 rice/foods	- -	Nepal
Urdu	+	9.6	6.0E	150	- -	884 (1970)	27	701 (1970)	cotton	6	Pakistan

COUNTRY	LAND			PEOPLE									
	Total sq mi (000)	Agricultural[1]		Population				Labor Force			Infant deaths per 1,000 live births	Life expect- ancy (yrs)	Average daily caloric intake
		Percent of total	Acres per capita	1970 (mill)	Growth rate (%)	Density per sq mi	Urban (%)	In agr (%)	In ind (%)	Literacy (%)			
Brunei	2.2	8	1.4	0.1	3.7	54	44	34	34	43	42	- -	- -
Burma	262	29	1.5	28	2.2	108	19	66	7	60	75	47	1,940 (1966)
Indonesia	736	12	.3	120E	2.6E	163	17E	70E	15E	43E	150	40	1,870
Khmer Republic (Cambodia)	70	16	1.3	7	2.2	98	12	80	5	55E	127	44	2,170
Laos	91	8	1.6	3E	2.4	32	13	85	- -	19	na	35	2,000
Malaysia	128	18	0.8	11	2.9	85	40	59	na	43	60	63	2,190
Philippines	116	41	0.7	38	3.4	332	34	57	15	72	83	55	2,010
Singapore	0.23	21	.02	2	2.0	9,165	100	7	35	75	21	62	2,440
Thailand	198	24	0.8	36	3.3	178	15	80	5	70	67	56	2,100 (1965)
Viet-Nam, North	61	14	.3	20	2.0E	328	15	70	10	95	na	na	1,700
Viet-Nam, South	67	33	0.8	18	2.6	277	24	65	2	75	37	35	2,140

[1] Consists of (a) arable land under permanent crops and (b) permanent meadows and pastures.

[2] GNP data in constant 1969 prices; unadjusted for inequalities in purchasing power between countries.
Growth rates: average annual growth rate, 1960-70, except as noted.

		ECONOMY									
		Gross National Product[2]				Imports		Exports			
Primary language of central govt.	Ethno-Cultural Heterogeneity above 15%	1970 ($ bill)	Growth rate (%)	1970 per capita ($)	Per capita growth (%)	1969 ($ mill)	Percent from U.S. 1970	1969 ($ mill)	1967-69 primary (%)	Percent to U.S. 1970	COUNTRY
Malay		.11 (1969)	--	950	--	72	14	85	96 oil	--	Brunei
Burmese	+	2.0	--	74	1.8	181	7	131	50 rice	1	Burma
Indonesian	+	12.8E	3.3	108E	0.9	993	22	995	40 oil 23 rubber	13	Indonesia
Khmer		.74 (1969)	2.7	111	0.5	122	3	78	34 rice 24 rubber	5	Khmer Republic (Cambodia)
Lao, Fr	+	.2 (1969)	na	73	na	51	20	2	57 tin	--	Laos
Malay	+	3.9	6.3	360	3.3	1,178	6	1,651	36 rubber 20 tin	15	Malaysia
Pilip Eng Span	+	8.5	5.7	222	2.3	1,254	28	855	24 wood 17 sugar	42	Philippines
Malay Chin Tamil Eng	+	1.7 (1969)	6	843	4.5	[3] 2,040	8	[4] 1,549	22 rubber 19 oil	11	Singapore
Thai		6.8	8.1	181	4.8	1,242	15	708	27 rice 14 rubber	15	Thailand
Viet-namese	+	1.6E	na	90	na	700E	--	60E	coal	--	Viet-Nam, North
Viet-namese	+	3.1 (1969)	4.4	175	1.8	853	39	33	80 rubber	.5	Viet-Nam, South

[3] Over 40% goods reexported.
[4] Almost 90% goods reexported.

Nations of the World   91

COUNTRY	LAND			PEOPLE								
	Total sq mi	Agricultural[1]		Population				Labor Force		Literacy (%)	Infant deaths per 1,000 live births	Life expectancy (yrs)
		Percent of total	Acres per capita	1970 (000)	Growth rate (%)	Density per sq mi	Urban (%)	In agr (%)	In ind (%)			
American Samoa	76	30	na	30	3.2	na	na	na	na	na	28.6	na
Australia	3 mill	64	na	12,550	2.1	4.1	84	14	32	98.5	18.3	68
Brit. Solomon Islands	11,500	6	na	161	2.0	na	na	na	na	na	na	na
Cook Islands	93	na	na	20	1.3	na	na	na	na	na	na	na
Fiji	7,000	30	na	520	2.7	67	23	50	47	64	24.5	na
French Polynesia	1,543	21	na	98	3.1	na	na	na	na	na	na	na
Gilbert and Ellice Islands	342	46	na	55	3.6	na	na	na	na	na	22.7	na
Guam	209	36	na	85	3.2	na	na	na	na	na	20.3	na
Micronesia[4] (Pacific Isl.)	712	40	na	102	2.2	na	22	na	na	50	32.6	na
Nauru	8	neg	na	7	3.8	722	0	na	na	na	55	na
New Caledonia	8,548	28	na	107	2.6	5	55	na	na	na	32.8	na
New Hebrides	5,700	na	na	84	5.0	na	na	na	na	na	na	na
New Zealand	103,736	51	na	2,820	1.4	27	64	13	36	98	16.9	71
Niue Island	100	na	na	6	na	na	na	na	na	na	25.8	na
Papua New Guinea	183,540	18	na	2,420	2.5	5	na	na	na	na	na	na
Pitcairn Group	18	na	na	(5)	3.4	na	na	na	na	na	na	na
Tokelau Group	4	na	na	2	na	na	na	na	na	na	na	na
Tonga Islands	270	80	na	87	3.0	116	16	75	na	95	9	na
Wallis Futuna	93	na	na	9	2.0	na	na	na	na	na	78.7	na
Western Samoa	1,133	na	na	146	2.4	139	23	75	na	86	25.5	na

NOTE—Reliable data for most of the island groups is unavailable; data included is meant to give a general indication of status in various categories.

[1] Total land area. Many of the island groups cover far greater land-sea areas. The many islands of Micronesia, for instance, are spread over 3 million square miles—approximately the area of the 48 contiguous United States.

[2] For dependencies, official language listed is that of colonial or protective power. Most native languages in Oceania are of the Malayo-Polynesian family.

Average daily caloric intake	Primary language of central govt.	Ethno-Cultural Heterogeneity above 15%	ECONOMY									COUNTRY
			Gross National Product[3]				Imports		Exports			
			1970 ($ mill)	Growth rate (%)	1970 per capita ($)	Per capita growth (%)	1969 ($ mill)	Percent from U.S. 1970	1969 ($ mill)	1967-69 primary (%)	Percent to U.S. 1970	
na	Eng		na	na	na	na	12.2	66	24.1 (1970)	95 fish	na	American Samoa
3,300	Eng		31,600	5.0	2,542	3.0	4,558	25	4,217	24 wool 17 mach	14	Australia
na	Eng		na	na	na	na	10.5 (1968)	6 (1968)	5.9 (1968)	68 copra 27 timber	--	Brit. Solomon Islands
na	Eng		na	na	na	na	na	na	na	na	na	Cook Islands
na	Eng		200	5E	370	na	89.6	na	59.2	50 sugar	na	Fiji
na	Fr		na	na	na	na	109	12 (1968)	14	14 copra 7 van	na	French Polynesia
na	Eng		na	na	na	na	na	na	na	na	na	Gilbert and Ellice Islands
na	Eng		220 (1969)	na	na	na	60	56	4	na	52	Guam
na	Eng		.38 (1969)	na	430	na	14	na	3	63 copra 10 fish	na	Micronesia[4] (Pacific Isl.)
na	Nauruan Eng		.25	na	4,500	na	5	na	17	phosph	na	Nauru
na	Fr		19 (1969)	na	1,900	na	124	na	131	98 nickel	6	New Caledonia
na	Fr Eng		na	na	na	na	10.2 (1968)	na	11.6 (1968)	na	na	New Hebrides
3,500	Eng		6	3.8	2,100	2.2	1,003	12	1.211	32 meat 20 wool	16	New Zealand
na	Eng		na	na	na	na	na	na	na	na	na	Niue Island
na	Eng		55 (1969)	na	225	na	168.5	13 (1968)	84.3	26 copra 25 cocoa	8 (1968)	Papua New Guinea
na	Eng		na	na	na	na	na	na	na	na	na	Pitcairn Group
na	Eng		na	na	na	na	na	na	na	na	na	Tokelau Group
na	Tongan Eng		na	na	310	na	5.7	na	3.8	46 bann 38 copra	na	Tonga Islands
na	Fr		na	na	na	na	na	na	na	na	na	Wallis Futuna
na	Samoan Eng		17 (1967)	na	250	na	10	13 (1968)	6	49 copra 32 cocoa	na	Western Samoa

[3] GNP data in constant 1969 prices, unadjusted for inequalities in purchasing power between countries. Growth rates: average annual growth rate, 1960-70, except as noted.

[4] Includes whole western Pacific Island area: Mariana District, except Guam, Marshall District, Palau District, Ponape District, Truk District, and Yap District.

[5] Pitcairn population is only 124.

Nations of the World   93

This chapter reports the findings of an empirical study of 100 of the 1,200 secondary bilingual education units that were located in conjunction with obtaining the information discussed in Chapter VI. The principals or bilingual education directors of the 100 schools selected for study were asked to provide a great deal of information (400 items in all) about their communities, their faculties, their students, their programs, and the languages used as media. Some of the information requested was factual. Some of the information requested was attitudinal. Every attempt was made to obtain exhaustive information in order to explore each of the above areas as fully as possible. The respondents knew that one in ten of the schools would subsequently be visited by the principal investigator—and that he would correspond further with them and with others knowledgeable about their schools—and this further tended to encourage full and accurate reporting.*

What Did the Study Want to Find Out?

Description in itself is not enough; description must have a goal, a purpose, a focus. Similarly, although there is still a great need for detailed information about secondary bilingual education, whether in the United States or internationally, description alone, without focus, is not well calculated to answer questions. What questions did the International Study of Bilingual Secondary Education (ISBSE) seek to answer? Briefly put, it sought to find the particular descriptive details and dimensions that were most useful (or powerful) in explaining (or predicting) three criteria that are of prime interest to all those concerned with bilingual education. The three criteria upon which all the ISBSE data were focused were as follows:

> *Criterion I: Absolute Academic Success,* i.e., what are the averaged grades awarded across all subjects and all years of study?
>
> *Criterion II: Relative Academic Success,* i.e., how do bilingual secondary schools compare to monolingual secondary schools in their immediate areas serving comparable populations insofar as averaged grades are concerned?

---

*For a complete technical presentation of the research procedures and findings discussed in this chapter, see Chapters V and VI of the detailed Final Report mentioned in the Acknowledgments section.

THE INTERNATIONAL SOCIOLOGY
OF BILINGUAL SECONDARY EDUCATION:
EMPIRICAL FINDINGS AND THEORETICAL IMPLICATIONS

CHAPTER VIII

Criterion III: Student Satisfaction, i.e., how pleased are students with respect to their bilingual secondary schooling in terms of its impact on their academic, personal, and social development?

In connection with *Criterion I* the ISBSE data sought to find the descriptive information that differentiates best between academically outstanding and academically less outstanding secondary bilingual programs. All bilingual programs cannot be excellent any more than can all monolingual programs. What kind of descriptive details and dimensions are most important in differentiating between secondary bilingual programs along a continuum of academic success—when academic success is measured in terms of the averages of all grades awarded across all subjects and all years of study? Certainly this is a question of wide interest and great importance.

Criterion II is similar to *Criterion I* except that it is concerned with academic performance on a *comparative* basis. Some bilingual education programs are as good as or better than monolingual education programs in their immediate areas serving comparable populations; others are not. What kinds of descriptive details and dimensions are most important in differentiating between secondary bilingual education programs in terms of their *relative* academic success in comparison to their monolingual "competitors." This criterion pertains to a question that is often asked of bilingual education and empirical data pertaining to it—particularly, empirical data on an international basis could be very revealing.

Criteria I and II both deal with the academic (cognitive) goals of bilingual education. However, our concern for bilingual education as a whole, and for secondary bilingual education in particular, cannot and must not be reduced to the cognitive domain alone. Accordingly, *Criterion III* deals with student satisfaction, i.e., with the affective domain of education, and does so relative to a very inclusive formulation of educational goals (academic, personal, and social development). What descriptive details and dimensions pertaining to secondary bilingual education programs will best differentiate between programs for which high student satisfaction is claimed and programs for which low student satisfaction is claimed? This was the third major question for which the ISBSE sought an answer.

All in all, therefore, the ISBSE attempted to utilize an exhaustive battery of descriptive information in order to differentiate between more and less outstanding secondary bilingual programs on three fundamental criteria of "goodness" of education. From the findings obtained, to be discussed below, we should be able to tell, first of all, whether these three criteria are really as separate as they appear to be. After all, it is at least theoretically possible that they are all one and the same, i.e., that the programs achieving absolute academic success, relative academic success, and high student satisfaction are one and the same, and that the descriptive details differentiating best brtween programs on one criterion are also the same as differentiate best between them on the other criteria as well. Or it may be that the three criteria are really substantially independent. It would be interesting to know whether schools must really aim at three separate goals, or whether success on one criterion brings the others automatically into range as well. Finally, it may be that the criteria are negatively interrelated and that schools must choose between them because too much of one is counter-productive with respect to the other(s).

If the three criteria are at least *substantially* separate it would certainly be enlightening to know what are the descriptive details or dimensions that are uniquely related to optimal differentiation with respect to each. Which criterion, e.g., is best predicted by *student* characteristics, and by which student characteristics? Which criterion, if any, is best predicted by *teacher* character-istics, and by which teacher characteristics? The same question must be asked about *program* characteristics, *community* characteristics, and *language* character-istics. Are all of these types of characteristics equally important in predicting all criteria, or are some more important for one criterion and others more important for another? Indeed, are the types of characteristics (of students, teachers, programs, communities, languages) really independent of each other, or are they really groupable into fewer and different clusters than those that appeal to us intuitively?

Let us see what was found in connection with these fundamental issues in the international sociology of secondary bilingual education.

How Were the Hundred Programs Selected?

This is not the place to enter into the many delicate and complicated methodological issues and procedures involved in gathering 400 bits of informa-tion from 100 bilingual secondary schools throughout the world and in processing and analyzing the data so obtained. However, there are a few such issues that must be addressed, albeit briefly and simply, and one of these is how the 100 programs were selected and how many of them replied. The latter part of the question is easier to reply to: ultimately, almost all (94, to be exact). As for the former question, let us consider the data that permitted the preparation of Chapter VII. The 1,200 secondary education units identified there were initially clustered according to the *intensity considerations* (transitional, uniliterate, biliterate), the *goal considerations* (compensatory, enrichment, group maintenance), and the *one population vs. two population* distinction, which have been commented upon in Chapters III and IV. The 100 units studied were then selected by sampling at random from the above 18 clusters ($3 \times 3 \times 2 = 18$) in such a fashion as to maximize the number of countries represented. All in all, this approach was utilized in order to locate a random stratified sample of bilingual secondary programs that would represent all the intuitive types and at the same time be as varied as possible on geographic-political-cultural grounds. Data obtained on such a sample should yield international findings that are not only interesting but also instructive, since the basic stratificational parameters (e.g., intensity type, goal type, country, etc.) also become possible descriptive parameters whose predictive potential can be empirically examined vis-à-vis the criteria we have just reviewed.

Are the Three Criteria Separate and Predictable?

Obtaining 400 bits of information from a stratified random sample of roughly 100 respondents relative to three criteria is in itself no guarantee that the information obtained will actually predict (explain, clarify, account for) those criteria. As every teacher (and researcher) knows, it is possible to ask countless irrelevant questions. Similarly, it is possible to gather much information that is of no explanatory value whatsoever, interestingly descriptive though it may be. How did the ISBSE fare in this connection? Quite well indeed. The data collected yielded cumulative multiple correlations of .89, .91, and .80 in conjunction with Criteria I, II, and III, respectively, which is to say that it succeeded in accounting for 79%, 83%, and 64% of the variation from one school to the other on these three criteria.

Thus, if we are interested in accounting for the differences in self-reported absolute academic success, relative academic success, and student satisfaction in secondary bilingual programs the world over (and we are), then we can safely say that the kinds of data we have collected go a long way toward doing exactly that. Indeed, it is rare to obtain cumulative multiple correlations as high as these in psycho- and socio-educational research, and since ours is but the beginning of research on the international sociology of bilingual education, we may conclude that the prospects for explanatory predictive power in this area are certainly promising.

Further encouragement in this connection is obtained from the fact that the intercorrelations between the criteria themselves are very low (from $-.03$ to $.05$). This fact assures us that we are dealing with criteria that are not only separate intuitively but functionally as well. The fact that one cannot predict one criterion from the other means that a secondary bilingual program's *absolute* academic success does not yet tell us anything about its *relative* academic success or about the level of *student satisfaction* encountered therein. Furthermore, student satisfaction with a secondary bilingual program does not yet tell us anything reliable about either its absolute or relative academic success. Inter-school differences on these criteria (and that is *what* we are trying to account for) are explained or predicted by appreciably separate and independent sets of descriptive information, and it is to a review of these sets that we now turn.

Four Hundred Measures: Ten Factors. How many different bits of information can you actively keep in mind at one time, in terms of the differences and interrelations between them? Whatever the answer may be in any individual case, it is definitely below 400. Can you imagine trying to understand, remember, and explain findings based upon 400 means and standard deviations, as well as upon the $[n(n-1)]/2$ or 79,800 intercorrelations between the distributions from which they were obtained? Can you imagine doing so not only once but *three times,* once for each criterion? Our mathematical statistical procedures have far outstripped our human mental capacity to make sense of the figures that computers spew out with such seeming effortlessness. Fortunately computers will also do what we ask them to do in order to help us understand and assimilate their massive outputs. Thus, after the computers had finished working with all 400 bits of information, in conjunction with each criterion individually, in order to answer the above questions regarding criterion separateness and predictability, they were then asked to composite by factor analysis these 400 measures so that ordinary human minds could work with them conceptually.

In effect we said to our servant the computer: "Although 400 measures were taken of each secondary bilingual program, it may well be that many of these were redundant or overlapping in greater or lesser degree. What then is the *smallest number of maximally different* measures or dimensions in our data?" These latter measures, composited out of the intercorrelations between original measures, are called factors. In our case "our servant" came back and reported that there were *ten* factors that could account for almost all of the variation in our original 400 measures. Now *ten* dimensions are far easier for human flesh and blood to assimilate than 400. Therefore, it is with these ten that we will continue our discussion of findings. First let us get acquainted with the ten factors themselves. Then let us see what they can tell us about each criterion, that is, how

Table 8.1: Review of Factors

Factor I:	Two different mother-tongue populations, neither resident in the immediate vicinity of the school, both appreciably represented in student body.
Factor II:	Stress on total ethnocultural value of *marked* language and commitment thereto.
Factor III:	Stress on total ethnocultural value of *unmarked* language and commitment thereto.
Factor IV:	*Marked* language represents literary ethnic emphasis while *unmarked* language represents ethnically neutral activity.
Factor V:	Language of a comfortable minority dominates education and is therefore *unmarked.*
Factor VI:	Bilingual education starts at secondary level, and therefore *unmarked* language must initially be used even for *marked* group-related courses.
Factor VII:	Stress on technological value of *marked* language.
Factor VIII:	Stress on economic and international functions of *unmarked* language.
Factor IX:	Numerically significant and modernized language already known by many students is instructionally *marked.*
Factor X:	Language maintenance stress on *marked* language.

they can help us understand the differences that exist between secondary bilingual programs in connection with absolute academic success, relative academic success, and student satisfaction.

Marked and Unmarked Languages

One of the most striking facts about the ten factors of Table 8.1 is that four of them (II, VII, IX, X) deal with what we will refer to as the *marked language,* four others deal with what we will refer to as the *unmarked language* (III, V, VI, VIII), and, finally, the remaining two factors deal, directly or indirectly, with both the marked *and* the unmarked language (I, IV). Since this distinction between marked and unmarked is obviously crucial in understanding the dimensionality of secondary bilingual education, let us stop for a moment to make it clear.

In earlier discussions of bilingual education much stress has been given to the difference between *mother tongue* and *other tongue*, as well as to the interaction between that distinction and yet another, namely, the difference between *major language* on the world scene (English, Russian, French, Spanish, Chinese, and Arabic) and *minor language* on the world scene (all others). The latter category is sometimes further subdivided between languages of established standardization and modernization, on the one hand (e.g., German, Swedish, Japanese) and languages whose standardization and modernization are still recent or yet to come (e.g., Amharic, Hebrew, Nynorsk). The entire import of the above twofold (or threefold) distinction is that while it may be true that "a rose is a rose is a rose," it is *not* true that "a language is a language is a language." Presumably students, teachers, parents, and politicians alike react differently to a language, in the classroom and outside of it, depending on whether or not it is their mother tongue, whether or not it is powerful on the world scene, and whether or not it has long been authoritatively codified and attuned to the needs of modern technology. Presumably bilingual education that involves languages with plus ratings on all of these attributes will have "easier going" than bilingual education involving language with minus ratings.

The *marked* vs. *unmarked* distinction is related to the foregoing three but is different from them in that it is basically more responsive to a very pervasive but subtle socioeducational fact, namely, that *every bilingual education setting involves languages of differential school-relatedness in that particular setting.* It is precisely because of the fact that in any particular vicinity one language is more likely to be the mother tongue of most students than the other, and precisely because one is more likely to be stronger than the other on the world scene (particularly for international technological and fiscal functions), and precisely because one is more likely than the other to be at a more advantaged stage of sociolinguistic development that the *marked* vs. *unmarked* distinction comes into being, since, indeed, it cuts across all of these more customary distinctions.

That language is *marked* in a bilingual education setting which would most likely *not* be used *instructionally* were it not for bilingual education, i.e. to say, it is precisely bilingual education that has brought it into the classroom. Conversely, that language is *unmarked* in a bilingual education setting which would most likely (continue to) be used instructionally, even in the absence of bilingual education. Many advocates (as well as critics) of bilingual education have focused their attention upon the marked language (as well as upon the marked speech community whose mother tongue it is). One of the most surprising findings of the ISBSE study is that the factor-analyzed data obtained from directors of a highly variegated sample of bilingual education programs throughout the world reveal that unmarked language and unmarked speech community considerations are probably equally important, if not more so, with respect to the criteria here studied. This has not received sufficient stress in the past.

The Factors as Descriptive Dimensions

Now that the marked-unmarked distinction and the crucial importance of both of its polar extremes are clearer to us, we can return to our ten factorial dimensions of secondary bilingual education, seek to understand them better, and ultimately put them to use in conjunction with the criteria that are the focus of this inquiry.

Each dimension calls to mind the bilingual education setting in a particular country or region, although, quite clearly, each school would necessarily have *some* loading on every factor. Thus, Factor I is evocative of well-known bilingual schools located in cultural capitals or in regional centers, which often have some boarding students as well, but which more usually serve students who have left their nuclear families and are living with friends and relatives near the school itself. University-connected schools of this type are not unusual in those African and Asian countries in which the vernaculars are used instructionally either alongside one another or alongside some Western language. Seemingly, what is of importance is the *combination* of two populations, each with its own mother tongue, *and* the fact that they are both living away from home. It is such a combination of two superficially *separate* items into a single dimension that factor analysis is peculiarly well suited to highlight.

As Table 8.2 below indicates, examples of school types that would doubtlessly be characterized primarily by each factor are not difficult to suggest, although it must be stressed that in reality few, if any, schools would be adequately describable on *one* dimension and on *one alone*.

However, the major achievement of factor analysis is not in the naming of the factors that have been mathematically derived to begin with. (The naming process *is* a bit of a conceptual achievement—not to mention a source of gratification in view of the fact that elucidative naming is not always conceptually possible—but it inevitably forces an element of verbal uncertainty or infelicity upon what is essentially an elegant product of a good deal of quantitative work.*) The naming

---

*For a sound nontechnical introduction to the quantitative side of factor analysis as applied to social research, see Rummel, 1967.

Table 8.2: Factorial Types of Bilingual Schools (Hypothetical)

Factor I:	University-affiliated Afro-Asian bilingual schools drawing to them two different mother-tongue populations.
Factor II:	Welsh-stressing bilingual schools, Hebrew-stressing bilingual schools in Diaspora.
Factor III:	German-French bilingual schools in West Germany.
Factor IV:	German bilingual schools abroad.
Factor V:	Most bilingual schools in Francophone Africa or in Anglophone Africa.
Factor VI:	U. S. bilingual programs admitting Anglos for the first time in junior high years and stressing ethnic studies.
Factor VII:	English-stressing bilingual schools in Latin America.
Factor VIII:	Bilingual-oriented programs primarily for minorities residing in LWC (Language of Wider Communication) contexts.
Factor IX:	French immersion bilingual programs in Quebec.
Factor X:	Irish-stressing bilingual schools.

and even the further verbal explication of these factors are of less importance than the utility of the factors as explanatory or predictor variables in conjunction with criteria of crucial concern. It is to this topic that we now turn our attention.

The Factorial Dimensions as Criterial Predictors

We have said earlier that our 400 bits of descriptive data did yeoman service in accounting for inter-school variation on each of the criteria under study. We now return to this topic in terms of the factorial dimensions involved. What dimensions are most significant in connection with which criteria? Table 8.3 answers this question very parsimoniously.

Table 8.3: Pattern of Most Productive Predictors: Factorial Classification

Average Order of Entry	Criterion I	Criterion II	Criterion III
First Most Powerful	Factor VIII − (U)	Factor X − (M)	Factor IV + (B)
Second Most Powerful	Factor II + (M)	Factor IV + (B)	Factor V + (U)
Third Most Powerful	Factor V − (U)	Factor III + (U)	Factor II − (M)
Entirely Absent	Factor I	Factor I	Factor I
	Factor VI		Factor X

Note: U, M, and B indicate whether the factor deals with the unmarked, marked, or both languages. + or − indicate whether factor is positively or negatively related to criterion.

For each criterion three factors are of greatest predictive significance. Interestingly enough, each criterion is best predicted by a *combination* of both *marked* language and *unmarked* language factors. Furthermore, some factors which are positively related to Factor I (which deals with absolute academic achievement) are negatively related to Factor III (student satisfaction).

Absolute academic achievement seems to depend on a delicate balance between the attention given to the marked and unmarked languages, such that the former is genuinely and vigorously accepted, curricularly speaking, while the latter, though clearly dominant in the larger society surrounding the school and even surrounding the nation, is nevertheless not overdone. The message seems to be clear: overall absolute academic achievement is a reflection of performance on *all* subjects, and it is particularly the marked language subjects and efforts that require extra attention (acceptance, encouragement, recognition) in order to hold up well academically.

For the purpose of greatest absolute academic success, the unmarked language subjects and related efforts may actually need to be played down somewhat at school since they get more than ample support from contextual forces that permeate the school as well as the major formal and informal institutions of society as a whole. Academic excellence in these areas is not as school-dependent (upon school budgets, school time, school personnel, school rewards, etc.) as is academic excellence in the marked language subjects and related efforts.

The most productive predictors pertaining to relative academic success provide a nicely complementary picture to that which we have just reviewed in connection with absolute academic success. If bilingual secondary education is not only to be of high academic quality in its own right, but also is to compete academically with the monolingual secondary schools in the same area and serving comparable populations, then a different set of predictors and, indeed, a different predictive constellation are involved. For the purposes of such relative-competitive success, it is the marked language subjects and related efforts that must not be overstressed. Obviously, it is precisely in connection with marked language subjects and the entire atmosphere pertaining to the marked language that bilingual schools differ from monolingual ones. If *too much* is made of this difference, bilingual secondary schools may not be able to compete with the monolingual ones in those areas in which they share common goals (e.g., achievement in unmarked language subjects and, perhaps therefore, achievement in college admissions examinations pertaining to such subjects).

Does the foregoing mean that there is an inevitable conflict between Criterion I and Criterion II goals for bilingual secondary education? Perhaps so, if either goal is carried to an extreme. That there need be *no* conflict is clear both from the fact that these two criteria are hardly related to each other in our data as well as from the thumbnail sketches given in Appendix 1 (see particularly the sketches dealing with the newer Welsh bilingual schools). That there *can* be conflict between academic goals is clear even from monolingual secondary schools in which a given area of excellence (science, music, art) is developed at the expense of all else. Thus, this *is* a matter to watch. If attention to the marked language "gets out of hand" (and let us remember, the marked language need not be an oppressed or disadvantaged minority language; in much of the world it may be English or

French or Russian), the price that will need to be paid, in relative-competitive terms, may be one that will ultimately redound to the disadvantage of bilingual education itself. Once again we note that what is involved is a matter of balance, of sensitivity, of judgment. Certainly we should expect no less from bilingual education than that it be mature in these respects, and certainly such maturity has been reached in many schools in all parts of the world. There is a built-in tension in bilingual education, a built-in proportionality requirement. This is fortunate: it keeps bilingual education on its toes and keeps it from becoming complacent. It is also a built-in self-corrective: it keeps bilingual education from becoming monolingual.

The built-in balance in bilingual secondary education is not only conceptually required, but it is also a desideratum for student satisfaction. Criterion III is best predicted by factors that overlap with each of the other two criteria (whereas the first two criteria are best predicted by totally different subsets of factors). The greatest overlap is with Criterion I (but note that the directional significance of each shared factor is opposite in connection with Criterion III from what it was in the case of Criterion I). The configurational upshot in the prediction of student satisfaction is that both curricular balance within the school and societal allocation of language functions in the community as a whole are highly desirable contexts for bilingual education in general and for bilingual secondary education in particular.

It is also noteworthy that student satisfaction is higher when the marked language represents ethnicity (literature, history, culture, tradition) than when it represents technology. Bilingual education yields more student satisfaction (as well as more relative academic success) when the minority mother tongue is marked and ethnically justified than when English, French, or another Language of Wider Communication is marked and is technologically justified (Factor VII) or is unmarked and is economically justified on other grounds (Factor VIII). Languages of Wider Communication may be desired and admired; only languages of ethnicity are loved. All languages can be hated because of their symbolic associations; only the languages of real or imagined intimacy can be loved. Bilingual education must arrive at or reinforce a *modus vivendi* between marked and unmarked languages (and often between ethnic and supra-ethnic languages). It cannot afford to become confused with self-indulgent romanticism and rejection of the "outside" world. That is not what either marked languages, ethnic languages, or bilingual education need.

Predictively Useless Factors

It should be clear from our discussion thus far that some factors are predictively less useful than others. Least useful of all is Factor I (which never contributes at all to the prediction of any criterion). Factors VI, VII, and IX never make a *major* contribution to the prediction of any criterion, although they do make more minor contributions of this kind. Obviously there are dimensions of bilingual secondary education which, although they *are* dimensionally significant, are *not* significantly related to the three criteria that we have investigated. However, because they *do* accurately reflect real characteristics of bilingual secondary schools in some parts of the world, they *are* needed in accounting for the differences between such schools on an international basis. Perhaps there are other criteria for which these dimensions would be predictively useful (e.g., community support, staff satisfaction, etc.). This possibility remains to be studied in the future.

Relating Criteria to Intuitive Item Types

Factor analysis often cuts across a priori intuitions. It sometimes brings together items that investigators did not initially realize were highly related to each other. It sometimes separates items that investigators assumed to pertain to the same topics. This is precisely the value of factor analysis. It is an empirical approach to confirming or disconfirming the preexisting dimensionality assumptions and hypotheses (conscious or unconscious) of the investigator. However, in the final analysis every good researcher is also a bit of an artist. He cannot work satisfactorily only with objectively and quantitatively separate dimensions, any more than he can, as a scientist, work only with intuitively constituted dimensions. All research consists of a fruitful and gratifying combination of both types of dimensions and of a creative tension system (hopefully not a conflict system) between the two. Thus far in this chapter we have dealt only with empirically and quantitatively derived dimensions or factors. Let us now take a glance at what our intuitive dimensions (program characteristics, student characteristics, staff characteristics, community characteristics, and language characteristics) can tell us about the criteria that are of concern to us.

Table 8.4:   **Pattern of Most Productive Predictors: A Priori Classifications**

Criterion	Most Powerful Category	Next Most Powerful Category
Absolute Academic Achievement	Comm/Lang Items	Student Items
Relative Academic Items	Comm/Lang Items	Program Items
Student Satisfaction	Program Items	Student Items

A glance at Table 8.4 reveals many interesting facts in this connection. On an overall basis, community-language characteristics loom most large. They are the major predictors for both academic achievement criteria. Program characteristics are next most powerful. They constitute the major predictors of student satisfaction and substantial predictors of relative academic success. Finally, student characteristics are of tertiary importance since they contribute substantially both to the prediction of absolute academic success as well as to student satisfaction, although they are not the primary predictors of either. Clearly it is the staff characteristics that wind up last on all counts since these seem to contribute importantly or substantially to none of the criteria we have studied .

The latter finding is not an artifact of asking too few or unimportant items dealing with staff characteristics. On the contrary: many questions were asked dealing with this topic, and these included all the facets of staff background, training, certification, remuneration, experience, and interests that have been mentioned either in the general or in the bilingual education literature. Neither was there any lack of variation in our data with respect to staff characteristics. The implication must therefore be retained that the other topics studied are generally much more powerful than are staff characteristics insofar as accounting for inter-school variation on the criteria we have studied. Perhaps this is because staff characteristics are akin to "a scalpel in a butcher shop," i.e., they are simply too delicate to make a difference when pitted against such powerful factors as the others under consideration. Perhaps we also need to reexamine our staff training efforts in order to give staff far greater technical expertise than they may now possess in the secondary bilingual education context.

The relative impotence of staff characteristics assumes greater credibility when we compare such characteristics with the community and language variables which seem to be of greatest predictive importance. Here we are dealing with such truly powerful considerations as the proportion of the population that have the unmarked language as mother tongue, whether the unmarked language is of importance for international communication, the proportion of parents of unmarked mother tongue who are professionals or semi-professionals, the proportion of the unmarked mother-tongue population that already knows the marked language prior to secondary school, etc. Clearly, educators must not despair of their role in bilingual education in general or in bilingual secondary education in particular. Rather, they must realize that in large part the success of such education is dictated by very powerful and pervasive societal and language considerations (language-in-society considerations, if you like)—macro-factors, we might call them—and that it is only after these can be controlled (as they are in many local situations) that staff characteristics can come to the fore and enjoy the prominence that they deserve. Perhaps educators have too often been expected to perform miracles under societally impossible conditions. To know one's limitations is the beginning of wisdom in capitalizing on one's strengths.

A Precautionary Note in Parting

How much stock can we put in the findings of the International Study of Bilingual Secondary Education, given two limiting considerations: its data is of the self-report variety and its sample is rather small? Certainly the findings should not be oversold. Indeed, it would be well to honor them more for provocativeness and novelty rather than in terms of any purported conclusiveness. Certainly, like most initial research, they raise at least as many questions as they answer—and that is as it should be.

Nevertheless, neither the small sample size nor the self-report nature of the data can be the *reason* for any of the findings we have reported. The respondents to the ISBSE questionnaire were not aware of the criteria being investigated since these were never identified as such to them. The reliability and validity of their responses were generally confirmed (and, indeed, the respondents were informed that these would be looked into via personal visits to a 10% subsample, as well as via further correspondence with them and with others in their areas). Neither small sample size nor self-reporting is conducive to the high multiple correlations obtained nor to the conceptual clarity of the factor analyses. Obviously, had more data of the same kinds been collected via more precise methods, even better predictions and clearer factors would then have obtained. However, the predictive-explanatory levels attained are already extremely high and, rather than requiring apology of any kind, are sufficiently solid to provide a good point of departure for detailed follow-up research.

Types of Bilingual Secondary Schools

One of the findings derived from our factor analyses serves the same reassuring function as do "marker factors" in factor analytic research more generally. Normally, factor analysis is utilized for fields of inquiry where a certain few dimensions *are* known but many others are *not*. If the analysis yields any of the known factors, then greater confidence can be placed in the newly derived but previously unknown ones. Thus, if numerous measures were taken of all the rooms in a hotel, a factor analysis of these measures should yield the factors of length, width, and breadth, in addition to any other factors that might be forthcoming (other dimensions might also obtain due to rooms with curved walls, with curved or open ceilings, with more or less window space, with more or less door space, etc.). The "marker dimensions" of length, width, breadth tend to engender confidence in the other, more unexpected dimensions. In our case, we built into our sample selection the dimensions of compensatory, enrichment, and language-maintenance program types. No such factors appeared when the 400 bits of data for each school were factor analyzed. On the other hand, when the nearly 100 responding schools were themselves factor analyzed (that is, when the question was asked: "What types of bilingual secondary schools are there?" rather than "What are the dimensions of bilingual secondary education across schools? "), three distinct groupings appeared which were easily characterizable as compensatory, enrichment, and language-maintenance in their factorial characteristics. This "marker" finding, reflecting as it does something built into our data collection, is not only reassuring; it is also a substantive finding in its own right. It implies that program types—real though they be—are themselves not definitive of criterial performance and not closely related to variation in community, staff, student, program, or language characteristics. This too is worth knowing, particularly at this early stage.

Conclusions

What have we learned from the International Study of Bilingual Secondary Education that we did not know before? Quite a few things.

1. The criteria of absolute academic success, relative academic success, and student satisfaction can be predicted with very high accuracy on the basis of socioeducational and sociolinguistic data.

2. The overall dimensionality of secondary bilingual education is almost equally related to the marked and the unmarked languages involved in such education.

3. Maximal prediction of the criteria studied by the ISBSE requires a very careful balance of attention to both marked language subjects and related efforts, on the one hand, as well as to unmarked language subjects and related efforts, on the other hand. This remains basically true even though both relative academic success and student satisfaction require somewhat greater attention to the unmarked language and absolute academic success to the marked language.

4. Student satisfaction is greatest when the marked language is related to ethnicity and its intimacy rather than to technology and its impersonal efficiency.

5. The most powerful characteristics for predicting the criteria of concern deal with community-language and program considerations. Least powerful of all are those characteristics of secondary bilingual education that deal with staff considerations.

6. Program types (compensatory, enrichment, language-maintenance) are not powerful criterial predictors. There are good and poor schools of each of these types.

Given the relative numerical infrequency of bilingual *secondary* education in comparison to bilingual *primary* education throughout the world, it must be asked whether the above findings apply equally well to the latter as to the former. There is no evidence concerning this question at the moment, and certainly such is greatly needed. Nevertheless, the findings enumerated above appear to be of such fundamental conceptual validity that their applicability to bilingual elementary education, at least in part, would seem to be very possible.

The bulk of the current bibliography on bilingual education is either *psychological* (Lambert and Tucker, 1972; Lambert, Tucker and d'Anglejan, 1973; Mackey, 1972; Macnamara, 1966), *educational* (Andersson and Boyer, 1970; Andersson, 1971b; Anon, 1971b; Gaarder, 1970; John and Horner, 1971; Lange, 1971; Noss, 1967; Special Subcommittee, 1967; Swain, 1972), or *linguistic* (section of Kelly, 1969; Saville and Troike, 1971). Although there has undoubtedly been *some* sociolinguistic impact on the field (particularly in Anon, 1971a; Cohen, 1970; Fishman and Lovas, 1970; Kjolseth, 1972; Mackey, 1970; Macnamara, 1973; Ramos, Aguilar and Sibayan, 1967; Spolsky, 1972), nothing has as yet appeared that is an avowed sociology of bilingual education. This volume represents an attempt in that direction, both theoretically and empirically. Among the by-products to be hoped for from the development of a sociological component in this field are improved understanding, practice, and evaluation with respect to the *thousands* of bilingual education programs now under way in the U. S. A. and elsewhere. However, a sociology of bilingual education should not only suggest better answers to some old questions; it should also enable us to tackle some new questions.

Historical and Comparative Perspective

The stress on *thousands* of programs immediately indicates that a worldwide perspective is in order if we are not to confuse *sociology* with *American society* and the particular constraints that it has imposed on bilingual education at various times in its own relatively brief history. Of course, we want to understand, implement, and evaluate American bilingual education better, but in order to do so we must first know how it differs from and is similar to bilingual education elsewhere in the world. There are countries in which bilingual education is omnipresent and there is no other kind (e.g., Philippines, Singapore). There are countries in which it is not very common but a recognized alternative (Ireland, Wales, parts of non-Russian U. S. S. R.). There are countries in which it is rare and viewed as enriching for elites (e.g., Belgium, Switzerland), and others in which it is rare and viewed as compensatory for the poor (e.g., U. S. A.). Certainly, such basic differences in the societies in which it exists must be built into a universally

INTERNATIONAL SOCIOEDUCATIONAL PERSPECTIVE
ON SOME UNCOMFORTABLE QUESTIONS
ABOUT BILINGUAL EDUCATION

CHAPTER IX

relevant sociology of bilingual education. Doing this will provide useful heuristic perspective on the *American situation*.

Diachronic perspective is also likely to be needed, in addition to the comparative synchronic perspective just mentioned, in any sociology of bilingual education. From the earliest records of education in all classical societies we find ample evidence of the predominance of bilingual education (Lewis, Appendix 3). Most often all formal education was elitist, and, therefore, so was bilingual education. Most often the target or textual language differed from the process of mediating language. But, in any case, the variation to be noted across time is as important to us as that to be noted across cultures, both in devising a sociology of bilingual education and in benefiting from it for the purpose of American education.

An Initial Sociological Typology

Reflecting this concern both for historical and comparative (i.e., diachronic and crosscultural) perspective, a beginning typology can be derived based upon the interrelationship among four dichotomies first to each other and then to rated success in the marked and unmarked languages employed.

Dichotomy 1: Language Given Primary Emphasis vs. Language Given Secondary Emphasis (LPE-LSE). Because languages are not functionally equal or identical, *almost all bilingual education programs devote more time to one than to another.* It would seem, on intuitive sociological grounds, to be important to distinguish between the bilingual education *inputs* and *outputs* for LPEs and those for LSEs.

Dichotomy 2: Mother Tongue vs. Other Tongue. Just as most bilingual education programs are "unbalanced" in the emphasis each language receives, so most classrooms within such programs differ in the mother-tongue-other-tongue status of these languages for the students receiving bilingual education. It certainly appears sociologically advisable to examine the impact of this distinction on bilingual education inputs and outputs.

Dichotomy 3: Minor vs. Major Languages. The six official languages of the United Nations (Arabic, English, French, Spanish, Russian, and Chinese) were considered "major" languages on the world scene. The distinction between smaller and larger (broader and narrower in an international sense) seems well worth considering in any sociological typology.

Dichotomy 4: Out-of-School Formal Institutions. A language of organized or official importance out of school (regardless of whether it is the mother or other tongue of students) obviously can have a far different claim on students, teachers, and school authorities than can a language that has no such out-of-school reinforcement. The sociology of bilingual education must be concerned with the power differentials of language in the real world. This is exactly what the marked-unmarked distinction attempts to do.

A Heuristic Grid

These dichotomies, in interaction with each other, result in 24 or 16 societal contexts for bilingual education. An even more complicated grid is possible, of course, but if we can control our typological passions we may reap the benefits of conceptual parsimony which are so needed by any fledgling field. That these 16 contexts are more than a mathematical artifact of four dichotomies is demonstrated by the ease with which we can locate examples of bilingual education in connection with each of them. Indeed, there is already quite a bit of literature about bilingual education in several of these contexts so that the would-be sociologist of bilingual education can begin with quite a bibliography,* which means: with intellectual perspective.

Our purpose in presenting this grid at the close of this volume is to aid us in commenting on a number of issues pertaining to bilingual education that have been particularly worrisome of late to American educators and to community leaders with educational concerns. Perhaps a comparative and sociolinguistically oriented sociology of bilingual education can shed some light on these issues and concerns.

Must One Language Always Be an "Other" Tongue?

The implication of an "other" tongue is frequently somewhat invidious relative to the mother tongue. It often denotes an out-group. It usually connotes foreignness. Can that be overcome? Yes and no.

There are societies engaged in bilingual education whose members consider both of the languages that are involved to be *their own*. Such societies are called diglossic (Fishman, 1967). The outstanding examples today are the use of vernacular and classical Arabic as media in parts of the Arab world, Yiddish and Hebrew as media in much of Jewish Orthodox education, Demotic Greek and Katharevusa as media in Greece. These examples are reported as part of bilingual education in Chapter VI, although they are *not* listed in Table 9.1 because of its own-other distinctions. Both languages may not be equally used, or may not even both be used for textual (reading/writing) purposes, but they are both definitely *their own* to the pupils, teachers, administrators, and parents. Nevertheless, even in this case only one of the two is the mother tongue of one and all. Thus, the lesson to be learned is that *foreignness can be overcome*—by dint of long and stable positive association, on a widespread societal basis, with the "other" tongue. Nevertheless, even when the "other" tongue is no longer societally foreign, it is still not the same as the mother tongue: not in intimacy nor in the whole range of functions for which it is considered appropriate. This is necessarily so. No society needs or has two languages for the same functions. As a result, no society, not even those whose bilingualism has been most widespread and most stable, raises its children with two mother tongues. There is always an "other" tongue, and the purpose of bilingual education is not to have the other tongue

---

*See Fishman (1974) for an empirical example of the use to which these contexts and the literature pertaining to them can be put.

compete with the mother tongue for its societally recognized functions. Nevertheless, the other tongue need not connote things foreign and fearful; indeed, given sufficient societal commitment in that direction, bilingual education can be a powerful assisting force on behalf of divesting the "other" tongue and the "other" group of its foreignness. That is exactly what bilingual education at its best is all about.

Can the School "Go It Alone" for Bilingual Education?

Definitely not, not even when there is a clear mandate to do so. One of the major conclusions to be derived from the International Study of Secondary Bilingual Education is that not only is community consensus needed if bilingual education is to succeed, but that the help of the unmarked language community is needed every bit as much as, if not more than, that of the marked language community. The main trouble with foreign-language learning thus far has been that it was entirely a school-dependent affair with no out-of-school contextual significance whatsoever. Bilingual education that is left to the schools alone will have the same sad fate. The school can provide instructional power for bilingual education but not functional power for it. The latter must be provided by the community itself in terms of either dignifying its own diversity or the diversity of the international community. Dignifying diversity can take many shapes. It can take the shape of "protecting neglected national resources" of the language-and-culture kind in our own back yards (for details see Fishman, 1966, Chapter 14, or Fishman, 1972d, Chapter 2). It can be related to visitors, travel, concerts, visits, exhibits, projects, jobs, student creativity, correspondence. But it should be tied as securely and as fully as possible to community-supported undertakings rather than merely to those that the school alone espouses and maintains. Most of the studies abstracted in Appendix 2 make this very same point. Note how many of the contexts enumerated in Table 9.1 reflect strong community support. Community interest and involvement on behalf of bilingual education is a must for a successful program. American educators have long sought ways of fostering closer school-community ties—even for the sake of history, mathematics, and biology instruction. Such ties are all the more necessary for bilingual education, and bilingual education itself can often contribute to the fostering of such ties.

Can Community Interest Be Too Divisive for the Good of Bilingual Education?

Yes, at times. If the unmarked language community is apathetic or opposed, and if all of the interest in bilingual education comes from oppressed minorities, bilingual education finds itself in a context of pressures, tensions, grievances, conflicts, and cleavages. Such developments frequently obtain at early periods of bilingual education, when it is wanted more by the "have-nots" than by the "haves." What is needed under these circumstances is a campaign to familiarize the "haves" with the benefits of enrichment-oriented bilingual education for them and for their children. Many of the chapters of this volume have this very purpose in mind.

Table 9.1: **Toward a Sociological Taxonomy of Bilingual Education**

	Language of Primary Emphasis	Language of Secondary Emphasis	Language of Major Instit.	Case No.	Examples	Reference
I.	Own Major	Other Minor	Own	1	Russian children studying certain subjects in English in U. S. S. R.	Lewis (1972)
				2	Puerto Rican children (in P.R.) studying certain subjects in English in private schools	Epstein (1970)
				3	Magreb-Arab children in part-French schools	
				4	Franco-Canadian children learning certain subjects in English	Royal Commission, Vol. II (1968)
II.	Own Major	Other Major	Other	5	American children at the J.F.K. School in Berlin (or other "American Schools" in France, Latin America, etc.)	Mackey (1972)
				6	Chinese children in primarily Chinese and partially English schools in Hong Kong	
III.	Own Major	Other Minor	Own	7	English-speaking Irish children attending a part-Irish school	Macnamara (1966)
				8	Ethnic-group schools in the U.S.A. (not Jewish Orth.) for 3rd-generation children neither Spanish nor French mt.	Fishman & Nahirny (1964)

				No.		Reference
				9	The Germanized Romansh child in a primarily German school	Weinreich (1951)
				10	English-speaking Welsh child attending a part-Welsh school	Dodson (1966)
IV.	Own Major	Other Minor	Other	11	Schools for expatriate Anglo-American or French children in Afro-Asian countries with indigenous official languages	
				12	Israeli-Arabs attending Arab schools	
				13	Chinese students attending primarily Chinese schools in Malaysia	
				14	English mt. students at the American College in Israel	
				15	Russian students in the Ukraine in primarily Russian schools	
V.	Own Minor	Other Major	Own	16	Israelis studying certain h.s. subjects in English	
				17	Gaeltacht Irish children attending primarily Irish schools	
				18	Afrikaans children studying certain subjects in English	Malherbe (1946, 1966)
				19		
				20	Bulgarian children in partly Russian-language schools	
VI.	Own Minor	Other Major	Other	21	Ukranian children in Canada or many (Orthodox) Jewish children in U.S.A., Latin America	

Table 9.1 (continued)

	Language of Primary Emphasis	Language of Secondary Emphasis	Language of Major Instit.	Case No.	Examples	Reference
				22	Dukhobors, German sects, other nonparticipant minorities in U.S.A., Canada, Latin America, etc.	Vanek & Darnell (1971)
				23		Kloss (1966)
VII.	Own Minor	Other Minor	Own	24	Telegu children studying certain subjects in Hindi (or vice versa: Hindi-Telegu)	
				25	Javanese children studying certain subjects in Dutch	
				26	Croatian children attending part-Serbian schools	
				27		
VIII.	Own Minor	Other Minor	Other	28	Yiddish-speaking ultra-Orthodox children studying certain subjects in Hebrew (in Israel)	
				29	Tsisho (Yiddish-Polish) or Tarbut (Hebrew-Polish) schools in interwar Poland	Kazhdan (1960)
				30	Tagrinye-Amharic and Galinye-Amharic school demanded by larger minorities in Ethiopia	Ferguson (1970)
IX.	Other Major	Own Major	Own	31	Franco-Canadian children in Quebec attending primarily English schools	Royal Commission, Vol. II (1968)

	Other Major	Own Major / Own Minor	Other / Own	No.		Reference
				32	Children of Russian aristocracy/German aristocracy attending primarily French schools (mid-19th century)	
				33	Magreb-Arab children in primarily French schools	
				34	Mexican children attending the "American school" in Mexico City	
X.	Other Major	Own Major	Other	35	Anglo-Canadian children in Quebec attending primarily French schools	Lambert & Tucker (1972)
				36	Hispanic children in the U.S.A. attending primarily English schools	Gaarder (1970)
				37		Rojas (1966)
				38	American/German children attending primarily French schools in Switzerland	Balkan (1970)
				39	Puerto Rican Nuyorquino returning to P.R. and studying in part-English program	
XI.	Other Major	Own Minor	Own	40	Pilipino or Swahili mt. (or Soviet minority) children attending primarily English (or Russian) schools	Davis (1967)
				41		Tucker (1970)
				42	West African children attending primarily English schools	Armstrong (1968)

Table 9.1 (continued)

	Language of Primary Emphasis	Language of Secondary Emphasis	Language of Major Instit.	Case No.	Examples	Reference
				43	Jewish children attending Alliance schools in pre-Mandate Palestine	
				44	Ukranian children attending primarily Russian schools	
XII.	Other Major	Own Minor	Other	45	Ethnic-group schools in the U.S.A. today for children of recent immigrants of neither Spanish nor French mt.	Fishman & Nahirny (1964)
				46	American Indian children attending primarily English boarding schools	Gaarder (1970)
				47		Spolsky (1974)
				48	Rural Guaraní children attending primarily Spanish schools	Rubin (1968)
				49	Quechua children attending primarily Spanish schools	Burns (1968)
XIII.	Other Minor	Own Major	Own	50	English-speaking Irish children attending a primarily Irish school	Macnamara (1966)
XIV.	Other Minor	Own Major	Other	51	Anglo-American or French children attending *local* schools (nor for expatriates) in Afro-Asian countries with indigenous official languages	

			52	Recent American, French, Latin American, and Russian immigrants to Israel	Malherbe (1966)
XV.	Other Minor	Own Minor	Own	53	English-speaking children in primarily Afrikaans schools	Pietersen (1971)
			54	Frisian children attending a primarily Dutch school, or Landsmål children attending a primarily Riksmål school in their home region	
XVI.	Other Minor	Own Minor	Other	55	Luganda children attending a primarily Swahili school	
			56	Jewish children attending primarily Hungarian/Polish/ Romanian schools (LSE: Hebrew)	
			57	Minority Filipino children attending primarily Pilipino schools	Davis (1967)
			58		Sibayan (1972)

There is absolutely no reason why bilingual education should be made all of one cloth (e.g., "compensatory") throughout any given community. There is no reason why it should be entirely oriented around the needs of one group of children (e.g., the disadvantaged). There is no reason at all why education as a whole should suffer as a result of bilingual education. There is no reason why monolingual teachers should lose their jobs as a result of bilingual education, and there is also no reason why most such teachers cannot slowly become bilingual themselves and thus of greater benefit to society, to the educational system, and to their pupils. There is no reason for community divisiveness in connection with bilingual education. Note how few of the contexts enumerated in Table 9.1 involve divisiveness or conflict. Where divisiveness obtains, it is not the fault of bilingual education but of lack of appreciation for the diversity of the community and the diversity of the world. That diversity will not go away just because it is ignored or covered up by unmarked paint. Quite the contrary. Under such circumstances it will continue to "crop out" unexpectedly and unproductively. When bilingual education is given the communitywide support that it needs and deserves, the diversity that it heralds will be unifying and gratifying, not only cognitively but emotionally and esthetically as well.

Does the World or Mankind Really Need All Those Ethnic Languages?

An era that has witnessed the genocidal massacre of millions can ask questions that were formerly too embarrassing to utter. Chapter I tries to answer this question and not to react overly to the unconscious death wishes that lie behind it. However, these wishes too must be revealed. Sometimes they are harbored by the strong against the weak. Sometimes, by the weak about themselves or others who are also weak. Sometimes, the strong themselves are the targets of such wishes, and the utter impossibility of such death wishes leads to the substitution of weaker targets. But it is all a useless wish as well as an ugly one.

Ethnicity is one of the inevitable attributes of social life, and new ethnicities arise, old ones alter, and others disappear. No aggregative future is possible for mankind without ethnicity and, therefore, without languages strongly related to ethnic experiences. To look forward to the death of ethnicity is to misunderstand man and society. It is a particularly modern misunderstanding, one not shared by the ancient Hebrews, Greeks, Romans, Church Fathers, or early Islamic thinkers, all of whom had a capacity for combining both ethnicity and supra-ethnicity in their theories or philosophies of desired social organization. Their more balanced view toward ethnicity and toward bilingualism and linguistic diversity was lost by Western philosophers from the eighteenth century onward.

This is a loss that badly and sadly needs to be corrected, for our modern pursuit of the rational and efficient mass-society, state and world is crippled as a result. No matter how much international One World awareness grows, and may it grow as much and as quickly as possible, the human need and capacity for subgroup membership on the basis of traditional intimacy will go on and on. Indeed, ethnicity grows stronger when denied, oppressed, or repressed, and becomes more reasonable and more tractable when recognized and liberated (Fishman, 1972b). One of the strengths of bilingual education is that it accepts ethnicity and brings it into the open as well as into contact with modern ideas and modern goals.

Finally, let it be acknowledged that the supposedly nonethnic and supra-ethnic Languages of Wider Communication and the modern, quantitative, technological pursuits and life-styles with which they are purportedly associated are themselves not free of ethnicity. They are reacted to as such (e.g., as being Western European or American) in many parts of the world by uncounted millions. Our espousal of them is self-serving rather than entirely altruistic. It leaves us "on top" and relieves us, at the same time, from acknowledging the ethnic-cultural coloration with which that life-style is suffused. We do not so much despise ethnicity as much as we are impatient with other people's ethnicity. In practice we are quite ethnocentric, every bit as much as "all those little peoples," but, unlike them, we try to hide it from ourselves and pretend that what we are is "above and beyond that," is panhuman, the wave of the future. If bilingual education can help save us from this disease that has not only blinded us (to ourselves and to the world) but caused us to try to spread it to others, then it will have served us nobly.

What About Subject Matter Achievement Per Se*? Isn't There Necessarily an "Educational Price To Pay" for Using as Comedium a Language Which Is Not the Child's Strongest Language?*

The very way in which this question is asked reveals an unconscious assumption as to the societal context of bilingual education, namely, that education in a marked language is being urged upon children for whom the unmarked language is the mother tongue. From the ISBSE results, and from all that was known about comparative bilingual education before the ISBSE results were available, it should be clear that the above-mentioned societal context is really only one out of many in which bilingual education operates. Indeed, a far more common context for bilingual education is precisely the one in which *it is the means of providing education via the mother tongue* for marked language communities whose children had heretofore received (and would otherwise still receive) their education entirely in an unmarked "other tongue." If bilingual education does nothing else, it at least equalizes the children of marked- and unmarked-language backgrounds by providing each of them some instruction via their own mother tongue as well as some via the "other" group's mother tongue. If this removes an advantage that the unmarked community's children previously had (since they previously received *all* of their education in their mother tongue, whereas the marked children previously received *none* of their education in their mother tongue), then at least the "price" is being paid (i.e., the "sacrifice" is being made) by those best able to pay it (Fishman and Leuders, 1972).

But the general question (rather than its unconscious overtones) must still be faced up to. The answer must be seen in terms of social class and academic-motivational variation. Controlling for such factors, the brunt of the current evidence is that children whose bilingual education starts early enough (e.g., *no later than* the beginning of secondary school and as much before that as possible) and continues at a sufficiently intensive level within a generally positive familial, communal, and societal framework *do not lose out at all in subject matter achievement* when compared with their peers receiving monolingual education (see abstracts of research by Bruck *et al.,* Paulston [1972], Riegel & Freedle, Segalowitz in Appendix 2). Their language acquisition apparatus is still flexible enough for them to be able to acquire rapidly facility in any new language toward which they are attitudinally positive and to be able to rather quickly begin using that new language for purposes of further subject matter acquisition. Thus, unlike older or more negative learners, their "weaker language" soon becomes strong enough (under "immersion" or "ulpan" methods of language instruction) to become a vehicle for receptive and active communication and learning. The level of such learning will then depend on other factors, e.g., on those that more generally influence subject matter achievement: home environment, community reward and societal recognition, personal interest and ability, peer-group reinforcement, etc. Children with better personal and societal endowments will continue to do better and disadvantaged children will continue to be *relatively* disadvantaged, but this will be due to out-of-school inequalities rather than due to bilingual education *per se.* In none of the countries in which bilingual education is common (see Chapter VI) is it in any way associated with lower achievement than in the monolingual schools serving comparable populations.

When all is said and done, bilingual education "gives" much more than it "takes away." The unmarked-language child has at least acquired entrée into a language and culture that would otherwise have been for him a closed book. His unmarked-language attainment need not be a whit lower than it would otherwise have been, provided familial, communal and societal support for bilingual education is there. The latter is equally true for the marked-language child vis-à-vis *his* unmarked-language attainments, but in addition he has been given the opportunity to experience the dignity of his patrimony within the secular sanctity of the school.

When My (Grand-) Parents Came to the U. S. A. They Learned English Without Getting Bilingual Education at Public Expense. Isn't That the Better Way? Why Do More Recent Minorities Deserve Special Handling?

More American grandparents received bilingual education at public expense than most of us realize. There was considerable public bilingual education in the U. S. A. in the latter part of the nineteenth and in the early part of the twentieth century (Fishman, 1966; 92-126, 233-37), and only the xenophobia of World War I days has erased that fact from our historical consciousness. Subsequent waves of immigration did not have such opportunities, until very recent years. Their Anglification, linguistically and culturally, was achieved by dint of great personal and collective hardship, and whatever social mobility they may ultimately have attained was less the result of Anglification *per se* than it was of general economic trends in American life. There is no good reason to force this hardship of self-denial upon newer and older Americans today. Not only are our economic circumstances and prospects far different from what they were in the years just after the First World War, but we are a different country socially and intellectually as well, and the world too is a different place than it was.

Democracies are not static. They mature and develop, morally and philosophically as well as socially and politically. We are more sensitive now than we were then to the evils of child labor, discriminatory hiring and firing practices, unconscionably long hours of work, and other such undesirable characteristics of the so-called "good old days" when our (grand-) parents were struggling to make their way in the U. S. A. Similarly, we are much more sensitive to the cultural struggles of our minorities, and to their educational struggles, than we were then.

We now realize the folly of "plowing under" our cultural and linguistic resources—only to expend untold hours and dollars later on in order to teach crosscultural appreciations and foreign languages to pupils who have first been forced to forgo those they were already in control of. We also realize that bilingual education for minorities does not mean less mastery of English. In the long run it means just as much mastery of English *plus* more vibrant cultural pluralism, both for the minorities and for the majority as well. In the physical world one cannot "have one's cake and eat it too," but in the cultural-educational world, pluralism is not only possible but stimulating and enriching too. This is the precise experience that scores of other countries have had with bilingual education. None of the countries engaging in it as a wholehearted educational alternative has found it to be an educational burden on the minorities involved. Nor, in the long run, has it led to political unrest or separations. These are all baseless fears, particularly in the American setting. Indeed, bilingual education may serve to counteract such tendencies wherever they exist, since it is an indication of good will, of recognition, of cultural partnership, and these often are among the conscious or unconscious goals of aggrieved minorities.

Basically, however, real bilingual education is not a political ploy. It is an educational advance. Our country has advanced and improved in many ways since the times of our (grand-) parents. Bilingual education is both old and new, both in the U. S. A. and throughout the world. We have never tried it in a major, wholehearted way before. It is now coming into its own in the U. S. A., and it is about time that it do so. It is the kind of "special handling" that we *all* deserve and that we will *all* benefit from.

Why Is It That Only the U. S. A. Has Compensatory Bilingual Education?

That is not so. While it is true that compensatory (or compensatory-transitional) bilingual education is disproportionately widespread in the U. S. A., it is found to a lesser degree on every continent. It is the common approach to bilingual education wherever populations hitherto barred or restricted or disadvantaged vis-à-vis education in the unmarked language are given greater access to it without being given simultaneous control over either basic or local educational policies and practices. When such control is finally obtained, as it more and more commonly is, compensatory-transitional bilingual education is usually expanded to one or another of the more demanding, more rewarding and more stable types. If bilingual education is to take hold as a stable alternative type of education available to American youngsters, it too will have to travel this developmental course. This is necessarily so since compensatory-transitional bilingual education is self-liquidating at best and self-frustrating at worst. It is patronizing, apologetic, invidious, one-sided and unidirectional. Whatever good it may accomplish is attained at a terrible psychological and societal price. Part of this price is to leave behind an inherently false picture of what bilingual education is, of what cultural diversity is, and of the potential that both have to stimulate and to enrich us all.

The above conviction underlies the choice of thumbnail sketches in Appendix 1. None of the cases presented there are of the compensatory-transitional curricular type. At the other extreme only one is of the enrichment-full biliteracy curricular type. By and large the cases dwell upon the enrichment-partial biliteracy or the group-maintenance-partial-biliteracy types which are most prevalent on the world scene and which represent the logical next developmental steps as far as bilingual education in the U. S. A. is concerned. Not all of the schools/programs sketched are exemplary by any means. Indeed, the qualitative range is rather broad, but realistically so. Nevertheless, there are a few noteworthy and promising threads that run through all of the sketches: the importance of experimentation, the dependence upon parental and societal support, the endless hard work required of students and teachers alike, the capacity of dedication to move mountains and to touch children's lives by inspiring idealism in them as well, the importance of regulating the admission of students so as to be able to achieve the results that are desired, certain kinds of goals being realistic only for certain kinds of students at any particular time. These threads confirm many of the empirical findings of the ISBSE (Chapter VIII). All in all, they should serve to set American teachers and parents alike to thinking about more vigorous and creative types of bilingual education than the compensatory-transitional one with which they are so familiar.

Can Education, Particularly Secondary Education, Really Be Conducted in All Those Little Languages?

In terms of potential the answer is, of course, "yes"; in terms of present realities the answer is often "no" or "only in limited fashion." Each and every language is fully adequate to express those concerns and activities that its speakers have followed for many years. When these concerns and activities change, then the languages too change (most usually and rapidly, lexically; but grammatical change too occurs), although the linguistic changes may lag behind the sociocultural ones by several years. To keep such lags from occurring, governmental authorities (including educational authorities) establish language planning agencies (Language Academies) to more rapidly provide the new terminologies that are societally required or desired. Such terminologies are then utilized in textbooks (so that they are learned by pupils as part and parcel of new subject matter) and taught to adults who are beyond formal schooling via special educational campaigns and devices (posters, word lists, radio programs, job/examination requirements, promotions and other rewards, etc.). Language planning takes time, of course, and money, and expertise, but in a relatively short period of time (varying from a few years to a full generation, depending on whether authoritarian or democratic decision-making and implementation are involved) any language hitherto utilized only for familial, agricultural, and religious pursuits can be provided with whatever it lacks for technological, governmental, and other modern pursuits. The question is not whether this *can* be done for Navajo, Guaraní, Somali, Xhosa, Tongan, Fijian, Frisian, etc., but whether it *should* be done. The answer to the latter question depends upon the functions that these languages are to be allocated within their respective societies. In what subjects they are to be used as media also depends on the very same societal allocation of functions.

One of the allocative patterns strongly indicated as desirable by the ISBSE findings relates the marked language to ethnically encumbered domains such as literature, history, civics, customs, etc. While such an allocation may still require a modicum of language planning, it certainly requires far less of such activity than where the marked language is to be utilized as the medium for mathematics, chemistry, physics, etc. Major scientific work is actually done in only half a dozen languages in the entire world. Most other languages that are related to science teaching probably possess no more than a high school or lower-division college vocabulary in these fields and get along quite well. Although major efforts have been mounted during the past generation or two to provide extensive technical nomenclatures for Hebrew, Hindi, Indonesian, Afrikaans, and other newly official languages of state apparatuses, these nomenclatures typically have no more than a few hundred to a few thousand basic terms in each field. The fact that these could be prepared—and rather successfully implemented as well—is an indication that the same can be done for Hopi, Yiddish, Nynorsk, and Neo-Melanesian as well. It is also an indication that with additional exertion both the former languages as well as the latter ones could be provided with nomenclatures in these fields as extensive as those now existing only in English, Russian, and French. That no such exertion will be made in either case is a reflection of the societal allocation of functions. Thus, advanced scientific work in all these settings is conducted in and written up in one of the Big Three languages (or Big Six at most). This allocation itself implies the need for bilingual secondary education, and the other newly developing languages of today will probably arrive at a similar allocation as well.

What More Can We Hope for from the Sociology of Bilingual Education in General and from the International (Comparative) Sociology of Bilingual Education in Particular?

The sociology (and particularly the sociolinguistic sociology) of bilingual education, whether focusing on a single setting or on several settings simultaneously, is still in its infancy. Its basic contribution is the societal-communal perspective that it can yield. This is an important perspective for understanding bilingual education since, even more so than for education in general, bilingual education is particularly dependent on forces and factors in the society and communities that surround the school. Bilingual education comes into being as a result of societal-communal pressures and counter-pressures, and its entire course thereafter is determined by these forces. To study bilingual education without insight into ethnicity-nationalism, social mobility and social class differences, language-maintenance and language-shift patterns, and the societal (or the speech community's) linguistic allocation of functions is to reduce our grasp of the topic almost to the extent of letting its essence slip through our fingers while concentrating instead on more comfortable but less consequential residual phenomena. To study the essential features comparatively/internationally is to see them in yet greater perspective.

The sociology of bilingual education pursues a different perspective, with different emphases, than do the psychological, pedagogical, or linguistic approaches to bilingual education. As such, in concert with the other approaches, it helps safeguard against the oversimplification of findings that might result from dependence on the more pedagogically proximate sciences alone. Thus, the sociology of bilingual education, when it is developed in full vigor over a period of years, should enable one and all to see bilingual education both in terms of its full range of variability as well as in terms of more encompassing regularities than would otherwise be the case. The types of variables that will be utilized in analyzing bilingual education, whether one will look at the classroom/school curriculum or at the community/society/nation, will be richer and more powerful than if only pedagogically proximate sciences were to be employed.

In order to understand and successfully modify educational phenomena sociology alone is not enough, but neither are the pedagogically proximate sciences. When they are utilized jointly, it becomes clearer that certain types of variables and forces, which are the normal concerns of particular disciplines, must be controlled first before other variables and forces can have their maximal effect. Bilingual education itself is not a discipline—it is an interdisciplinary activity. The *sociology* of bilingual education is one of its most basic and most powerful contributories. When it is better understood and better utilized, then the full and proper potential of other contributories will be more evident as well. This volume is but a first step in that direction, and its partisan stance is an attempt to underscore the importance of the entire bilingual education enterprise as well as the sociology-of-language-contribution to it.

APPENDICES

PART III

Happy Immersion: Montreal

The entire school is devoted to seventh-grade Anglophone students who have volunteered to do their high school work in French (except for the study of English and English literature), although previously they had only studied French as a second language for 20-30 minutes a day (from the first grade on). Classrooms and offices are nicely decorated, and almost all notices, posters, labels, etc., meant for student eyes, are in French. The student population is clearly comfortably middle-class—a self-selected sample from the universe most likely to succeed at anything academic. After five months of immersion, students are obviously speaking French to each other in the hallways and dining room. They are pleased with themselves and with their teachers. Their teachers view themselves as successful pioneers.

In all four classes that I visited, the teachers, most of whom were imported native speakers, spoke only in French and that volubly, with no apparent restraint as to structures or vocabulary. The phonology of the students was quite often obviously Anglo (their immersion had begun at ages 13 or 14, when their articulatory patterns were already largely set), but their answers, questions, and comments were full and free. If errors in syntax or in grammar occurred, they were not corrected (except in the class teaching French language *per se*), and most students seemed eager to participate and be completely involved in every class. In part this must be due to the mixture of playfulness and seriousness with which teachers approached the target of each class-hour and their stress on concepts to be discussed or argued, rather than facts or structures to be remembered. Communication-with-feeling comes first!

The science class dealt with explaining what snow was (something quite evident in Montreal in January) to children in Malagasy. Homework assignments required use of encyclopedias and other references. The teacher stressed that only French references should be used (in school or at home) because only such references would convey how science and all the world are viewed through French eyes!

The texts used in the classes teaching French language *per se* are ones prepared for continental French monolinguals. The students may be a year or so behind continental French students in what they are covering in grammar, but they are

THUMBNAIL SKETCHES OF TEN BILINGUAL SCHOOLS
OUTSIDE OF THE UNITED STATES

APPENDIX 1

not behind their Francophone counterparts in Montreal. (Elementary school immersion students use specially prepared materials as well as Canadian adaptations of continental French materials.)

Some Anglophone students in Montreal are involved in French *sub*mersion programs. In these a very few well-prepared Anglophones attend schools in which the rest of the student body is Francophone. This requires more sociocultural adaptation than does *immersion,* but, if submersion continues to succeed (in school, at home, and in the press), it too may become quite popular.

Working-Class Immersion: Montreal

The Anglophone working class in Montreal is even more in need of French mastery than is the middle class, which, if it desires to do so, can still escape from a good deal of daily interaction in French. Nevertheless, French immersion experimentation began not only with *volunteers,* but with *middle-class* volunteers who had good-to-high academic averages. Now, after a few years of recognized success with such students, it is finally being attempted with working-class volunteers whose averages are distinctly lower. Some of them find the program too difficult. In this school, 14 out of 116 incoming seventh-graders returned to regular English programs after a few months of trying to make the switch to French. Nevertheless, the teachers and principal claim that those who remain do better in French immersion programs than they would have done otherwise. "They know they have to do their homework and hang on to every word the teacher says if they want to get an education and stay in the program." Seemingly, volunteers—whether Hawthorne effected or not—tend to be promising material for successful academic endeavors.

In the same building there is also an elementary-level immersion program. Here the phonology is much more native-like. When these children reach the seventh grade (junior high) they will be able to function as teaching assistants in the elementary grades, thereby further assisting and motivating working-class students to like the immersion program and to succeed in it.

Thus far, there seem to be more girls than boys in the immersion programs, whether at the elementary or secondary levels and whether in the middle-class or working-class schools. This may be a reflection of self-selection (or parentally guided self-selection) in which girls feel more confident with their verbal skills, and more attracted to the stereotype of things French ("fashions, foods, poetry") than do boys.

It is obviously harder to hold student interest and to marshall student participation in the working-class school than in the middle-class school. Fewer of the teachers are foreign-born native speakers. The immersion programs, elementary and secondary, occupy only one wing of an entire building. It seems harder to establish an all-French atmosphere under such circumstances, even in the French wing, given that students of the entire school eat and play together or do so in shifts unrelated to whether or not they are in the immersion program. Nevertheless, even under less than ideal circumstances, a very substantial degree of language facility is being attained.

Boys Boarding School: Dublin

A famous school, but one that has seen better days. When it was in its glory it offered an all-Irish program. Now it is a bilingual school, and almost none of its students have had instruction via Irish in their prior elementary schools. The school makes a somewhat "institutional" impression; it is down to essentials insofar as equipment, facilities, staff, and decorative decor are concerned. Student-teacher relations seem formal, businesslike. A boys' school in Ireland is serious business, not meant to be fun.

Most teachers are native speakers of Irish—not necessarily all from the same dialect area—but all, native speakers or not, intersperse their comments with English interjections ("so," "well," "right"). Indeed, some English terminology is used in almost all classes taught via Irish, and in some cases the mixture of Irish and English, or the switching from one to the other, is quite extensive and uninterrupted. One factor that seems to contribute to this is the lack of Irish textbooks for many subjects and at many levels. It is obviously harder to keep English from forcing its way into an Irish discussion when the material being discussed has only just been read in English.

Nevertheless, quite a few students in every class conducted in Irish participate very eagerly. Indeed, the Irish of a few reveals not only nativeness, but even distinctive regional markers. On the whole, however, the phonology of most of the boys is that known as "Dublin Irish," i.e., non-native in phonology, terminology, or structure, although fluency is certainly not lacking. Finally, there seem to be a few in each class who are having difficulty keeping up with the others or with the material that the teacher is presenting. For these the Irish medium is a deterrent to academic progress, given the fact that their grasp of the language is still too weak for it to be of much use to them for serious academic work. Unfortunately, the school does not have the staff to give these boys additional or separate attention.

Several teachers are obviously wholeheartedly dedicated to Irish instruction. Others seem to regard it as a necessary burden for a few more years, by which time it should be possible to dispense with it as a medium or, at most, to restrict its use to students who really want it and know it. However, with "mandatory Irish" being increasingly undercut at the elementary school level by the party that has recently come into power, it is hard to imagine where such students will come from in the future. It is obviously hard to accomplish much in a language that few really want and that fewer yet really use out of school. This is particularly so if funds are lacking for textbooks and for staff, and if society at large is ambivalent as to whether to be sad or happy at the twilight of its long embattled ethnic tongue.

Girlish Enthusiasm: Dublin

The school itself is lovely, and the decorative love lavished upon it by staff and students alike is obvious the moment one steps inside. Like the boys' boarding school it is conducted by a religious order, but, unlike the boys' school, it is still "all-Irish" (except for English language and literature).

In most respects, except for the sex difference, the two schools involve similar teacher and student populations. Once again there are a few teachers whose phonology is English rather than Irish. Once again there are frequent English interjections in Irish talk. Once again most students (at least two thirds) have not had instruction via Irish in their elementary education. Nevertheless, there is a huge difference between the two schools.

The girls do not board at school. Perhaps living at home with their own families enables them to enjoy school more when they arrive. Perhaps this also helps diminish the institutional flavor of the school. Perhaps the fact that the students are all girls means, at least at this stage in Irish life, that the school can be somewhat more relaxed academically, somewhat more enjoyable, more arts- and humanities-oriented than science- and career-oriented—more fun.

As in the boys' school, a high proportion of the texts employed are in English. Nevertheless, the average fluency of the girls seems to be greater. Perhaps this is a spill-over or fringe benefit from the large amount of time that they spend in Irish singing, choral recitation, and drama. Perhaps the fact that the girls seem more interested, attentive, orderly, and better motivated in their Irish-medium studies is also, at least in part, attributable to these same Irish activities—although the fact that they are girls is doubtless also an important factor in their fluency, in their school behavior, and in their obvious enjoyment of singing, reciting, and acting in Irish.

Nevertheless, with a matriculation examination in Irish no longer being required for high school graduates, and with other types of "easing away" from mandatory Irish being predicted for the near future, the value of stressing emotional bonds and noncognitive experiences with the marked language, particularly given its extremely limited out-of-school functional load, should not be underestimated. A language's symbolic functions can be highly motivating even when its other functions are slight. There are many other bilingual education programs in which the marked language is little more than an ethnic symbol (of great—or potentially great—emotional value but of little worth in the world of everyday practical affairs), and where the unmarked language is one of worldwide significance. The Irish experience should be pondered carefully by all of them.

On the Bilingual Frontier: Wales

Some 5,000 students in the more Anglicized parts of Wales, some 10% of the entire secondary school population in those areas, are now in attendance in recently established bilingual schools. Relatively few of the students are of Welsh mother tongue, although many have had some Welsh as a medium in their elementary schooling. Thus, most of these students attend these new bilingual high schools out of parental conviction. The increasing evidence that the schools are doing a good job educationally, and the growing occupational advantage for bilinguals over monolinguals among those who remain in Wales, are also powerful magnets attracting students to these schools.

The Welsh phonology of students at this particular school seemed very native. On the other hand, their Welsh, as well as that of their teachers, was heavily interspersed with English connectives and interjections as well as with English technical terms (although Welsh terminology cards and posters lined the walls). Teaching-learning materials are just *now* becoming available, as are complete terminologies, in many of the subject areas, and it will be a while before new technical terms are fully mastered by both teachers and pupils. Until this time arrives, teachers, inspectors, and parents alike are pleased to note the Welsh fluency of the students and their ability to handle very advanced material in a very personal and innovative fashion.

Linguistically and conceptually, students from "good backgrounds" seem to be doing every bit as well academically at these schools as similar students in the country's best monolingual English schools. The secret seems to be in the excellent young teachers and principals being assigned to these new schools, as well as the community interest in seeing to it that they are well supported. In addition to its full complement of teachers, this particular school, as well as the other visited in Wales, has a translator and a Welsh typist on its staff to help in the preparation of learning materials in Welsh. These materials are then inexpensively reproduced for classroom use and shared with other schools via a central coordinating bureau.

The male students in this school seemed somewhat subdued, nevertheless, with the girls finding schoolwork much more satisfying. On the whole, the language hurdle seemed to have been fully overcome, perhaps at the price of somewhat more concern for language versatility than for educational achievement as a whole. Clearly, the school was everyone's pride and joy, including many who had thought that it "couldn't be done," and it was set to prove its excellence in every possible way.

Re-greening the Valley: Wales

This school, another of the newer type of Welsh-English bilingual schools, devotes some 80% of the time of the sixth form (the graduating class) to work in Welsh. Nevertheless, students must be equally good at their schoolwork in English in order to do the bulk of their university entrance examinations in that language. Therefore, although graduating students may be writing and discussing most of their work in Welsh, much of what they are reading is in English, in order to be sure that specialized English terms and phrases are not unknown to them.

This particular school has a very varied program and student body. It attracts both middle-class and working-class youngsters and provides both academic and commercial/industrial courses for them all. It is experimenting with a variety of student grouping-patterns and a large number of its teachers are utilizing the services of the school's translator and Welsh typist in order to create novel materials for student use. The general orientation is that the school will succeed with its Welsh mission only if it is an exciting place intellectually and really helpful in terms of the students' subsequent employment or higher education. Working-class and modest ability students are given particular attention, assistance, and encouragement. Indeed many of the very best teachers in the school, whether in Welsh or in English, are focused entirely on these students for whom the school very definitely provides a far superior program to that available monolingually (in English) in the area.

Thus, by striving first and foremost to provide a superior intellectual, interpersonal, and vocational program, this school is able to relate the symbolic functions of Welsh and the community's concern for these functions to even more generally worthwhile goals and consequences. Graduates of these schools are helping to strengthen the demand for increased Welsh instruction at the university level and, all in all, show a lesser dropout rate than those in monolingual schools. For these several reasons, some of them highly practical and others at least somewhat ideological, the continued growth of schools such as these in largely English-speaking areas of Wales is to be predicted.

Tradition: Bnei Berak (Israel)

This school is conducted by an ultra-Orthodox community of Hungarian origin, disciples of the late, great rabbi of Presburg (Bratislava), the Chatam Sofer. The school offers eight years of instruction for boys (a similar girls' school is also found in the vicinity), and refuses any aid or supervision from secular educational authorities who, in turn, "tolerate" it but do not "recognize" it or other schools of the same kind (serving some 50,000 students in all).

The students come to school at age six, speaking mainly Hebrew, but understanding some Yiddish and even some Hungarian as well. Yiddish is first introduced as a second language (direct method teaching), is then used as the language of religious texts and translation, and finally, by the sixth grade, as the language of instruction for most religious or traditional subject matter (e.g., Pentateuch, Prophets, Talmud, Commentaries, Mishna, Rashi, Dinim, and Halacha). Former pupils, now engaged in more advanced religious studies at more advanced schools, help tutor youngsters who are having difficulties with the heavy academic program (which also includes Hebrew, mathematics, biology, geography—taught in Hebrew—and English). The entire program is under the supervision of an Educational Committee of local rabbis.

Classes tend to be somewhat noisy, by Western standards, but teachers and students are fully involved and hard at work. The emphasis on Yiddish as the language of instruction is a difficult hurdle, but one which ultimately defines the unique nature of this type of school and its particular link with tradition and with its immediate community. Approximately 80% of the pupils go on to a programmatically similar senior high school and by dint of great effort and devotion become very proficient in Yiddish (as well as in Hebrew), even though its out-of-school functions are shrinking and its out-of-community functions in Israel are meager indeed.

Obviously, Yiddish functions not merely as a group symbol (it is that too), but as a traditionally indispensable medium of intensive study. It is not overtly ideologized, advocated, or defended; it is simply used so much, in connection with every traditional subject of study, as to become completely bound up with its target. Neither interest nor enjoyment nor ease are permitted to enter as considerations, and the cost in effort and time is viewed as the necessary and inevitable price of piety and scholarship. Only a supremely dedicated community willing to pay any price for its basic values, and having minimal cognitive and affective interaction with the society and culture about it, could maintain this approach over generations and across continents. However, as Hebrew increasingly becomes the work-a-day language of this community and the everyday language between parents and children, additional pressures for curricular change may come into being.

Bilingual Education for Israeli Arabs: Haifa

Although the Arab students are taught in separate classes from those for Jewish students in the same building, they have common "breaks," clubs, and social events. In dress and manners, the two groups are indistinguishable, and Hebrew is their lingua franca. Arab students study history, geography, Arabic and Arabic literature, and have a free discussion period with the teacher in Arabic. The rest of their program (Hebrew, Hebrew literature, math, sciences, and English) is in Hebrew. Thus, these students receive rather more of their high school program in Hebrew than is usually the case even for Israeli Arab students engaged in bilingual education. Indeed, next year this experiment in maximizing the Hebrew exposure of Arab students will begin to offer them history and geography as well in Hebrew, thus becoming the reverse mirror image of the usual bilingual education program for Israeli Arab youngsters.

Those pupils who are residents of Haifa itself come to the secondary program with rather good elementary school preparation in Hebrew as well as in other subjects. They have also had substantial prior social experience with Jewish youngsters. Those coming from Arab villages in the Galilee tend to have much poorer academic preparation or mastery of Hebrew, and hardly any prior social experience with Jewish youngsters. With the passage of time, few unprepared Arab students have been admitted, both because more villages have introduced bilingual education, and because more and more Haifa Arabic families want to send their children to this school.

The major complaint expressed in connection with this program is that the Arab students make insufficient progress in Arabic languages and literature. Living in a predominantly Hebrew-speaking environment and seeing their future in terms of occupational success in that environment, their Arabic studies appear to them to be overly difficult and insufficiently motivated. When students have difficulties with other subjects, e.g., math or any of the sciences, they are offered additional tutoring and given intensive review and remedial classes, free of charge and during regular school hours. This extra attention, which is very popular with the students and much appreciated by their parents, is not available in connection with Arabic studies.

On the whole the Arab students do not perform as well on their course or matriculation exams as do the Jewish students on theirs. Nevertheless, with the exception of their Arabic studies, these students are generally doing better than their counterparts attending monolingual or more conventional bilingual programs for Arab students. Next year, when the Arab students will actually be in a Hebrew immersion program, their academic performance is expected to improve further. There is even some interest in Hebrew *sub*mersion programs for some students, and, given further improvements in the overall political situation, such may come into being in the not too distant future.

Yanqui Feel at Home: Mexico

The school is big and obviously successful. It has been in operation many years and is very popular among the American colony, other foreigners wanting their children to learn or maintain English, and a good portion of the local Mexican gentry as well. As a result of applications from non-Spanish-speakers for admission into every year of the program, two different Spanish tracks are required. One is the "continuing bilingual education" track for all those who have been sufficiently exposed to Spanish before coming to high school. The other is really a programmed language laboratory course for students arriving without sufficient Spanish mastery to be able to catch up well enough to participate in Spanish-medium classes. One third of the students are of Spanish mother tongue and one fifth of the high school courses are in Spanish. The Spanish-medium curriculum tends to be skewed toward ethnic material (language and literature), although this is not invariably so.

There is some tendency for English-mother-tongue youngsters to be more active in the English-medium classes and for Spanish-mother-tongue students to be more active in the Spanish-medium classes. On the whole, however, the latter classes tend to be somewhat more subdued anyway because of the Latin American "professional style" which expects teachers to lecture and students to take notes. Nevertheless (although it is difficult to tell who is of what mother tongue, since all students dress with equal informality), both the English and the Spanish of participating students seems to be of native or near-native phonology, fluency, and informality.

Both sets of teachers are native speakers of the medium they utilize and are also fully proficient in the "other tongue." When Spanish names or terms come up in an English-medium class (or vice versa: English names or terms in a Spanish-medium class), the teachers and students pronounce them as they would be pronounced by native speakers. With those not conversant with Spanish streamed off, and with Spanish not utilized instructionally during most of the day, the Spanish-medium classes proceed at a very fluent pace, as they might in a Spanish immersion program for English-mother-tongue students. However in truth, this school, at the high school level, tends to be offering an English immersion program for English-mother-tongue students, and this seems to be agreeable to all. The American students can relax and not "waste" too much time on Spanish. The Spanish-mother-tongue and other non-English-mother-tongue students learn a lot of English. There is considerable socializing between the two groups and a good time is had by all.

Chocolates and Cheeses: Mexico

The Swiss school functions in German and Spanish, with courses being taught in German to the extent that teachers are available who can do so. The particular courses that German mother-tongue teachers are qualified to teach are the ones that are taught in German. This varies from year to year, depending on the available staff. What is invariable, however, is the fine building, the well-scrubbed students, and the high educational standard. Only one third of the children are of German mother tongue (although another third are of German or Swiss-German ancestry which has by now been linguistically Hispanified). Parents would send their children to this school "if it were conducted in Russian or Swahili," says the principal, "as long as the educational program remained as good as ours currently is."

There is little, if any, *Swiss cultural* aspect to the school's program, although children rise when the principal (or a teacher) enters the classroom, and their attire and grooming are somewhat more restrained than in the American school in the same city. Students and teachers mostly speak Spanish to each other, almost as a matter of course, and most notices throughout the school are in Spanish as well. Indeed, the school seems to be aiming at little more than passive or receptive bilingualism. Students appear to understand all that they hear or read in German, but they speak it only haltingly. There is next to nothing in the out-of-school environment that either requires or reinforces German, and as a result, the mass media and tourism reinforcement enjoyed by English is entirely lacking. All of these minuses (symbolic as well as functional) are reflected in the students' spoken German. Indeed, most students speak English better than German, although English is *not* a medium of instruction and is given little formal attention.

Nevertheless, the school is doing a fine job in terms of educational achievement more generally. Its bilingual component is viewed as a broadening intercultural experience that tops off an educational program that would be considered excellent even without it. The school is small (no more than about 120 children in the entire high school). Teachers know their students well and can give them a great deal of time and attention. Thus, a school which originally served the needs of a particular cultural minority has made the transition (as has the group itself) to orientation to the needs of the more general community. Its distinctive language program is considered to be a part of a valuable educational experience rather than something to get "hung up" about in and of itself, or anyone's "priceless heritage" that cannot be set aside when it is no longer needed.

Auslandsschulverzeichnis '72 (Register of Schools Abroad '72). Ismaning bei Munchen, Max Huber Verlag, 1972.

"This register provides information about schools abroad which provide instruction via German or which offer special emphases with respect to the teaching of German." Updated every few years, the register is not only an excellent source of information concerning scores of bilingual schools utilizing German as one of the media of instruction, but it can also serve as a model for the registers that we still lack pertaining to English, French, and other Language of Wider Communication schools all over the world. Such registers would not only be extremely useful tools for furthering the international sociology of bilingual education, but they would certainly also further bilingual education *per se* by making its availability (particularly vis-à-vis LWCs) more widely known to the families of businessmen, government representatives, military personnel, UN personnel, tourists, and expatriates abroad. With typical thoroughness, the German educator or layman interested in bilingual education abroad involving German as a medium also has available a special journal devoted to this topic, *Der Deutsche Lehrer im Ausland.* Note also that Vol. 23, No. 3, 1975, of *Pedagogik und Schule im Ost und West* is entirely devoted to pedagogics in the German school abroad and provides a huge bibliography on this topic.

Bruck, Margaret, Wallace E. Lambert and G. Richard Tucker. "Bilingual Schooling Through the Elementary Grades: The St. Lambert Project at Grade Seven." Mimeographed (McGill University), 1974, 44 pp.

After seven years of study (and of equally constant research and reporting on the part of the investigators) the major findings first spelled out in detail in Lambert and Tucker's *Bilingual Education of Children* (Rowley: Newbury House, 1972) still seem to hold. Not only have the experimental pupils (the first to be involved in an "early immersion program") mastered near-native French, but their English-language skills have not suffered at all in the process, their attitudes toward French Canadians are more favorable than those of French-Canadian

COMMENTS ON RECENT REFERENCES

APPENDIX 2

control students, and their cognitive behavior reveals significantly greater flexibility. (For counterpart findings pertaining to French-Canadian children attending English programs primarily or entirely, see John Macnamara's "What Happens to Children Whose Home Language Is Not That of the School" [Montreal, McGill University, 1975. Dittoed].) All in all, this work lays to rest all of the old bugaboos concerning possibly deleterious consequences of bilingualism and bilingual education with respect to intelligence, phonology, self-identity, etc. Indeed, the only danger now would seem to be from those who may not realize that positive findings with highly motivated, self-selected, middle-class students, living in the midst of two world cultures and two languages of wider communication (indeed: international communication), will not necessarily apply to very different and academically less favored sociolinguistic contexts. Thus, there is much to learn from this work, including the limitations of its applicability.

Campbell, Russel, Donald M. Taylor and G. Richard Tucker. "Teachers' Views of Immersion-type Bilingual Programs: A Quebec Example." *Foreign Language Annals,* 7 (1973), 106-10.

Both English-speaking and French-speaking teachers have been studied as to their views about the traditional program of English-language instruction (for Anglophone children) with French as a second language, on the one hand, and the newer French immersion programs, on the other hand. Both French-speaking and English-speaking teachers agree that the traditional program provides Anglophone children with a firm base in English—but not in French—language arts and in content subjects, and with a sensitivity to their own—but not to the other group's—cultural heritage. Notwithstanding all of the above agreement, the two groups of teachers did not agree either on the attainments or on the desirability of the immersion programs. Whether or not these differences are due to job-security fears among English-speaking teachers (in case immersion-type programs were to spread dramatically beyond their current experimental and demonstration confines), these findings should remind us all that bilingual education programs of *whatever* kind can stir insecurity feelings among traditional administrators, teachers, and parents as well. Such feelings are part of the social context of bilingual education and may well determine the success or failure of any program, even if not of the immersion type.

Coffman, William E. and Lai-Min Paul Lee. "Cross-national Assessment of Educational Achievement: A Review." *Educational Researcher,* 3 (1974), 6, 13-16.

A preview of the forthcoming nine volumes of the latest phase of the IEA (International Association for the Evaluation of Educational Achievement) studies. These students have encompassed science, literature, reading comprehension, English and French as foreign languages, and civic education and have involved some 258,000 high school students and 50,000 teachers in nearly 10,000 secondary schools in 14 different countries.

Many of the findings will be of interest to bilingual educators, particularly those dealing with differentials in English and French achievement. However, rather than spell out those differentials here it seems even more to the point to stress several more general conclusions that pertain not only to language instruction, but to all of the areas of instruction studied. Thus, it was found that prediction of student achievement in subject matter areas can be made almost entirely from achievement in reading, and that prediction of achievement in reading can be made substantially from home background variables. Thus, the importance of home and community in school achievement is, once again, confirmed. Thus, rather than view bilingual education as a means of changing home and community characteristics (as many American spokesmen and educators are inclined to do), it would be much more realistic to view it as governed by these characteristics and therefore requiring home and community support for its success.

Cohen, Andrew D. "Bilingual Schooling and Spanish Language Maintenance: An Experimental Analysis." *Bilingual Review,* 11 (1975), 3-12.

In contrast to the fears of Kjolseth, below (and earlier, to those of Gaarder, 1970), relative to the U. S. A., and in contrast to the dangers to minority languages inherent in bilingual education in the U. S. S. R. (see below: Lewis, in press; Hall, 1973), Cohen finds evidence that even a traditional bilingual education program can continue to have measurable and positive language-maintenance impact a few years after the program has ended. How long such impact will continue cannot be predicted, nor is it clear *why* the particular program studied did have this impact whereas other programs might not. Nevertheless, this is an important paper because it helps focus upon *out-of-school* criteria in conjunction with which bilingual education programs should ultimately be evaluated. Without such out-of-school criteria, bilingual education fails to take seriously the family, neighborhood, community, national, and international goals that are often mentioned in connection with it. How can such goals be operationalized and studied? What program variables, student variables, teacher variables, and community variables are helpful or harmful to the attainment of out-of-school goals (such as language maintenance)? This paper does not provide all of the answers, but it does provide some, and in general it encourages others to begin to probe this crucial area that merits far more attention than it has received.

Cohen, Andrew D. "Bilingual/Bicultural Education Re-visited: A 'Minority' Viewpoint." Mimeographed (University of California—Los Angeles—and Consultants in Total Education, Inc.), 1974, 13 pp.

The process of testing the limits of immersion programs continues with the derivation of a general theoretical position: literacy should first be taught in the non-native language. This view is advanced even for a context in which students are minority-group members whose mother tongue has little if any institutional support outside of the immediate family context. Those for whom the assimilationist consequences of such an approach is abhorrent (or, at least, highly problematic) should not fail to note the many less doctrinaire and distinctly positive suggestions advanced in this paper on behalf of minority-group students. Actually, the goal of the author is not really to espouse English literacy over literacy in the mother tongue, but rather to foster emotionally sound programs that help produce functionally bilingual and actively bicultural minority-group members. As for the initial issue (with respect to priorities in education for literacy), perhaps it should be viewed in terms of the literacy functions of the languages involved, and, in addition, in terms of the marked-unmarked distinction. Perhaps if literacy is likely to come about in a particular language *only* if the bilingual program stresses it (therefore, *marked* literacy), then it should be given priority, particularly if such literacy has an established societal function, or if the introduction of such a function is the express goal of the school and its community of support. The latter approach would also be in agreement with the findings of Politzer and Hoover (below).

Cohen, Andrew D. "The Culver City Spanish Immersion Program: The First Two Years." *Modern Language Journal,* 58 (1974), 95-103.

This early attempt to try out the immersion approach in the U. S. A. finds that many of its purported benefits *do* transfer to the Anglo-Chicano context of Southern California. However, certain local innovations were found to be available. Thus, since Anglo children in Southern California are not exposed to nearly as much Spanish in *their* environment as Anglophone children are exposed to French in Quebec, about a quarter of the children in the experimental grades were native speakers of Spanish. These children were looked up to as models of good speech among the Anglo pupils, many of whom ultimately succeeded in doing better than the models themselves. Other differences between the Culver City and St. Lambert approaches pertain to teacher strategies. All in all, this will be an important project to watch. Hopefully, it will also include community, attitudinal, and cognitive style variables. In any case, American educators may soon begin experimenting widely with the immersion approach (which is actually merely a variant of the full-bilingualism approach to bilingual education) and, thereby, begin to discover the range of innovations that are necessary in order to adapt it to the variety of widely different minority contexts with which its Canadian originators did not need to be concerned.

Erickson, Frederick. "The Politics of Speaking: An Approach to Evaluating Bilingual-Bicultural Schools." *Division Generator, American Educational Research Association,* No. 3 (1974), 9-13.

The major contribution of this paper lies not in its political rhetoric but in its sociolinguistic sensitivity. What the author proposes is a possible *goal* for bilingual education rather than an "approach" to the evaluation of this goal. The goal is derived from the sociolinguistic concept of language repertoire (see Fishman, 1972c). An accomplished member of a speech community controls a repertoire of situationally appropriate varieties of the language of that community. If an accomplished bilingual is a member of two communities, then he should have a linguistic repertoire encompassing the language of each. The author of this paper suggests that the control of a repertoire of varieties in each language should be a goal of bilingual-bicultural programs and that evaluation procedures should be designed for evaluating progress toward this goal. Whether the communities involved really recognize as valuable or schoolworthy all of the varieties in their active repertoires, or whether they will have any use for varieties corresponding to roles not in their role-repertoire is not discussed. However, the notion merits consideration by all those hoping for more than two formal language varieties in the bilingual education now coming into being.

Ferguson, Charles A., Catherine Houghton and Marie H. Wells. "Bilingual Education: An International Perspective." In Bernard Spolsky and Robert L. Cooper (eds.), *Current Trends in Bilingual Education.* Rowley: Newbury House, in press.

The authors arrive at four clear and sound conclusions:
"1. Bilingual education—in the sense of explicit recognition of the use of two or more languages in the formal educational system of a society—is very widespread in space and time.
2. Bilingual education—in the sense of the use of a different variety of language in the classroom from that used in ordinary conversation (in more extreme cases a different language altogether)—is universal.
3. Bilingual education may have many possible implicit goals, and these goals may overlap or be in conflict.
4. The success of bilingual education depends primarily on the attitudes and expectations of people, not on such language factors as the degree of difference between languages or language varieties or the nature of the pedagogical methods."

Points 1 and 4, above, are in direct agreement with this volume. Point 2 is further documented in Fishman and Lueders, 1972, and in Fishman, 1973b. However, Point 3 takes up the lion's share of the paper here under review, and it is well worth further systematization. This might be helped along somewhat by greater contact with the extensive taxonomies of educational goals dealing with the cognitive, affective, and conative realms.

Frasure, Nancy E., Wallace E. Lambert and Donald M. Taylor. "Choosing the Language of Instruction for One's Children." Mimeographed (McGill University), 1974, 30 pp.

"It is not unusual in Quebec to find English-Canadian parents sending their children to French language schools and French-Canadian parents sending their children to English language schools. Why some parents decide on this form of language experience for their children was the focus of this investigation. It examines in some detail the ethnic identity patterns and motivations of selected subgroups of French and English Canadian parents and compares those who send their children to 'other' language schools with those whose children attend schools where the home language is used as the medium of instruction. Although all parents agree on the benefits of bilingualism in occupational and educational matters, only particular subsets of parents, depending on their ethnicity, the community they come from, and their distinctive constellations of personal motivations, decide to send their children to other language schools. Clearly, people perceive different costs and rewards associated with choice of language of schooling. This decision furthermore has implications not only for the relationship within the family but for the established network of social relationships within the community." All of which means: The same social pressures that impinge on the students (see Bruck *et al.,* above) and on the teachers (see Campbell *et al.,* above) involved in bilingual education also impinge on the parents involved. Ultimately their interest, support, assistance, enthusiasm, dedication, and conviction may be the deciding factor, more crucial by far than method A or method B, sequence A or sequence B, time allotment A or time allotment B. A devoted and powerful community is one of the greatest assets that a bilingual education program can have and can help compensate, at least temporarily, for many deficiencies along psychoeducational lines.

Hall, Paul R. "Language Contact in the USSR: Some Prospects for Language Maintenance among Soviet Minority Language Groups." Ph.D. dissertation, Georgetown University, 1973.

A painstaking statistical analysis of Soviet textbooks during the decade of the sixties reveals that "instruction through the mother tongue has been maintained in all grade levels for only 18 non-Russian languages. Of the other 49 (larger) non-Russian language groups, instruction through the mother tongue exists only in the subject area *Native Language Literature* for 28 language groups, and in random subject areas and . . . grade levels for the remaining 21 groups. It is concluded, therefore, that the USSR employs a variety of models of native language schooling and that a pattern of limiting such instruction through the mother tongue is clearly evident from [data for] 1960-1969 . . . The patterns of increasing emphasis on learning . . . literature . . . printed in the native language and a consequent decrease in native language accessibility to technical topics are evident both in general publications and in school textbooks. Together, these facts support the general conclusion that at least one aspect of (the larger) non-Russian cultures—the native language itself—is being strengthened or at least maintained; and that there is strong pressure to rely on Russian (alone) in technical areas which are themselves more closely tied to modernization needs."

Inclán, R. G. "Can Bilingual-Bicultural Education Be the Answer? " *Educational Horizons*, 50 (1972), 192-95.

A popular report of one of the earliest and most successful (as well as famous) bilingual education programs in the U. S. A. Starting a decade ago, the Dade County (Florida) program has shown good academic results (see Rojas, 1966; Richardson, 1968), including the transfer of skills learned in one language (e.g., in Spanish) to learning processes involving the other (e.g., English). In addition, the author, who has long been involved with this program, believes that it has had desirable affective results as well, strengthening intercultural relationships as well as feelings of self-worth among Cuban newcomers to this country. Finally, the author pleads for expanded bilingual-bicultural programs in the U. S. A. and for more widespread recognition that the country is really multilingual and multicultural.

It is worth pointing out that the Dade County program now feeding students into local secondary schools began with middle-class (professional and semi-professional) Cuban refugee and Anglo children, i.e., with children that were already predictably "good material" as far as educational motivation and achievement were concerned. After a few years, disadvantaged learners were involved as well, but by then the program was well established in terms of personnel, materials, and community support.

Kjolseth, R. "Bilingual Education Programs in the United States: For Assimilation or Pluralism? " in B. Spolsky (ed.), *The Language Education of Minority Children*. Rowley, Mass.: Newbury House, 1972, pp. 94-119.

Bilingual education programs may be seen as distributing along a continuum, from maintenance of ethnic languages and cultures concurrent with the dominant culture ("pluralistic") to encouraging the assimilation of ethnic cultures into the dominant culture ("assimilation"). A review of the ERIC literature reveals a trend in the United States, in that most (over 80%) bilingual education programs "closely approximate the extreme of the assimilation model, while the remaining few are only moderately pluralistic."

The fundamental question (for sociolinguists and educators alike) is: "What are the *social* consequences of particular bilingual education strategies upon the changing patterns of *community* language *use*? " (p. 116). Only after answering this question can an enlightened approach be taken to bilingual education.

La Fontaine, H. "Para-professionals: Their Role in *ESOL* and Bilingual Education." *TESOL Quarterly,* 5 (1971), 309-14.

Para-professionals are community members who assist teachers ("profession-als") in various ways. The author believes strongly that such assistants are desirable not only as a temporary palliative for the critical shortage of trained bilingual teachers, but that they are needed even where no such shortage exists. Para-professionals who are really members of one or another of the language communities bring to a bilingual education program contacts with reality. Community holidays, poetry, song, dance, art, drama, foods, personalities—all those things that make a language worth *learning* and *using*—may become more accessible to the learners via the involvement of such personnel. Not only can community members help bring the community's riches into the classroom, but they can help make arrangements for bringing the classroom into the community. The personal relationships and communicational needs that are stimulated by such interaction may be every bit as important as what the teacher is doing in a more "professional" capacity.

Leckie, Dan (Chairman). *Draft Report of the Work Group on Multicultural Programs.* Toronto: Board of Education, 1975.

Until recently most Canadian work on bilingual education came from Montreal and highlighted the French-English accommodation. Now other, more Anglified, parts of Canada too are coming to the fore with their own formulations and emphases. This publication details the need for cultural pluralism in general and discusses curricular approaches to third languages (i.e., to ethnic languages in addition to English and French) in particular. It is but one of a series of Board of Education publications on this topic and should well repay the interest of American readers concerned with the "why" and the "how" of cultural and linguistic pluralism in schools situated within an Angloculture. A similar benefit can be derived from J. J. Smolicz's "Ethnic Languages in a Plural Society: A Humanistic Sociological Perspective" (Adelaide: University of Adelaide, 1975, mimeographed), whose point of departure is Anglo-Australian. (Also note the collection on "Bilingual Education" edited by Marta Rado and published by La Trobe University, Bundura, Australia.) Slowly, too slowly perhaps, this perspective is returning to America where it long seemed to have been forgotten, although Horace Kallen had given it a firm philosophical basis here over half a century ago (*Culture and Democracy in the United States: Studies in the Group Psychology of the American Peoples.* New York: Boni and Liveright, 1924; Reprint Edition: New York: Arno Press, 1970).

Recently many agencies and media that had only or primarily been sensitive to the special educational needs of black Americans have recognized the corresponding needs, including the linguistic ones, of other American ethnic groups as well. Among the very recent outcroppings of this kind are: Judith Herman, *The Schools and Group Identity: Educating for a New Pluralism,* New York: American Jewish Committee, 1974; A. Harry Passow, "New Curricula for Multi-Ethnic Schools," *Equal Opportunity Review: ERIC Clearinghouse on Urban Education,* 1975, June; Ray C. Rist, "Race, Policy and Schooling," *Society,* November-December (1974), 59-63. All of these, and yet other similar American publications now becoming quite numerous, tend to realize that just as it is not enough to be "color blind" in order to do justice to the rights and needs of black children, so it is not enough to be "ethnic blind" vis-à-vis white cultural minorities. They all attempt to encourage positive recognition of ethnic diversity. However, they all fail to realize sufficiently that it is not the ethnic child alone who needs this recognition but that this is also needed by the de-ethnicized Anglo majority and by American "Culture and Democracy" more generally. The Canadian and Australian publications cited above are in advance of the American ones in that they are aware of the ethnic contribution to society at large rather than viewing ethnicity as a type of democratically permissible special pleading.

Lewis, Glyn. "Bilingual Education and Social Change in the Soviet Union." In Bernard Spolsky and Robert L. Cooper (eds.), *Current Trends in Bilingual Education.* Rowley: Newbury House, in press.

Bilingual education in the USSR is simultaneously "dynamic" (i.e., promoting the Russian language) and "conservative" (i.e., a safeguard for the minority nationality languages). Educational planning seems geared toward the former, though "integrated" schools (or "parallel medium" schools where Russian is *one of several* languages used as media) are maintained (mostly) outside of Russian language strongholds (i.e., outside of the Russian Republic and the Ukraine). A difference between *unilateral* and *reciprocal* bilingualisms is posed, and it is suggested that if the present trend toward the former continues (whereby Russian speakers do *not* learn the minority languages, whereas speakers of the minority languages *do* learn Russian), the product will be a "linguistically homogenous state" and bilingual education will have been a factor in creating it. (Compare with Kjolseth's views on similar dangers in connection with most bilingual education in the U. S. A.)

Mackey, William F. "The Evaluation of Bilingual Education." In Bernard Spolsky and Robert L. Cooper (eds.). *Current Trends in Bilingual Education.* Rowley: Newbury House, in press. And Macnamara, John. "The Generalizability of Results of Studies of Bilingual Education." Mimeographed (McGill University), 1973, 9 pp.

Both these papers present important cautions against assuming that enough is known about bilingual education *in general* to really enable us to derive useful guidelines for *particular* new programs that are about to get under way. The uniqueness of each program is stressed, particularly insofar as goals, personnel, materials, methods, and the interactions between all of these factors are concerned. Certainly, the wholesale borrowing of evaluative techniques and of teaching methods from one program for use in others is unfounded and reveals a lack of understanding on the part of those preferring to do so. Nevertheless, as experience with bilingual education accumulates, the thoughtful administrator, teacher, and layman should not be discouraged from exploring the implications of that experience, particularly as it is seen within a social context, for his own complex situation. Undergeneralization is as foolish as is overgeneralization. As always, we must learn from the past and from one another, or we are hopelessly lost, but we must add to the foregoing our own thought and our own sensitivity.

Paulston, Christina Bratt. "Las Escuelas Bilingües in Peru: Some Comments on Second Language Learning." *IRAL,* 10 (1972), 351-56.

Many of the bilingual schools in Peru are supported by the Instituto Linguistico, a missionary organization. Since its goals are genuinely bilingual (rather than merely transitionally so for the purposes of ultimate Hispanization), its efforts and the schools it supports were often stymied by the Ministry of Education, which primarily pursued monolingual and monocultural goals (see also Burns, 1968). Nevertheless, both formal and informal data indicate that bilingual school achievement in subject matter fields is fully as good as that attained in monolingual schools in comparable areas. Moreover, proficiency in Spanish is, if anything, greater in the bilingual school, perhaps more as a result of the lower absenteeism and smaller dropout rate than of instructional factors *per se.*

Reports, such as this one, from Third World nations, are much needed in order to balance the flood of research and other publications dealing with American and Canadian bilingual education efforts. As this volume has revealed, bilingual secondary education alone is ongoing in over 1200 schools in more than 100 countries. More reports from a variety of localities are needed so that American-Canadian provincialism will not dominate in this field under the guise of advanced and impartial thinking.

Paulston, Christina Bratt. "Ethnic Relations and Bilingual Education: Accounting for Contradictory Data." In *Proceedings of the First Inter-American Conference on Bilingual Education.* Arlington: Center for Applied Linguistics, 1975.

We can all think of unresolved questions pertaining to bilingual education. What sets this paper off from others of the question-asking kind is that it focuses on the need to *systematize* the minority-majority relations context in which much (but not all) of bilingual education is embedded. Many educators and concerned laymen treat intergroup relations as a field that they are "naturally" familiar with as a result of their exposure to black-white or Chicano-Anglo issues. Professional students of ethnic relations realize that the above represent only two out of a large number of different *kinds* of interaction contexts, and they also realize the dimensions to utilize in order to discuss and analyze *kinds* of ethnic relations. Paulston's chief contribution is to relate many unsolved problems in bilingual education to one of the major theoretical systems pertaining to ethnic relations (Schermerhorn, 1970). Fishman (1966) and Verdoodt (1968 and 1971) had also previously made use of the very same system for other types of sociolinguistic inquiry, and educators too may find it useful in opening up their own awareness to the comparative complexity of this topic.

Other papers in this same volume also merit careful perusal, particularly those that provide further international perspective to the Swedish perspective that Paulston brings to her own paper. This volume, of course, is inter-American in its focus (Mexican, Canadian-Indian, French-Canadian, Chicano, American-Indian, Bolivian, Peruvian, Ecuadorian, Guatemalan). What is now needed is a truly international collection of papers organized within the framework of Schermerhorn's system or some other systematic approach to the various types of bilingual settings or bilingual education approaches.

Politzer, Robert L. and Mary Rhodes Hoover. "On the Use of Attitude Variables in the Teaching of a Second Dialect." *IRAL,* 12 (1974), 43-51.

The ultimate triumph of those concerned with engendering sensitivity to sociocultural factors as important determinants in the evaluation of psychoeducational alternatives comes when those who are most concerned with pedagogical methods come to similar conclusions on the basis of empirical evidence. In this paper, one of the world's most outstanding teachers of language teachers concludes that "lack of attachment to the native language and/or high integrative motivation will favor success of an approach that excludes use of the students' language, while high attachment to the native language and/or low integrative motivation will militate against such an approach." This approach is particularly well founded because it does not give across-the-board advice, but rather indicates the dimensions that must be considered before decisions are made as to which language should be used/taught first or most. It definitely indicates that psychoeducational expertise is needed in bilingual or bidialectal education, but that such expertise can be most effective only after the necessary sociocultural expertise has been brought into play in conjunction with the broader, all-pervasive considerations that such expertise is peculiarly qualified to handle. The proper sequencing of expertise can be as crucial as calling upon expertise at all.

Riegel, Klaus F. and Roy Freedle. "What Does It Take to Be Bilingual or Bidialectal? " In D. Harrison and T. Trabasso (eds.), *Seminar on Black English.* Hillsdale, N. J.: Erlbaum, 1975.

In our concentration on sociological issues and approaches to bilingual education we have tended to overlook the psychological factors that pertain to bilingual cognitive functioning and, therefore, to bilingual education *per se.* This paper is a very useful and a very positive review of monolingual-bilingual comparisons with respect to thinking, learning, remembering, and forgetting. A similar purpose is served by Norman Segalowitz's "Psychological Perspectives on Bilingual Education," in B. Spolsky and R. L. Cooper's *Current Trends in Bilingual Education* (Rowley: Newbury House, in press). The latter is a more detailed review as well as a more extensive one since it also covers personality, affective and motivational comparisons between bilinguals and monolinguals.

Once again, and quite in contrast to findings a generation ago when socioeconomic differences were often uncontrolled, the comparisons are overwhelmingly favorable to bilinguals, bilingualism, and bilingual education.

Rubin, Joan. "Bilingual Education and Language Planning." Honolulu: East West Center-Culture Learning Institute, 1974, mimeographed.

Besides providing a useful and brief introduction to various facets of language planning, this paper is especially attentive to the problems of policy makers and executors (implementors) vis-à-vis language planning in general and bilingual education in particular. It points to the need to be clear about the goals that such persons have in mind in order to avoid frustration in the local application of mandated programs. It also points to the fact that planners, policy makers, and implementors are not always in touch or in agreement with one another, leading to further difficulties in local interpretation and application. It stresses that the introduction of bilingual education is part of a general social change trend, and, therefore, that it both benefits by as well as suffers from the goals and values being fostered and opposed by that more general trend. Finally, it stresses the difference between bilingual education and the other kinds of language planning being conducted by the Federal Government of the United States. When viewed in this perspective, bilingual education is much more population-focused (rather than being focused inward on government agencies *per se*), more client-centered, more permissive of local variation, and more visible to public scrutiny than is the bulk of other language planning going on in the U. S. A. today. These differences may account for some of its peculiar strengths and weaknesses.

Spolsky, Bernard. "Speech Communities and Schools." *TESOL Quarterly,* 8 (1974), 17-26.

A powerful argument for sound school-by-school study of the needs and aspirations that bilingual education is expected to serve. One of the most striking cases of ignoring the local school-and-community context of bilingual education is the failure to distinguish between programs that stress the *unmarked* language of the broader community (as in most schools for on-reservation Indians, particularly those in relatively inaccessible areas) and those that stress the *marked* language of the narrower community (as in most urban and semi-urban schools for Indian tribes whose children no longer speak their parents' language). "Confusion of these two arguments leads to false and irrelevant claims, easily demolished by intelligent critics, and seriously damaging the cause of those who aim to make schools more sensitive to community language needs." The factorial and predictive findings revealed in the International Study of Bilingual Secondary Education merely lead to the further argument, beyond that so forcefully made by Spolsky, that separate though these two considerations may well be, both of them, nevertheless, need to be pursued in almost every bilingual education program.

Spolsky, Bernard, Joanna B. Green and John Read. "A Model for Description, Analysis and Perhaps Evaluation of Bilingual Education." *Navajo Reading Study Progress Report No. 23.* University of New Mexico, 1974, 35 pp.

A very detailed discussion of six factors relevant to any consideration of bilingual education: psychological, sociological, economic, political, religio-cultural, and linguistic. Each of these is further subdivisible in accord with whether its primary relevance is at the very *outset* of a bilingual education, during the *operational* period of the program, or in connection with the *effects* of the program *per se.* The second and third contexts of the factors discussed are of primary concern to those interested in the sociology of bilingual education. The potential of this model is examined relative to bilingual education programs in the Navajo, the Micronesian, and the St. Lambert student-teacher-parent-community constellations. The model as such is still a preliminary one as well as a nonquantitative one. However, in view of its detail and its inherent crosscultural and societal concern, it would seem to have great potential, at least for overall orientational purposes. Its utilization with actual data will doubtless lead to changes and refinements in the model.

Titone, Renzo. *Bilinguismo Precoce e Educazione Bilingue.* Rome: Armando-Armando, 1972.

Although dealing primarily with psychological issues that have been largely resolved in the American and Canadian settings (e.g., the once feared negative consequences of bilingualism for cognitive development), and although concerned with the primary level of education, this volume is still well worth scrutinizing. It constitutes a marshaling of evidence (450 pages!) on behalf of bilingualism and bilingual education, as well as a plea and a plan for the revitalization and reform of all elementary education in Italy on a bilingual model. This would not now be as far-fetched a goal as once appeared to be the case. Italian education is currently being changed and modernized in many respects, and the bilingual nature of elitist education all through Italy and of indigenous minority-group education in various northern provinces is becoming better known. The arguments and findings of American and Canadian advocates of bilingual education are thus being given increased recognition. Unfortunately, bilingual education in Italy is faced with a difficult choice between French and English as "the" second language. Hopefully, this split in the ranks of bilingual education protagonists can be overcome before long.

Verdoodt, Albert. "Erster Bericht der internationaler Untersuchung uber zwei-sprachige Universitaten and Hochschulen" (First Report of the International Study of Bilingual Colleges and Secondary Schools). In Rolf Kjolseth and Fritz Sack (eds.), *Zur Soziologie der Sprache.* Opladen: West Deutscher Verlag, 1971.

(Also appeared as Sonderhefte 15 of *Kölner Zeitschrift für Soziologie und Sozialpsychologie.*)

This precursor of the ISBSE is an expanded German version of the original French report listed in Appendix 4 (Verdoodt, 1969). It still stands virtually alone insofar as attention to bilingual higher (i.e., tertiary) education is concerned and deserves to be replicated and expanded at this level. This pioneering study makes some interesting and useful distinctions, e.g., between bilingual institutions serving two populations with separate cultures and those serving only one population requiring two languages for different purposes; those institutions of the former type that attempt to facilitate the interaction between their two populations and those that deal with two solitudes; those institutions that seek to foster cultural pluralism and those that seek to foster assimilation; those that consider bilingualism as a desired outcome and those for whom it is merely a concomittant of more basic and pervasive educational goals. All in all, this study points toward much needed further research on the international sociology of bilingual education at levels much higher than those commonly thought of in the U. S. A.

Introduction

(a) *The significance of bilingualism.* Polyglottism is a very early characteristic of human societies, and monolingualism a cultural limitation. It is doubtful whether any community or any language has existed in isolation from other communities or languages. At all times in Europe and elsewhere, there have been bilingual groups and this is reflected in the regard with which the possession of more than one language has been held in even remote countries and undeveloped educational systems. For instance, a Norwegian Speculum Regale of the Middle Ages claimed that mastery of many languages, especially Latin and French, was necessary to an educated man (Sommerfelt, 1954: 25). In New Guinea and in vast areas of South America and Africa languages, though they belong only to individual villages or groups of villages, are held to be mutually intelligible over varying distances—one-day languages or one-week languages (Hocket, 1958: 326). Many tribes, like those of the North American Indians, were so small that voluntary or obligatory intertribal marriages were encouraged or made obligatory to ensure survival, and the complexity of the linguistic patterns which resulted must have been formidable. Nor was the condition of Europe in earlier times different from what we may observe today in many parts of the world. Indo-European was not a single homogenous language but a congeries, a reticulation of several dialects and languages. Furthermore the speakers of those languages conquered and settled lands in the Middle East, for instance, where non-European languages in equal diversity were spoken (Atkinson, 1952: 8).

Contact of languages and consequent changes in personal and group attachment to particular languages result in a proportion of the population becoming bilingual, invariably for so long as it takes to complete the shift of attachment and usually longer. Nor is it only those parts of the population actually in contact which become bilingual: at all stages the need to become bilingual is brought home to those who are far from the point of contact but have need for social intercourse with those who have become bilingual (Meillet, 1951: 77). The specifically linguistic consequences, especially the problems of "substratum," "which it is now the fashion to minimize" (Tovar, 1954: 221), have not been ignored to the extent that the social and historical contexts of language contact

BILINGUALISM AND BILINGUAL EDUCATION:
THE ANCIENT WORLD TO THE RENAISSANCE
(E. Glyn Lewis)

APPENDIX 3

have been.* Yet, because of the frequency of such contacts in the past, as well as the current fluid social and linguistic situations of many communities—products of the history of those contacts—we need to encourage a study of the history of languages in contact and of the attempts of those interested in the education of children in their efforts to cope with consequent bilingualism.

Because of bilingualism in medieval Europe, it is argued, "people were forced into perpetual approximations in expressing their thoughts . . . forced as they were into an incessant movement to and fro between the two planes of languages" (Bloch, 1961: 78). It is difficult to conceive how such an allegation can be validated or what criteria should be employed in any attempt to do so. Bilingualism has rarely been absent from important levels of the intellectual and cultural life of Europe, and nearly all European languages have had long and, in some instances, several successive periods of language contact. Bilingualism has been and is nearer to the normal situation than most people are willing to believe. Imprecision of thought and expression, if it is a consequence of bilingualism, following Bloch's argument, is a normal rather than a pathological condition. Such generalizations, and many like them, are commonplace, but the authority behind them makes it necessary that we should understand the historical roots of bilingualism if a realistic policy for bilingual education is to gain approval.

The study is made even more imperative by some of the characteristics of the present age. On the whole, the apotheosis of language loyalty during the last two centuries has not been uniformly advantageous. Language is peculiarly endowed to enable communities to assert the separateness as much as the identity of their interests. Of the various ties that bind mankind a common language can claim no privileged status: other bonds protect the language rather than vice versa. Those who press the national inviolability of a language are usually an elite or intelligentsia for whom "national languages constitute a huge system of vested interest which sullenly resists critical enquiry" (Sapir, 1949: 118), and it is easy to underestimate the power of such mental insularity. Sapir could hazard the guess that "revivalist movements" and the investment of great emotional and intellectual capital in the effort to save languages from the consequences of contact "would come to be looked upon as little more than eddies in the more powerful stream . . . which set in at the end of the medieval period" (Sapir, 1949: 88). But these eddies are still strong and may still turn out to be highly significant.

(b) *Linguistic pluralism or exclusiveness?* Though it has profound social and educational importance the identification of language with national or group self-interest is, if not peculiar to the modern era, far more characteristic of it than it was of an earlier age. Little is more alien to ancient or medieval tradition than such views as were attributed by Daudet to the schoolmaster in his "La Dernière Classe," prompted by the substitution of German for French in Alsace Lorraine:

---

*For a useful summary of the issues involved and the current consensus see Cassano, whose treatment is broader than is suggested by the title.

"We must keep it alive amongst ourselves and never forget it: because when a people is imprisoned, as long as it looks after its language it is as if it holds the key to its cell." Such views have their origin to some extent in the growth of nationalism at the time of the Renaissance, as Sapir implied. Ronsard was among the first to speak of the "treachery" of abandoning "le langage de son pays ... c'est un crime de leze majesté." Du Bellay argues that "la même loi naturelle qui commande à chacun défendre le lien de sa naissance nous oblige aussi de garder la dignité de notre langue." This novel consciousness of the national associations of a language was reinforced in the Age of Enlightenment as well as by "Romantic particularism" conjoint with the idealization of the "folk" exemplified in the writings of von Humboldt, for whom the essence of ethnic identification is the associated language—"The spiritual characteristics and the linguistic structure of a people stand in a relationship of such indissoluble fusion that given one we should be able to derive the other from it entirely" (von Humboldt: vol. VII, 42). It is but a short step to the identification of language with political nationalism such as we find in the Irish nineteenth-century writer Thomas Davis—"a people without a language of its own is only half a nation" (Davis, 1914: 173). The Romantic (Idealist) aspects of philosophy, linguistic nationalism, and the development of modern philology are not only linked historically but draw their strength from the same epistemological roots.*

Elitist nationalism and exclusive attitudes to languages, derived from the views of Romantic philosophers about the uniqueness of ethnic groups, were necessary but not sufficient preconditions of the present identification of national self-interest and language, an identification which justifies bilingual education in the eyes of many. They needed to be reinforced by those factors which put a premium on the growth of interest in the vernacular, namely the rise of a powerful and self-conscious middle class, the invention of printing which made the vernacular a viable literary language, the rapid growth of industrialism which required a proletariat which was literate (necessarily to begin with in the vernacular), and an advanced process of social integration which fed on national self-consciousness as a means of ensuring acquiescence in the discomfort of social change. This combination of circumstances may have made linguistic nationalism inevitable, but inevitable or not it certainly did result in a profound change in mental attitudes which have had vital implications for education. It is not unfair to say that the *refusal* to accept a pluralistic philosophy toward language in society determines the philosophy of education in most of those countries where the consideration is relevant; and what is more disturbing, a unitary linguistic philosophy is taken as the most natural state of affairs by many educationists. Suppression of a language is assumed to be a necessary condition of the political integrity of the state. No doubt the first obligation of the state is to itself, and because of that it will seek to maintain untrammeled the paths of communication.

---

*For a full review of language and nationalism see Fishman, 1972b.

However, its survival is simply the means to ensure the well-being of its constituents. Its "esse" is only the precondition of the "bene esse" of the groups of which it is composed: its integrity is justified solely by its capacity to accommodate diversity.

It would be patently absurd to argue that peoples and nations had never until now regarded their languages with pride and affection. But it was not until well after the Enlightenment that a sense of a group's identity was commonly tied to the maintenance of its language, or that attitude to language became an ideology, thus ensuring that attitude to language not only reflected certain beliefs about that language but was transformed into a powerful tool for social action which was often only slightly associated with language. As late as the end of the Middle Ages it often happened that writers would abandon their native language in favor of another with higher claims to cultural or esthetic preeminence. Bruno Latini did so, as did the Catalan troubadours. Roman Vidal chose to write lyric poetry in French because it was the convention that the choice of language was determined by *genre* rather than the nationality of the author (Chaytor: 29).

In the Classical world, group differences, especially those relating to cultural activities, were not thought to require different languages for their expression. In the older empires, problems affecting choice of language were determined empirically and pragmatically rather than on grounds of fixed principle. The Greek language was claimed by barbarians, semi-barbarians, and civilized alike. The Greek-speaking population on the Struma and Isker rivers were not brought into the Hellenistic political system until the advent of Claudius. Conversely there were thoroughly Hellenized peoples whose languages were Carian and Lycian, Lydian, or Messapic. Claudian in the days of Honorius could write, "We who drink of the Rhone and the Orontes are all one nation," and language was never the criterion of membership. Convenience might indicate the desirability of using a particular language for the administration of large territories; but beyond convenience there were few if any other considerations that might affect the suppression of a local language or the promotion of an intrusive one. While Latin became the acknowledged medium for the transmission of Greek culture in the West, the Romans refrained from dislodging the Greek language in any country where it was either the native tongue or a lingua franca. This was true of areas like Sicily and the northwest coast of Africa, which were nearer to Rome than to Athens. Africa remained a Greek-speaking country through the seventh century A.D., and in accordance with strict Roman practice the Edicts of Cyrene, even under Roman rule, were written in Greek.

Between the phase of Classical indifference leading to tolerance of diversity and our own sensitivity to diversity associated nevertheless with intolerance, there was an age also tending to intolerance, but in that instance arising from linguistic universalism rather than diversity. The extent to which Latin was a universal language is a matter of controversy, but it cannot be doubted that compared with the diversity and acceptance of "pluralism" of the Classical world, the Middle

Ages not only tended toward but pressed for uniformity in theory and practice. Compared with the encouragement which the Byzantines and the Eastern Church gave to the vernaculars, the Western Church was singularly restrictive. It is true that within Greece itself the Byzantine policy was to Hellenize the Slavs, but outside Greece they not only tolerated but did what they could to promote the vernaculars. Not till the eleventh century did the Roman policy of centralization succeed in uprooting that tradition of tolerance. The slavophil policy pursued by the eastern imperial regime "contrasted with the uniform imposition of Latin upon Western Christendom in the Middle Ages" (Obolensky, 1971: 147-51). Even as late as the Carolingian Empire educational and cultural enactments were intended to ensure total subjection to an authoritarian policy (Heer, 40). Latin, the sacred language, was the sole safeguard of man's store of culture, science, and faith. In the whole period down to the twelfth century, though it was associated with a beleagured culture which found its refuge in monasteries and elitist and aristocratic schools, Latin was virtually the only vehicle of communication on an intellectual level. The world of Western Europe, unlike that of pre-Classical and Classical times, or of the Byzantine Empire, was "a closed world of grand forms," the frontiers of which were defined by the currency of Latin. Our own era prefers "closed national worlds of limited forms."

Once a policy favoring uniformity was articulated and a highly cogent rationale for it argued at the highest levels, any divergence from it would also need to be formalized and made explicit, so that attitudes to language became polarized. Once the political will and the economic power to maintain a universal regime (linguistic, ecclesiastical, or political) were enervated, what was proposed as a substitute had also to be rationalized and presented as an alternative ideology. However, just as there were undercurrents of conflict in Classical and medieval times, so today the grounds for linguistic exclusiveness are being eroded. The accelerating diffusion of several languages has tended to "denationalize" them. English, Spanish, and Russian (at least in the vast complex of the U. S. S. R.) have tended to loosen their historical associations with their native and historical cultures. They and others have come to be adopted by other nations with their own important traditions and languages, not for the historical and national associations of those languages but as vehicular languages of wider communication. For instance, at the inauguration of a new medical school in 1838 the Ottoman ruler reminded the students: "you will study scientific medicine in French. . . . My purpose in having you taught French is not to educate you as French men; it is to teach you scientific medicine and little by little to take that into our language" (Lewis, 1961: 83). Any system of education has to attend to this ambivalence if the tension which so frequently characterizes the discussion and formulation of policies for bilingual education is to be avoided or resolved. Thus, attitude to English in Wales is distorted by failure among many of the Welsh intelligentsia to acknowledge that English need not in all situations be regarded as a "national" language. It might then cease to be associated so ineradicably in their minds with English cultural dominance.

1. Language Contact and Linguistic Unification

The historical study of contact cannot in theory, or very well in practice, be limited to any one area of the world, however extensive. Nevertheless some areas and the languages native to them represent an identifiable and close-knit web of contacts which are very well recorded. In some cases, too, these contacts have influenced the world far beyond the geographical location of speakers of those languages. Prior to the Christian era there had been three periods of linguistic unification and of consequent widespread, though not always "mass" or "popular," bilingualism. Moreover, each of these periods necessitated bilingual education for those minorities who were required to operate the machinery of political and administrative unification. The three periods correspond to the ascendancy of Akkadian (the Babylonian language), Aramaic, and Greek. The successive moves toward unification and the pattern of language contact and consequent bilingualism occurred in areas of considerable linguistic diversity. In Asia Minor there existed a substratum of ancient languages such as Lydian and Lycian over which flowed a series of linguistic influences from the south represented by the Semitic languages, and out of which emerged Babylonian, Hebrew, and Aramaic. From the north and northeast came the Indo-European languages—Hittite, Phrygian, Thracian, and Armenian. During the Christian era we can recognize the continuing influence of some of the earlier languages on unification, especially Greek, as well as newcomers to the category, for instance Latin and Arabic. In all these phases of unification, early and late, bilingual schools were an important formative factor, though they involved only a minority of those who were bilingual. Upon the East Mediterranean, during successive historical periods, a large number of different linguistic influences converged, which interacted to produce a variety of contact situations and types of bilingualism. In fact the history of the Mediterranean constitutes a key to any study of bilingualism and bilingual education not only in Europe (Western, Central, and Eastern), Asia Minor, Russia, and by association with Russia and Iran, parts of Central Asia, but in large areas of the New World—Latin America and the United States as well. Whether the direction of linguistic movement and influence is from the north with Celtic, from the east with Greek, from the south with Latin, or from the west with Latin influence on the Slavs, all forces appear to converge upon the Mediterranean: it is "the sum of the individual voices of Europe."* And these multifarious voices are heard not only in the total European context, but in many small localities. Because of the convergence of linguistic influences down the centuries there is hardly a bay that is not a unique complex linguistic community. And to that complexity contributed not only the languages of the Mediterranean peoples but those of the Portuguese, Normans, Bretons, Dutch, Flemings, and English who were drawn to it. This fact suggests an important conclusion about the bilingualism of the Mediterranean: it was of two

---

*No one who is acquainted with Baudel's seminal studies will fail to recognize the indebtedness of this section to his researches. It is not only a duty to record that debt, but a pleasure to express gratitude for many exciting hours following the paths he has pioneered.

kinds, or rather it existed on two levels. First there is the bilingualism which results from "maritime contact"—a series of contacts with considerable influence but tending to lack continuity. Contacts are brought about quickly but are impermanent, for instance western penetration by the Greeks, the establishment of Phoenician centers, the later extension of Venetian influences to the east, and in the Aegean Archipelago the confluence of the Byzantines, Venetians, and Genoese. The story of the Corsican and Sardinian complex is that of a succession of Etruscan, Greek, and Carthaginian contacts; and Sicily exemplifies the same interrelationship of Greek, Arabic, Norman, Angevin, and Spanish languages. Maritime contact produces a "conjuncture" of languages in contact, and this is due to the fact that while the sea promoted such contacts, the Mediterranean lands are regions isolated by high mountain ranges, obstacles which had to be overcome before language contact could be consolidated.

The second level of bilingualism in the Mediterranean is "territorial," reflecting the gradual appropriation of a firm and expanding base. It is slow in developing and permanent in its historical influence—it creates a "structure" rather than a "conjuncture" of linguistic contacts. The maritime contacts tended to be motivated by trade and commerce, and for that reason produced a "reciprocal" bilingualism where both groups had to learn of each other. "Territorial bilingualism," resulting from conquest, displacement of native populations, or migration, tended toward assimilation and the creation of "unilateral bilingualism" which hardly affected the newcomers. The Celtic and Germanic penetration to the west and the Latin domination of Italy, Gaul, and Spain—so far as permanence of linguistic influence is concerned—compare very favorably with the influence of Greek.

The Mediterranean area constitutes a unity in the sense that the sea and the associated mountains provide a frame, or a set of limitations to the constant flux of peoples and languages. The sea promoted, or at least facilitated movement as well as the means whereby trading colonies were constantly reinforced. The mountains placed constraints on such movements and ensured the concentration of the intrusive languages in limited areas. Furthermore the mountains provided the "proletarian reserves," a countervailing linguistic influence in any particular area—in Southern Italy, or in Massilia, or on the eastern shores of the Mediterranean where Greek and the local languages, for geographical reasons, coexisted for several centuries. The Mediterranean, because of this interaction of mountains and sea, constrained the contact of languages so that the influences of Aramaic, Greek, Latin, and Arabic in turn were not dissipated. It is true that these constraints did not work so effectively inland so that we cannot speak of a similar coherent pattern of contacts for the whole of Europe, but what coherence there is derives in considerable part from the influence of the Mediterranean.

This appendix is based on the belief that while we cannot wholly break with the tradition which seeks for the origins and derivations of contact, it is more profitable to understand how people have achieved their unity: starting as heterogenous elements and moving into a new and coherent pattern. Bilingual education is only partly, and to my way of thinking only secondarily, concerned with simple maintenance and conservation. If it is to be worth anything it needs to make certain that out of the discrete cultural elements a new unity is born. This is what we witness in the history of bilingualism in the Mediterranean.

(a) *Akkadian.* The Semitic languages belong to several closely related groups. The main division separates West and East Semitic. In the former West Semitic group are the Ugaritic, Canaanite languages (Phoenician, Carthaginian, Moabite, and Hebrew) and the southern "Aramaic" languages (Syriac, Samaritan, and Nabatean among them). The West Semitic also includes Arabic, and the ancient languages of southern Arabia. The members of the other main group, East Semitic, are the ancient languages of Mesopotamia—Assyrian and Babylonian, the general name for the two almost identical languages being Akkadian, derived from the old Sargonic Kingdom of Akkad.

It is clear that two cultures, Sumerian and Semitic, were found in close association from the earliest historical times and the two languages were not used exclusively by each ethnic group. For instance in 2,600 B.C. Sumerians in southern Mesopotamia wrote inscriptions in Semitic on votive tablets, and there were Semitic names on Sumerian tablets (Moscati, 1959: 48). The distinction of languages was made according to locality and to some extent according to the subject of communication—Sumerian being the language of learning, religion, and literature. During the first half of the third millenium before Christ this civilization reached a high level, enriched by a literature employing the newly invented cuneiform syllabic script. Akkadian, when it emerged as the heir of this political dominion, introduced a new element into an already richly varied pattern of contacts. The result of a fusion of Sumerian and Semitic cultures in Mesopotamia, and hitherto the tongue of a minority of Mesopotamian Semites, Akkadian spread rapidly, partly because its literature became associated with the court and ruling classes. Between 2350 and 2150 it is attested over the whole of Mesopotamia from south to north, coexisting with South Sumerian, the other language of unification, as well as languages of local provenance (Moscati, 1960: 50).

In 1595 Babylon fell to the Hittites, and Hammurabi's dynasty ceased. Until that time speakers of Sumerian or the Semitic languages dominated Mesopotamia; thereafter Akkadian had to contend with a "host of proletarian vernaculars—Hyskos, Hittite, and Kassite" (Toynbee, 1950: 484). Northward, the land between the Zagros Mountains and Lake Van was inhabited by the Hurrians, who even before the Akkadian period had infiltrated quietly into areas bordering on Mesopotamia and as far as the Mediterranean, submerging Assyria and sweeping through Syria. On their southern flank they were in close contact with the Semitic Hyskos, Hittite, and Kassite" (Toynbee, 1950: 484). Northward, the land Anatolia. In spite of their numbers and their military power they formed no lasting political unit, and though there is evidence of the influence of Hurrian on the languages of that area, they were assimilated. Many diverse peoples who were literate in Akkadian settled in Assyria, Phoenicia, other territories of Asia Minor, and Egypt. By means of the Akkadian script the contributions of other language groups, Hittites, Hurrians, and Cretans for instance, were disseminated widely. The native lore of many peoples was transcribed and translated so that the Akkadian language came to serve a vast polyglot urban population in many lands.

Thus the contact between Akkadians and Hittites was mediated partly by the Hurri of the South Caucasus. There is linguistic evidence in the Tell Amarna Letters of the Hurrian contacts with Egypt. The Akkadian-Hittite contact was strong, and the latter language assimilated many Sumero-Akkadian loanwords, and, more significantly, countless Akkadograms—words taking Akkadian form but meant to be pronounced as Hittite translations. It has been claimed that it was the Akkadian impetus that carried Anatolian culture and the Hittite language over into the Aegean (Gordon, 1962: 59-63). The Hittites were unlike another of the mountain people who came down from the northeast, bringing their own language, namely the Kassites who usurped the rule of Babylonia for 400 years but nonetheless assimilated the language and culture of the local people. The Kassites had also been infiltrated by the Hurrians in the Zagros Mountains, and this fact is attested by the occurrence of Hurrian elements in Kassite names.

The Hittites were an independently minded people who preserved their culture and maintained their linguistic identity. There are bilingual Hittite-Akkadian documents of the reign of King Hattuclis X; and Hittite scribes composed glossaries of Sumerian, Akkadian, and Hittite words in parallel columns (Sturtevant and Hahn, 1951: 2-4). The situation was further complicated by the fact that in addition to two methods of writing, cuneiform and heiroglyphic, the Hittites had two native languages—Hittite and Khattish. Hittite was the dominant language of the empire, and its sphere of influence spread from Halicarnassus to Zion. A Hittite enclave flourished around Hebron in the days of Abraham. They dominated an important section of the polyglot populations of Ugarit. A long bilingual inscription in Phoenician and hieroglyphic Hittite discovered in eastern Cilicia is evidence of this (Sturtevant and Hahn, 1951: 6). Ugarit had accommodated a Mycenean settlement, and the whole area, including Alalakh, was a cultural entity with an overlapping pattern of languages. Through Cypriot Myceneans the population of Ugarit was in linguistic contact with the mainland Greeks (Webster, 1958: 66) as well as Mesopotamia. Ancient Syrian literature is completely identical with Ugaritic (Moscati, 1959: 213). Though Akkadian was the language of international communication, diplomacy and law, and Hurrian was the language of religion, the normal language of local and everyday affairs was Ugaritic (Gordon, 1962: 131ff).

The writing of the cuneiform script and knowledge of Akkadian as a lingua franca (together with Sumerian and/or Hurrian) meant that educated people were bilingual and possibly trilingual. But though large numbers of the ordinary population needed some oral command of more than one language, formal instruction was restricted to a privileged and specially selected group of young people. Trilingual vocabularies, used in the education of the scribes, have been discovered at Ugarit, and at least two examples of vocabularies in four languages—Sumerian, Akkadian, Hurrian, and Ugaritic—have been discovered (Gordon, 1962: 60). In the royal colleges of Babylonia and Assyria students received a very efficient linguistic education during a period of three years, after which they were expected to be proficient in several languages. Like other captive Hebrews in Babylon, the prophet Daniel, for instance, after being selected for such an education by Nebuchadnezzar, was able to communicate in the most important languages of the empire as well as in his native tongue. The linguistic requirements of those graduating from the royal colleges varied considerably, but the course was intensive, well-organized, and uniform. Even those who confined themselves to writing the business documents and so-called "letters" received some instruction in the ancient Sumerian language as well as a thorough grounding in their mother tongue. No one could read or write cuneiform otherwise. In addition to this, their work demanded a considerable knowledge of Semitic dialects other than their own. Those who were occupied in copying or writing literary or scientific texts needed a good linguistic training, and a whole corpus of texts exists to show how this was obtained. From copying out personal names the pupils proceeded to write phrases, first in Sumerian and then in Akkadian. Instruction proceeded to the translation of long continuous passages of Sumerian into Akkadian line by line. The translations were not required to be literal: the main intention was not to inculcate scholarly accuracy but to render the sense well enough for practical purposes. The acquisition of other Semitic dialects did not require the same prolonged discipline, and for them bilingual lexicons seem to have sufficed (Smith, 1937: 103).

(b) *Aramaic.* Before moving to the next phase of linguistic unification, the Aramaic, some mention should be made of the influence of Phoenician (later Punic), if only because it is a good example of the impermanence of "maritime bilingualism." The actual start of Phoenician history coincides approximately with the event which more than all others created the linguistic complexity and flux of the ancient Near East—the invasion of the "peoples of the sea" around 1200 B.C. Restricted to the strip of land between the Mediterranean and the mountains of Lebanon, hemmed in by the arrival of powerful states (the Hebrews and the Aramaens), the Phoenicians were compressed into a unified people and simultaneously compelled toward the Mediterranean (Moscati, 1959: xxii). Thus the civilization of the Phoenicians emerges partly as a consequence and partly as a component of the cultural and linguistic complex of the Near East, as well as the intermediary between Eastern and Western Mediterranean thought. Their language is undoubtedly closely related to other Semitic languages of the Syro-Palestinian area, though its remarkable geographical distribution and history of contact with non-Semitic languages helped to create dialects which correspond to different phases of the development of the Phoenicians.

After the collapse of the Mycenean empire in the twelfth century the Phoenicians made sure that eastern influence—linguistic, cultural, and economic —did not flag. Classical writers ascribe the Phoenician colonization of Cadiz to 1100 B.C. and of Utica to 1101. They preceded the Greeks in Sicily. From the sixth century B.C. it was the Phoenicians in concert with the Etruscans who defended the trading depots of the west against Greek colonization. It is a fact that the history of Etruscan culture begins with an orientalizing phase which has usually been attributed to Phoenician influence. At the same time inscriptions in Zincirli and Karatope show the spread of the Phoenician language into southern Anatolia. In the territory of Carthage, the zone closest to the city was in the hands of Punic settlers. Cultivating their vines, orchards, and olive groves, they had very intimate contacts with the native Libyans who remained in possession of the hinterland. Consequently we observe a marked divergence between the conservative official language and Vulgar Punic in which there are clear divergences from the Semitic norms, especially in syntax, due to the influence of the languages with which it was in contact.

However, the almost exclusively maritime communication network of the Phoenicians limited the possibility of permanent linguistic and cultural influence, so that the second great phase of linguistic unification belongs to the Aramaic language.

Pressed by Aramaic, during the eighth century Akkadian was on the retreat as a spoken language (Moscati, 1959: 70). The Aramaen nomads radiated into Mesopotamia where at first they adopted Akkadian. Masses were transplanted by Ashur-nasirpal into Assyria. They established a series of Aramaen cultural zones with their own written language using the Phoenician script. Aramaen-speaking merchants came to replace Phoenician traders, and, eventually supported by Assyrian military power, Aramaic became the vernacular of the whole Fertile Crescent, including Palestine and Phoenicia. In Nineveh, the capital of Sennacherib's empire, men from the northwest jostled with Medes and Elamites, and the royal scribes were hard put to transcribe the strange words from so many languages. In fact the keepers of the royal records added Aramaic glosses to facilitate interpretation later (Smith, 195). By the end of the eighth century Aramaic had supplanted Akkadian after coexisting with it for three centuries as the diplomatic language of southwest Asia and Egypt. Since the two languages were of the same Semitic family it was comparatively easy for speakers of Akkadian to learn Aramaic. The transfer was made easy also because of the superiority of the Aramaic alphabet over cuneiform. This facilitated the development of Akkadian/Aramaic bilingualism, exemplified by bilingual inscriptions dating from the reigns of the Assyrian Shalamanaser V, Sargon, and Sennacherib (Dupont-Sommer, 1940: 82, 84, 86, 88).

The Achaemenian monarchy established a universal empire stretching toward India in the east and Libya in the west, a single empire built up of diverse peoples among whom Aramaic, a well-tried lingua franca, coexisted with a large number of local languages which it was the policy of the empire to tolerate. Aramaic was the official language in all provinces, certainly west of Iran. It was used extensively in Egypt, and it appears at the same time in Anatolia. Eventually Aramaic came to be the dominant partner in a large number of contact situations. The kind of bilingual patterns so created is illuminated by a fresco of the ninth century showing an Iranian imperial official dictating to two secretaries, who, simultaneously with the dictation, translated onto clay and parchment (Dupont-Sommer, 1940: 86-189). The area within which Aramaic supplanted the local languages was not so extensive as that in which it was used simply as a lingua franca, but even so, people over the whole of the northern fringes of the Arabian steppe gradually transferred their affiliation to it. The Nabataean inhabitants of Petra were Arabic-speaking, but the official language of their inscriptions was Aramaic. The Jews first adopted Aramaic as an auxiliary language, but after a lengthy period of transitional bilingualism abandoned their own native tongue in its favor, retaining Hebrew for the sanctified texts originally composed in it, although finally Aramaic, too, was admitted to the pale of sanctity.

The Nile and the Aegean, the Indus and Jaxartes, the African desert and the frontiers of China were the limits of the expansion of the Achaemenian Empire and it might be expected that the Persian language would have been promoted as the language of unification in that area—an adstratum to Greek, Egyptian, Hebrew, Phoenician, Assyrian, Phrygian, Lydian, Median, Armenian, and Aramaic. However the Persians had no lingua franca of their own to help consolidate their hold on so vast a territory with such varied vernaculars. They depended upon the liberal recognition of languages of limited currency, the official recognition of Aramaic as the major international language, and localized official support for Persian at Persepolis, Assyrian at Babylon, and Neo-Susan in Elam. The coexistence of Aramaic, Greek, and the local languages is evidenced not only among the denationalized inhabitants of Babylon and the towns of Syria but in remote and backward areas as well, where cities were rare and village life the rule. Scribes and administrators were brought up in specialized "government schools," which used bilingual lexicons and texts, to be literate in Aramaic as well as the local vernacular, though the emphasis was mainly on reading and writing Aramaic. Consequently, it has been claimed that Aramaic could carry those who knew it northward as far as the Amanus, eastward as far as the Zagros, and westward as far as the Nile, in the certain assurance that whatever the vernacular of any area might be, there would be sufficient speakers of Aramaic with whom to communicate.

Just as Phoenician exemplifies a category of impermanent maritime bilingualism, Aramaic is an excellent illustration of "territorial bilingualism," slow to develop and enduring for centuries. It was not until the Babylonian exile (586 B.C.) that the Jews, for instance, began to replace Hebrew with Aramaic as the language of normal conversation. And after the return of the exiled Jews, Aramaic continued to exert an important influence on Hebrew. Indeed, the existence of Hebrew/Aramaic bilingualism lasted a long time in some few cases, into the modern period. Meanwhile Aramaic came to be challenged by Arabic, and though it is difficult to determine the period of the shift to Arabic it is probably true that Aramaic was still spoken up to the middle of the eighth century. Some claim that a variant of Aramaic is still spoken in Syria, Azerbaijan, and Kurdistan. Others insist that after a prolonged period of Arabic/Aramaic bilingualism the latter was completely replaced by Arabic in the fifth century A.D. In any case Aramaic had a long history of contact with other languages and contributed to a significant phase of unification.

(c) *Egyptian.* The Egyptians, though they exercised nothing like the imperial sway of the Persians, were similarly involved in a complex pattern of linguistic contacts from early times. The Egyptians were an amalgam of African linguistic groups, wandering Semites and Asiatics. The Helu-nebu who made recurrent appearances in Egypt were, it has been claimed, Greek in origin (Montet, 1964: 131). After gaining independence from Persia, Egypt opened its doors to the outer world; large numbers of Greeks entered, some of whom settled in Egypt as merchants, and some possibly as artisans. Beside those immigrants who were elevated to the upper strata of Egyptian society, there were large numbers who earned their living in agriculture and as clerks. Consequently different immigrant bilingual groups came to be significant in Egyptian society (Rostovtseff, 1941: 82, 331). Furthermore, the attitude of the Egyptians encouraged the injection of these new influences, because they valued their contacts with other nations:

"The North wind is a life giving wind,
He has been given to me and from him I derive life."

(Quoted in Montet, 1964: 208)

From as early as 3000 B.C. they had regular contacts with Byblos where a temple served a permanent settlement (Gordon, 1962: 104). Relations between Cretans and Egyptians were close for several centuries, and their contracts, treaties, and diplomatic communications were bilingual (James, 1920: 58).

Sometimes their contact with other peoples and other languages was not of their seeking. Invasions by the Hyskos are a case in point. Egypt was invaded and occupied by these Asiatic hordes, and the period of their domination witnessed the movement of Semitic tribes into Egypt. The biblical account of Joseph probably refers to the end of the Hyskos era. During the eighteenth Dynasty, the language of these invaders was used widely, a fact which was responsible for changes in the Egyptian language which were not unlike, though they were less radical perhaps, than those which saw the transformation of Latin into the several Romance languages after similar periods of bilingualism (Montet, 1964: 201). Contact between Egypt and the Hebrew people became increasingly important during the period of the decline which followed the New Kingdom. Later, in the seventh century, a colony of Jewish mercenaries was established near Aswan, and this continued until the end of the fifth century. From this site as well as from Suggura, Edfu, and Hermopolis have come a great mass of letters and business and legal documents written in Imperial Aramaic, revealing considerable Egyptian influence. After 301 B.C. Ptolemy brought back many Jews from his Palestine campaigns, and he employed Jewish soldiers in Egypt, giving them land and so establishing a semi-permanent Jewish influence. Solomon's reign witnessed considerable economic expansion as well as many social and political innovations. Because of these he required an enlarged and better-educated cadre of administrators whose training was influenced by Egyptian models on account of Solomon's ties with Egypt through marriage.

Egypt had a long tradition of didactic treatises designed for the sons of officials who were trained to enter government service. These treatises, entitled "Teachings" in Egyptian were the textbooks of the scribal schools and were used to teach reading and writing together with the habits of correct speech. The tenth century, which witnessed the rapid development of the Israelite state under David and Solomon, owed much to the introduction of scribal schools patterned on those of Egypt and they adapted Egyptian "writings" into the Hebrew language. Nevertheless, in spite of these known developments and the fact that the Egyptians were from time immemorial in contact with Semites who have left written records almost as old as Egyptian ones, it is noteowrthy that the "Egyptian language made only a relatively slight impact on the languages of the ancient world" (Cerny, 1971: 197). This may be due to the "impermanency" of Egyptian contacts. For instance, from the Greek standpoint Egypt was "used" rather than Hellenized (Preaux, 1971: 322). The Egyptians used rather than incorporated the Jews. The lack of Egyptian linguistic influence to the west and south is not remarkable, for the languages of those areas left no written records, and were superseded by the languages of invaders or immigrants (Cerny, 1971: 197).

Another reason for this slight impact of the Egyptian language is the Greek reluctance to admit Egyptians to the privileges of citizenship. This served to keep the Egyptian element in the population separate. Even in the time of Caracalla, those who infiltrated into Alexandria could still be distinguished easily by their "rustic" language. Yet under Greek rule Egypt became the most important mixing place of East and West, for the Ptolemaic Empire at its high point included not only Egypt but Cyrenaica as well as parts of Ethiopia, Arabia, Phoenicia, and Cyprus. Although it drew elements of its population from all these countries, the bulk of the people were Egyptians while the top strata of society consisted of Greeks and Macedonians. It is no wonder, therefore, that the large cities, Alexandria for instance, were polyglot. Greek dialects predominated there, though in the native quarters Egyptian was the language of the inhabitants. In the Jewish wards, Hebrew and Aramaic were the prevailing languages. Other Semitic languages and even some Indic dialects could be heard as well (Rostovtseff, 1941: 418). These facts were reflected in the linguistic aspects of the school curriculum of the middle- and upper-class children of all ethnic groups.

(d) *Greek.* (i) *East Mediterranean*—The Greeks who represent another of the main waves of the linguistic influence with which we are concerned were themselves the products of prior linguistic contacts and mergers, which began as far back as the second half of the twelfth century B.C. with the arrival of the "new people" in what had been the Mycenean area. These series of intrusions resulted in the merging of populations and in the close contact of their languages and dialects (Nesborough, 1964: 259-60). Meanwhile, the northwest corner of Asia Minor was the scene of similar incursions from Thrace. During the beginning of the first millenium, that area became the home of the Phrygians and related populations, who maintained close linguistic contacts with the native peoples. A second wave of Thracians followed and settled in the land to which they gave their name, Bythynia (Magie, 1950: 303). There is ample evidence of the contact established between the various linguistic groups of Mesopotamia and the Aegean area, arising partly out of the existence of mediating groups of Greeks who established themselves on the Bosphorous and the shores of Euxine Sea, as well as of Ionians who colonized areas of the Propontes. The Near East became an area of special colonizing interest. At Mina, at the south of the Orontes, existed the most important Greek settlement, led possibly by the Euboeans bringing with them slaves and setting up regular trade.

The Greek colonizers must have been a minority, and because of this they had to learn the local language. These mediating expatriates involved in normal trade and commerce helped to spread the results of linguistic contacts over the whole of Asia Minor. As the language grew in importance with the rise of Greek political influence, it was confirmed as the bond between the different linguistic groups of the Eastern Mediterranean and Asia Minor, and consequently as the one common factor in very many different bilingual situations. It would be unwise to exaggerate the currency of the Greek language. For instance the discovery of a substantial funerary inscription in Greek and Georgian near Tbilisi dating to the second century A.D. does not permit us to extend Greek linguistic influence so far. Nor does the use of Greek in official documents in Inner Asia (for instance in Mylasa) argue that the language was firmly established in that area. However there are cases enough of the use of the conquering Greek tongue in places where there can have been no Greeks or very few to speak it (Tarn, 1950: 226).

Of all these languages and cultures it is about the Phrygians, the heirs of the Hittites, that we know most. They seem to have exerted the main influence in Anatolia in the eighth century. But really close contacts between them and the Greeks do not appear before the seventh century, by which time the Phrygians were able to adapt to their own language the recently developed Greek alphabet. By the sixth century the Phrygians, defeated by the onslaughts of the Cimmerians, handed on their political and cultural supremacy in that area to the Lydians, whose capital, Sardis, lying very much closer to native Greek cities, became an important focal point of linguistic contact (Cook, 1961: 27). The Lydians during their period of ascendancy employed many Greek mercenaries, against Egypt for instance, and thus helped to spread language contacts. Like the Phrygians, the Lydians also adopted the Greek alphabet.

At about this time, too, the Aeolian Greeks arrived among the Thracian population of Samothrace, and the Carians were also brought into close contact with them. In Greek tradition the latter were regarded as natives of the Aegean, though they themselves claimed to have arrived from Asia Minor. It is now thought that their language belonged to the Luvian group. There are many references to their contact with and displacement by the Greeks, together with evidence of intermarriage between Greeks and Carians. This is not surprising in view of what Xenophon called the "mixo-barbarous" character of the small towns along the coast (Cook, 1961: 22-23). The most important of these communities which welcomed Greek cultivators and industry was at Halicarnasus, reputed to be the scene of the first regular meeting place of Greeks and Carians, and where, from the beginning, Greek as well as Carian was spoken. The Carian population of the settlement, witnessed by the proportion of personal names recorded by Herodotus, was as numerous as the Greek. This was an example of a thoroughly bilingual community, one which had absorbed a considerable native element without diminution of its Hellenism. Furthermore, because of the traffic between Greek and Carian settlements and cities, it is not surprising that some Carians were residents of Greece itself, as the Carian-Greek bilingual inscriptions on an Athenian statue suggest (Boardman, 1964: 101). Even before the fourth century the West Carians had taken to the Greek way of life and its language. By the end of the fourth century most Carians had followed their example. Consequently the Greek language dominated the pattern of contacts (Cook, 1961: 22-23), partly because the Greeks themselves, like the English in the nineteenth century as well as present-day Russians in Central Asia and elsewhere in the U. S. S. R., were reluctant to learn local languages. They might not insist on others learning Greek, but they had a high regard for their native tongue. The monoglot Greek possessed the superior culture, and the fact that he did not seek to understand the language of Phrygians or Syrians or Carians made for unilateral bilingualism on the part of the latter. Their urban proletariat had good opportunities to acquire a smattering of Greek, and though the class was small, their Hellenization was remarkably thorough. Greek rapidly became the universal language of polite society, and most Hellenized orientals were bilingual insofar as they could talk to their humbler compatriots in the local languages (Jones, 1939: 32).

(ii) *West Mediterranean*—Almost simultaneously, with the consolidation of their relations with the peoples of the East Mediterranean seaboard and its hinterland, the Greeks penetrated to the West Mediterranean. The Greek colonization of Southern Italy, Sicily, and the coasts of Gaul and Spain constitute the third and perhaps the most important of the unifying influences in the Mediterranean. It began in the Tyrrhenian, as it did in the Aegean and Black Seas, during the eighth century, and under the same economic and social causes which compelled populations to seek their fortune abroad (Glotz and Cohen, 1955: vol. 2). The colonists belonged to several dialect groups, Chalcidians, and Eritreans of Euboea for instance, and they established their first colonies at Cumae and Naxos, their aim being not so much the acquisition of territory as the development of a market, and the safeguarding of their trade routes. From there they dominated the Hellenization of the Etrurian coasts. There is evidence, according to Pliny, of Greeks living in Etruria, marrying Etruscans and becoming prosperous merchants there. After the sixth century (and the Ionian trouble), many Greeks emigrated and settled in Etruria, while Etruscans in their turn came to work among the Greeks at Cumae (Boardman, 1964: 102).

The Etruscans, little though we know of their origins, contributed a novel and undoubtedly extraneous element to the pattern of contact in Italy. On the one hand there was admittedly some emigration from the east, which produced a dynamic minority to work on the indigenous culture. On the other hand, whether it was trade or colonization, the Western Mediterranean from the Mycenean onward was constantly furrowed by ships coming from many directions. By 700 B.C. they were established in Central Italy, their centers of civilization being the towns. Etruscanization of Northern Italy coincided with the progressive acquisition of Etruscan consciousness—"a sense of political, cultural and linguistic affiliation with the Etruscan world" (Heurgon, 1973: 41-45). Their sea power limited Greek colonization to Southern Italy until about 600 when the Phocaeans opened up their lines of communication, only to be parried by a combination of Phoenician with Etruscan forces. Etruscan is not an Indo-European language, though some have thought it might be so derived by way of Hittite. It borrowed from Greek and from Italic dialects, but its own contribution as a non-Indo-European language may have been far more considerable. It was the Etruscans who taught the Romans to read and write by introducing them to the alphabet. Etruscan influence beginning at the end of the seventh century expanded throughout the Provence, Languedoc, and Catalonia. It was broken off about 580 with the foundation of the Greek city of Massilia in 600 B.C.

The Euboeans who settled on both shores of the Sicilian straits and in eastern Sicily were followed by other Greeks—Dorian, Megarians, Corinthians, Achaeans, Lacedaemonians, Rhodians, Cretans, and Ionians—so that Sicily was colonized by a variety of Greeks and to a very considerable extent. As in South Italy, some of the native population worked and lived in Greek cities, and Greeks may have lived in native villages—Tore Galli for instance. The Hellenic influence was not limited to the coastline. Morgantina in the center of the island was a Hellenized city. The two populations intermarried, for they got on together well enough in spite of the basic master-slave relationship. The Sicels took to writing their own language in the Greek alphabet: they used Greek names and ultimately shifted their linguistic attachment from Sicel to Greek after a considerable period of bilingualism. The inscriptions to Motye, a half-Greek town in the fifth century, were probably cut for half-Greek inhabitants (Woodhead, 1962: 22). Consequently, bilingualism is claimed as being responsible for the replacement of Latin /d and g/ by /t and k/ in the Messina region of northeast Sicily and in South Apulea (Jungeman, 1959: 475). The linguistic complexity arising from Greek colonization was not limited to the interaction of Greek and the native languages. Sometimes a city together with some of the surrounding area might be colonized by more than one Greek dialect group—Chalcidians and Miscenians in Rhegium, Achaeans and Troezenians in Sybaris, Rhodians and Cretans in more than one city. Himera spoke a mixed language halfway between Dorian and that of the Chalcidians. In Sicily this mingling gave rise to a Doric koiné in which Rhodian elements predominated. On mainland Italy the original dialects maintained themselves more distinctly (Heurgon, 1973: 85).

Hellenization came about gradually by contact and by import trade. Instead of taking over an area inhabited by natives the Greeks let them live as neighbors, leading a life that was altered only by commerce with the colonists (Adamesteanu, 1957: 20-46, 147-80). Nevertheless there are differences between Greek colonization and its linguistic consequences in Southern Italy and Southern France, at Massilia for instance. There the impact of the Greek language was less permanent than in either Southern Italy or Sicily, though it provided a center from which Greek influences radiated widely into Western Europe. Phocaeans colonized

Massilia around 600 B.C. under pressure of their own small and poor land, together with the threat of the Persians under Cyrus. Their foundation of Marseilles was only one point in an ambitious program which many think may have begun in the south of Spain, moving to the coast of Provence because of the antagonism of the Phoenicians already established there and controlled as well as reinforced from Carthage. The establishment of Marseilles not only exemplified the comparative impermanency of Greek influence in that part of the world but was the cause of continuing struggles between the Ligurians and later the Gauls. In spite of these struggles it was from contact with Massilian Greeks that the Gauls learned "a more civilized way of life and abandoned their barbarity. . . . Their progress was so brilliant that it seemed that Gaul had become part of Greece rather than that the Greeks had colonized Gaul" (Dunbabin, 1948: 187). It is well known that the Gauls were called "trilingues" speaking Greek, Latin, and Celtic. The example of Massilia encouraged the establishment of colonies like Nice, Nomaco, and Antibes, which still retain their Greek names. Consequent on the social intercourse of Greeks and Gauls, Provence came to inherit Greek linguistic influences, and the same applies to Southern Italy. It has been argued that Greek enclaves in the west did not survive the third century (Jones, 1964: 986). Yet observers in the sixteenth century A.D. claimed there were 22 Greek-speaking localities there, and as late as the nineteenth century there were still 12 such localities. There were, even more recently, Calabrian and Apulian villages which remained partly Greek in speech. These very late survivals were small and very scattered. Nevertheless, the existence of considerable Greek bilingualism, especially in Southern Italy, and of a Greek substratum is not to be doubted.

(iii) *Hellenic language policy*—Gradually as the various Greek dialects leveled themselves in the direction of a uniform koiné, the influence of the language deepened and spread; and with the imperial advance of the Hellenes it penetrated far into the east and Egypt, where there was a considerable Greek social and linguistic element from early times, witness the story of the Samian merchant who about 638 B.C. made regular runs to Egypt. Herodotus records the use of Greek mercenaries by Egyptian kings. After such early beginnings, Herodotus claims, the Greeks settled down to close relations with the Egyptians. By about 575, Naucrates, at the mouth of the Nile had accumulated a considerable polyglot population, including all sorts of Greeks—merchants, artists, poets, and a variety of professional people and skilled workers. Such settlements, however large, were isolated and it was not until the arrival of the Macedonian kings in Egypt that the use of Greek became widespread. The dissemination of the Greek language is recorded in thousands of administrative documents drafted by village officials and thousands of private letters written by persons of quite humble station. This is because the elaborate bureaucratic regime established by the Ptolemies required scores of minor officials with at least an adequate knowledge of Greek. It became worthwhile for the better class of peasant to learn enough Greek to justify a government post. Furthermore, apart from the inducements which fraternization with the Greeks held out to the fairly well-to-do Egyptians, almost everybody's affairs, at some time or another, were matters of concern to the government and involved some discussions in Greek. Consequently there must have been a fairly large number of Egyptians and Greeks who were bilingual, particularly for the purposes of administration. Many of the rural clergy, too, were bilingual (Rostovtseff, 1941: 882). The upper classes received a good education in Latin as well as in Greek and Egyptian. In the courts the judges and advocates, though local men, insisted on evidence being given in Greek. It is not unlikely that Greek was the normal language of town life for many people (Jones, 1937: 995).

The nature of Greek influence in Egypt, as elsewhere, was determined partly by the attitude of the Greeks to their native language. They were liberal in their acceptance of other languages, especially in religious affairs. It was certainly this attitude which enabled the Jewish temples to perform their own services in Aramaic. But however they might react to the speaking of local languages by others their purpose was to maintain the Greek language and to secure a Greek upbringing for the younger generation. In the larger villages and the capitals of the provinces the Greeks established their own enclaves. The Greeks in their long history scarcely tried to Hellenize anyone; the notion was generally foreign to them partly because it was unnecessary. If Greek colonization produced a certain amount of Hellenization, that was the result of a natural symbiotic process: natives became Hellenized and Greeks orientalized. On the other hand, Greeks were intent on preserving their own language and avoiding complete assimilation. Consequently the new members of the Egyptian ruling class saw the advantage of acquiring the Greek language and conforming to some degree with a way of life which gave significance to the acquisition of the Greek language (Rostovtseff, 1941: 502).

An important item in the budget of any community was the cost of the gymnasium and of public education (Jones, 1960: 220). Many inscriptions show that the cities of the Greek east were extremely eager to secure for the youth of the cities an education on Greek lines, which though good was expensive. Huge sums of money were required to pay the teachers and to provide and keep in good repair the schools and athletic grounds. Nevertheless, wherever any significant number of Greeks congregated they made the gymnasium the focal point of their civic existence, and there are recorded petitions that they should be allowed to establish schools. Even the Greeks who lived in rural Egypt and who apparently had no state-recognized self-government had their own educational institution. Other communities under Greek rule aspired to obtain the same facilities. The progressive party in Jerusalem petitioned Antiochus IV to be allowed to establish a gymnasium at the same time as they requested that they should be incorporated as a city (Rostovtseff, 1941: 147). The Attalid kings provided Pergamum with three gymnasia, and cities like Salamis in Cyprus and Miletus had the same distinction (Jones, 1960: 220). To have pursued a course of instruction in a "palaestra" or to frequent a gymnasium was the distinguishing mark of an educated man. In Egypt those who had profited from the experience inevitably became bilingual and in consequence entered a special class of the population which enjoyed privileges and rights of a high order. The youths of Alexandria who had been educated in this way were considered by the Emperor Claudius to be qualified for Alexandrian citizenship.

Such educated men lost interest in their local culture, and though their native language remained for them a necessary means of communication with the majority of their own people, they gradually shifted their attachment in favor of Greek, at least so far as the more sophisticated aspects of life were concerned. Within their own class they normally spoke Greek and were able to read and write that language only. Some texts have survived which refer to schoolmasters and their pupils, and they bear witness to the popularity of the Greek schools among the Hellenized natives, as well as to the efforts that were made to teach children the Greek language in order to qualify them for the gymnasium. On the other hand, many Greeks became acclimatized to Egypt and, taking an active interest in Egyptian affairs, learned the language also. The bilingualism of Egypt ran both ways, though there was, naturally, a much stronger flow in the direction of Greek (Jones, 1960: 220).

Large numbers of Greek settlements were established throughout the oriental parts of Alexander's empire. Some of these, like the seaports of Gaza and Tyre, became centers for trading and industrial interests. Such settlements were found throughout Iran, Bactria, and the Punjab; and it has been emphasized that the size of the Greek-speaking elements of these populations, which kept in touch with the rest of the Greek-speaking world and were constantly reinforced by Greek-speaking groups, ought not to be underestimated. Initially the native and Greek-speaking populations might be segregated. The fact that at Thyateria the "Macedonians" are described as "around" the city, while those at Cobydele are noted as being "from" the communities, suggests that though the language groups were at first segregated they were later in much closer contact (Magie, 1950: 972).

Although an exception was made in the case of Judea, the underlying principle of the policy of Antiochus (Ephiphanus) IV was not to Hellenize the oriental towns by force but to legalize a process of amalgamation between orientals and Greeks. But by spreading over their dominions a network of Greek settlements whose inhabitants belonged to the same nationality and spoke the same language as themselves the Seleucids inevitably made Greek the *de facto* official language of the empire. Greek became the lingua franca. Trade with the west and north was conducted on the acceptance and official recognition of Greek documents: transactions in which one party was Greek and the other native were regulated by Greek law and recorded in Greek legal documents. Perhaps more important than commercial and administrative uniformity was uniformity in the mode of life. Boys were educated in Greek schools. There were Greek private elementary schools in all Greek settlements, and the gymnasia were as fundamental an institution in the eastern monarchies as they were in Greece and Asia Minor (Rostovtseff, 1941: 521, 1047).

Consequently the Greek settlements never lost their original character, and even in the farthest outposts of Hellenism, in the Parthian kingdom, they kept their Greek tongue. Alexander arranged that 30,000 youths in Bactria should go to school to learn Greek. It is a fair assumption that many of the native population as well as many of the Greeks in India were bilingual in Greek and Prakrit; and Greek was alive there in the reign of Kajula Kadphises in the first quarter of the first century A.D. An Indian who was a citizen in a Greek polis was bound to be Hellenized to some extent: he would have to learn enough Greek for the purposes of daily life and understand something of Greek civic forms, and the educated had been taught to read some Greek literature. Conversely the Greeks knew some Indian languages. But the effects were not long lasting, nor did they penetrate the system of Greek education in India (Tarn, 1938: 375, 387). The sphere of Greek linguistic influence embraced Babylonia too: Herodicas' epigram to the effect that Hellas and Babylon were equally his homelands is well known. A Babylonian would add a Greek name to his own. He learned Greek and wrote the Babylonian language in the Greek alphabet. Some wrote their books in Greek because of the prospect of a better distribution throughout the whole of the eastern territories (Tarn, 1938: 56). The Greek city of Sileucia had a large Babylonian population outside its walls with which it was in close communication. In Syria, Greek and Aramaic were closely intertwined, both languages being familiar to the more or less educated and denationalized inhabitants of that region.

(e) *Preservation of Local Languages.* So far we have described the spread of Greek and other languages of unification, but bilingualism, if it is to be more than a temporary and superficial phenomenon, involves the continued long-term existence of the local languages. Partly because of the permissive linguistic policy the Greeks pursued, partly because of the class structure of the society which made linguistic stratification possible, and partly because of the simple facts of geography and the comparative inaccessibility of the majority of the people to an intrusive language, this was the case in the Mediterranean area. Western Asia Minor was a land of great natural contrasts with fertile river basins and highways terminating in busy ports where the Greek was at home with his commerce and industry, his complicated political machinery involving the Hellenized and urbanized natives. On the other hand, there were almost inaccessible mountain groups, into which neither trade nor the Greek language penetrated deeply. For a long time the Greek population of pioneer settlements, Smyrna even, was quite small. Not more than a thousand free Greeks lived in the city, matched by an equal number outside. Miletus may have had a somewhat larger Greek element. This fact ensured the demographic, if not the functional supremacy of the local language. Greek influenced the masses because of its prestige, but the number of those who spoke Greek was small to begin with. Then again, the physical contour of the land, while it allowed for the Greek settlement of the fertile river basins in western Asia Minor, preserved the comparative inviolability of the local languages in the mountainous interior. Though the Greeks built cities in which the indigenous were offered a Greek education, these were along the coast, and Greeks did not proceed into the interior for a long time. Lycia's population of highland folk remained isolated in spite of their contacts with the ring of

Hellenized countries along the coast (Magie, 1950: 144, et seq.). If, as was certainly the case, native languages survived well into the Byzantine age in some localities and among certain social strata, it is plain that Greek never completely dominated them.

Greek-based bilingualism was a matter of the cities and towns, therefore, and these were truly and remarkably bilingual. For instance, according to Strabo, in Cibyratis four languages were in use—Greek; the language of the original Cabalians; Lydian, introduced by the first colonizers of Cibyra; and Pisidean, spoken by invading tribes from the east. Pontus had such a heterogeneous population that it is not surprising to read that 22 languages were spoken within its walls. In Rhodes, freedmen and foreigners, including natives of Asia Minor, Syria, Phoenicia, and Egypt, as well as a slave population drawn from a large number of language groups—Lydian, Phrygian, Cappadocian, Galatian, and Armenian—formed the bulk of the population. But of all the polyglot communities, perhaps Dioscurus, in Colchis at the eastern end of the Black Sea, was the most remarkable. According to Pliny "it was once so famous that as many as 300 different languages were spoken in the settlement." Subsequently business was carried on there by the Romans with the help of a staff of 130 interpreters.

As has been suggested already, the attitude of the Greeks to their own language and to the languages of the various localities was an important factor in producing long-term bilingualism. They were intent on remaining Greek, but they were not interested in displacing the languages of the areas into which they penetrated. Some of the languages, Lydian for instance, were superseded, but not as a result of any deliberate policy. Carian seems to have become obsolete before the beginning of the Christian era, but here too, there was no noticeable attempt at extermination or suppression. Other languages, such as those of Pamphylia, became unrecognizable because of Greek influence which was fortuitous and unplanned. The Lycians preserved their distinctive national culture, language, and script down to the fourth century B.C. In the third century, Lycian inscriptions disappear, though the people did not lose their national pride when they succumbed to superior Hellenistic forces (Jones, 1937: 97, 289). The Thracians, on the evidence of John Chrysostom, retained their language until the first century of our era (Chrysostom: 501). Although by the second century the Hellenization of the Galatian upper classes appears to have been widespread and Celtic names are not found thereafter, the peasantry continued to speak their ancient language, and Jerome recalls that the Celtic Galatians still spoke their language in his day. It probably survived until the end of the fifth century A.D. Cappadocia remained on the whole a very backward country by Greek standards, and the Greek language made very slow headway there. Philostratus in the third century notes the influence of the mother tongue of the Cappadocians on their second language, Greek. They spoke it with a thick utterance, confusing the consonants, shortening the long vowels and lengthening the short ones.

Phrygian, like Galatian, was spoken in the time of St. Paul and persisted to the end of the fifth century A.D. Its preservation, until that time, shows that a native tongue may continue to be spoken for some purposes after the major responsibilities for communication have devolved on an intruding language. The city of Iconium was considered Phrygian, even when Greek had taken over the transaction of public business, and many of the Iconians were bilingual since they retained a command of Phrygian (James, 1920: 69). As Greek education spread among the towns and villages of eastern Phrygia, radiating from the centers of Seleucid and Roman government, and reinforced by the extension of Christianity, Greek killed off the use of Phrygian eventually, but the two languages coexisted for a long time. There is evidence of this in the Neo-Phrygian texts which have survived. There were many Greek borrowings—many more than has generally been supposed, and Greek influenced Phrygian syntax as well (Calder, 1911: 164).

The same Greek influences were brought to Egypt and Syria. There the survival and use of the vernaculars together with Greek are attested by the fact that in those countries the national churches adopted Coptic and Syriac as the literary and liturgical languages, the government-supported Orthodox church language being Greek (Jones, 1960a: 293). East of the Euphrates, in Osrhoene and Mesopotamia, Syrian survived not only as a spoken but as a written language as well, with a corpus of original literature. It was taught in the schools of grammar and rhetoric of Mesopotamia with Latin and Greek, and it was possible for even an educated man not to be inconvenienced if he know no Greek provided he spoke Syriac and Latin. Mesopotamia was socially orientalized, and Syriac early established its supremacy there, though in political sentiment the population remained Greek. Harmonius laid the foundations of a vernacular literature in the third century with his Syriac hymns. Greek education declined with the emergence of Syriac as a literary language (Jones, 1937: 223). Syriac was, therefore, more successful than Egyptian, which did not maintain a continuous literary tradition and could not contribute to the education of the young. The demotic script was less and less used in Egypt and died out before the end of the third century with the result that Egyptian became the illiterate peasants' patois. Even when Coptic appeared after a long period of contact with Greek and adopted a modified Greek alphabet, Egyptian remained the language of the less-educated lower classes. No educated Egyptian chose to write in Coptic if he could help it, and Coptic literature was limited to translations and lives of the saints (Jones, 1960b: 992).

Greek became a unifying language from Travancore to the hinterland of Marseilles, but it did so in partnership with a large number of languages which had a remarkable gift for self-preservation. Though where bilingualism did exist the degree of oral competence was adequate for all practical purposes, the amount or the spread of Greek literacy among the various classes of society should not be exaggerated (Tarn, 1950: 226). In some areas, indeed, the Greek language made very little headway: in Iran and Babylonia the Seleucids elicited only a limited response from the natives and little Greek influence has been found in Babylonian documents of the period (Tarn, 1938: 55). It has also to be recognized that few of the vernaculars provided for literacy, though Syriac, as we have noted, survived as a written language. It was used for translating Greek theological works, as well as for original writing, mainly religious. In the Latin zone of the empire, the only rival to Latin in ensuring any degree of literacy was Gothic, together with Hebrew among the Jews. But though the local languages could not compare with the languages of unification, the bilingualism of these centuries and in these areas, especially among the upper classes, cannot be underestimated. It is because of the inclusion of Greek in a number of bilingual partnerships that the Septuagint appeared in Greek, that Greek as well as Hebrew and Latin appeared at the Crucifixion, and that St. Paul could communicate freely in the different lands through which he traveled. He could address a Roman governer in Paphos because the one had learned Greek with Aramaic and the other Greek with Latin. He could stand before the Areopagus at Athens and address that distinguished body in its own language because it was, as it was for many of his countrymen, a well-cultivated second language. In fact, though large numbers of various populations became bilingual to some degree or other, the contribution which language contact has made to a unified civilization, to a shared sensibility and a set of common assumptions and practices in education, derives from the existence of literate bilinguals, the elites who learned the dominant language in addition to their native tongue, whether for theocratic or administrative purposes, or simply because they belonged to a certain class.

2. Bilingualism in Western Europe

(a) *Celtic and Other Languages.* (i) *Italy*—Whitney suspected "the prevalence of a peculiar and strongly marked linguistic disease known as Celtomania which is apt to attack students of the subject, especially those of Celtic extraction . . . leading them to exaggerate . . . the importance of the Celtic civilization, language and literature." This is a point of view, which at the time when Whitney wrote, may have been received sympathetically. However, later linguistic and archeological research justifies a less cynical note. Indeed it has been claimed recently that Celtic contacts with Germanic and North Italian dialects introduced "barbarian Europe into the advanced Mediterranean cultures and civilizations of the maturing ancient world" and that the "significance of the Celts in European civilization has no parallel in the early history of Europe" (Filip, 1960: 191).

How the pre-Roman and Greek languages and dialects of Italy with which Celtic was in contact came to be there, whether as the result of three separate waves of migration moving from east to west as some have suggested, or as the result of slow, uninterrupted and almost unperceived infiltration, it may be impossible to decide. What we know is that up to the time when Latin became the official language in peninsular Italy the many ethnic groups possessed different languages. Some of these were Indo-European—Latin, Faliscan, Venetian, Umbrian, and Oscan for instance. Others were non-Indo-European, like Ligurian (though strongly influenced by Celtic), Messapic, Iapygian, and Etruscan. "For at least 40 centuries the Peninsula witnessed the constant arrival and intermingling of currents of immigration, a successive and gradual displacement of groups infiltrating where the land was sparsely populated, establishing themselves near the local inhabitants and being assimilated wholly or partly: sometimes taking to the local culture, and sometimes exerting a great influence of their own so that not only in culture and religion but in language we witness a long and complex evolution." Right up to the fifth century there was a continuous arrival of elements that were new demographically and culturally (Francisci, 1959: 129). What is equally certain is that the speakers of the languages maintained long periods of contact and coexistence with each other. The result is that we have layers of languages across Italy and various indications of bilingualism (Pulgram, 1959: 345). The Celts had established very intimate contact with several Italic languages, and this cannot have occurred much later than the fifth century B.C. Those who came down into Italy came from the banks of the Rhine or at all events from Central Europe. Because of the same pressures other Celtic hordes surged toward the Danube (Grenier, 1943: 212), plundered Greece, and penetrated Asia Minor where they established themselves in Galatia. Various Celtic groups mingled with the Ibero-Tartessian, non-Indo-European indigenous groups in Spain, and so helped to form the Celtiberi (Bosch-Gimpera, 1961: 245). The Celts occupied almost the whole of Central Europe and affected the eastern parts of France as well as Northern Italy.

They were in extensive contact with Scythians, Thracio-Dacians, and Illyrians. That the Celts migrated in large bands is unquestionable since a few stragglers could not have had even the short-term immediate influence they undoubtedly did exert. "Had they behaved not like the Etruscans before them but rather like the Romans, their successors, they might . . . have become masters of Italy and altered the history of the entire world," including its linguistic heritage (Pulgram, 1959: 204). Even so they did have an enduring influence. Long before the end of the fourth century the Ligurians had been overrun, and Ligurian came to be spoken by a people whom it is difficult to distinguish from Celtic-speaking tribes. In other words an area was recognized in ancient times in which the two linguistic groups, an early Ligurian and an invading Celtic one, were indissolubly intertwined (Whatmough, 1933: 65).

The Augustan period was the principal time of Celto-Ligurian and Latin contact. Towns like Augusta Praetoria were founded by garrisoned soldiers, and the speakers of the native languages had their quarters there. Many of the inscriptions which witness to the Ligurian language came from town centers, so that it would be safe to assume that Ligurian speakers took an active part in city life. The evidence of Latin in these inscriptions increases as the people became bilingual. At first they were written in Celtic script and from right to left. As the contact of the two languages became more intimate, there is an approximation to Latin forms and styles (Chilver, 1941: 70). There are a number of Celtic borrowings in Latin, and Celtic names in the inscriptions of Cisalpine Gaul are frequent (Palmer, 1954: 13-15). However, the importance of this Celtic contact is restricted to its influence on Ligurian and other northern dialects, showing itself perhaps as a substratum influence on some modern "Gallo-Italian dialects" (Pulgram, 1959: 204).

Along the valley of the Adige in northeast Italy, another Celtic language, Raetic, was spoken, its speakers having intermingled with those of Venetic and Illyrian, a language which survived both Celtic and Latin contact to form the base of Albanian. Raetic shows the results of considerable contact with Etruscan, the consequence of an Etruscan overlordship. The bilingual inscription of Voltino on the western shore of Lake Garda is an indication of Raetic contact with Latin also. The contact of Latin with another Alpine language is revealed by the bilingual inscription found at Todo (Tuder), which reveals the existence of Lepontic in Apulia (Whatmough, 1933: 175). This was where, as Horace illustrates (*Satires*, 1.10.30), the contact of Latin, Greek, and another Italian language, Oscan, was made. The latter derived from the conjunction of Umbrian and Sabittic, a dialect spoken by the Samnites after their conquest of Campania (Pallatino, 1955: 25-26).

By the end of the Second Punic War, the Romans had overrun the Celtic-speaking areas of Northern Italy and founded Placentia and Cremona. What remained of the Celtic dialects of the Alpine area was overlaid by the Latin speech of the conqueror. By the end of the second century the Romans had taken control of the whole of Italy and had established their linguistic hegemony. Though practical measures were never adopted with the view to Latinizing others, Roman soldiers, Roman officials, and teachers carried the language of public administration throughout Italy so that their language found access into homes and market places where, nevertheless, the local languages continued to be spoken. Large sections of the population who were conquered by the Romans passed through longer or shorter periods of bilingualism according to the local language they spoke. They adopted Latin as a second or third language at different times.

The ultimate shift to Latin lasted about 500 years, and it is interesting to note that for centuries after the ethnic and political assimilation of the conquered people bilingualism between speakers of Celto-Italic dialects, and between Latin and other Italic dialects, was still strong. At a later point this bilingualism expanded to include Latin with Greek, as in the case of Tarent after the Roman conquest in 272 (Honnyer, 1957: 415-20). This widespread Latin-related bilingualism led to several linguistic consequences—the adoption of a foreign alphabet for instance, considerable place name changes and much lexical borrowing, accompanied by radical phonetic changes to accommodate these new lexical items. Furthermore, as Plautus and Lucilius witness, grammatical interference of several languages with each other occurred quite frequently. A bundle of isoglosses running east and west from Lucia to Ancona separates the Gallic-Italic dialects of Emilia, Lombardy, Liguria, and Piedmont from Tuscan in the South. North of a line from Rimini to La Spezia is an area which shows the influence of Latin and Venetic phonology (Pulgram, 1959: 162).

(ii) *Spain*—In our ignorance of the demography of pre-Roman Spain we are unable to map the distribution of the indigenous languages or even to distinguish many of them with any confidence. It was not a question of the indigenous ethnic groups living as separate entities. The Celts intermixed with many such groups to produce a mixed race of Celts and Iberians who possessed in the fifth and fourth centuries a living unity of culture and language, fertilized by Greeks and Phoenicians. The influence of Celtic on the language of Spain was reinforced later from association with Gaul. Contemporary Greek and Roman writers in Spain distinguished the languages of the Tartessians in the south and southeast, Iberian in the east, Celtic in the extreme northwest, and in the center Celtic and Iberian in mixed and bilingual communities. We are confronted with a multilingual pre-Roman Spain in which the Celtic language as an element in Ibero-Celtic played a significant role and did so until contact was established with Latin. Celtic had probably ceased to play an independent role by the time the Romans arrived, having been absorbed socially and linguistically by the earlier inhabitants (Malbert, 1961: 72). By the end of Augustus' reign (14 A.D.) Latin was fairly well established, and it was spoken throughout the peninsula except by the Basques. When the Empire came to an end (476 A.D.) Spain was as Latin as Italy, and surviving linguistic evidence of the existence of Celtic is even more tenuous than it is in Italy. It has been claimed that only one word of proven Celtic origin is peculiar to the peninsula (Etnwistle, 1936: 39-40).

(iii) *Britain*—It is to Britain and mainly to the fate of Welsh that we must look if we are to find contemporary evidence of strong Celtic influences and a long surviving Celtic tradition in spite of contact with other dominant languages. Bosch-Gimpera speaks of a Celtic invasion of the whole of the western province of the Hallstatt civilization amounting to a military occupation. Though the establishing of the Gallic peoples in Gaul spread over more than a thousand years, it was the fifth century which marked the decisive turn in the peopling and the linguistic development of France. Then occurred a new influx of settlers who, like those who crossed to Britain about the same time, were undoubtedly Celts. While the greatest proportion of the speakers of Celtic dialects remained on the continent (Gauls), two waves descended on Britain, the first in the sixth century B.C., speaking a variant of Brythonic from which Welsh, Cornish and Breton derive; followed a considerable time later by Goedelic-speaking Celts, from whom are derived Irish, Scots Gaelic, and Manx.

Of the languages spoken in Britain before they arrived we know as little as we know of the pre-Roman languages of Spain, but Celticists would have no objection to admitting that "the more securely the Celtic invasions are anchored within the half millenium between 600 and 100 B.C. the more incumbent it becomes upon them to admit the existence of some prior language, let it be non-Indo-European or an earlier form of Indo-European than that which we recognize as Celtic" (Adams, 1940: 21). When the Romans arrived in Britain, therefore, Celtic and possibly some vestiges of a non-Celtic language in the far north were spoken throughout the islands. To the end of the Roman occupation Celtic continued to be spoken by the vast majority of the population either as their sole language or in conjunction with Latin. It has been argued that there is "ample evidence that Latin was spoken by all classes of the population, not only in the towns but also in the rural country houses and the farms" (Zachrisson,

1927: 25). Celtic was presumably the mother tongue of the Romano-Britons, and there is no clear evidence as to what proportion of the population was bilingual or mainly Latin-speaking. However there can be no doubt that speakers of Celtic were in close contact with the Latin language and considerable bilingualism resulted.

The Latin language must have been used in government and in the administration of the law. The native upper classes, who came to play an increasingly important part in local government and official life, were encouraged to learn Latin. Latin was the language of the army and its Celtic recruits. Those who ministered to its needs would need to know some Latin. The language of all large-scale trade and commerce would be Latin, though the local markets would probably be dominated by Celtic. In the lowland zone all education and writing would be in Latin. The cities and towns in the same zone were always very strong buttresses of Latin since they were the centers of administration and government. As time went on their influence spread in ever widening circles into the surrounding countryside. It has been shown that the great expansion of town life in the Flavian and later Antonine periods had considerable influence on the contact of the languages (Collingwood, 1937: 194-95). The language of the Church was Latin, and with the advent of Christianity it became to a large extent the quasi-official language of the country. Elsewhere in the agricultural lowland zone (apart from the villas) and the whole of the highland zone, where Latin was confined to the military encampments and garrison areas, there was very little Latin (Jackson, 1953: 97-105).

In Britain the system of education was very similar to that of Gaul and Spain. The sons of the nobility were gathered together and educated as Roman citizens, and eventually local initiative may have carried on what was started officially. The process is well known from Spain where it started early in the first century B.C., until by the end of the first century A.D. even small mining centers had elementary schools, and grammatici and rhetors were at work in most towns (Liversidge, 1968: 150). The children who passed through such schools were taught very conservatively by schoolmasters who insisted on strict speech habits, unlike the Vulgar Latin spoken by traders and lower-class townsfolk. The families of these children provided many of the *decurions* who would have to speak in the *ordo* on public occasions, and many of the children completed their studies with professors of rhetoric, many of whom were Gauls. Juvenal (*Satires* XV. 112) ridiculed the fact that "the whole world has its Greek and Roman. . . . Eloquent Gaul has trained the pleaders of Britain and distant Thule talks of having a rhetoricum."

With the collapse of the Roman occupation in the fifth century A.D. the Celts, whom we may now conveniently identify as Welsh, were overrun by Germanic invaders speaking dialects with phonological and morphological systems which differed considerably from Welsh. By the seventh century the "linguistic divide" between the Welsh and English had been established on a line which is virtually identical with the present day administrative boundary between England and Wales. The *whole* of Wales as well as parts of England, especially the southwest, remained Celtic in speech for the following five hundred years. Since the Welsh who had not already been pressed into Wales were not exterminated, as was once claimed to be the case, the Saxon occupation of all except the eastern areas of England was a gradual process, so that, though a change of language took place, one eminent Celticist claims that the Celtic element is dominant in the speech of the present-day population of England itself. Undoubtedly there was a long period of massive bilingualism, a fact which is evidenced by the considerable English influence on Welsh during this period (Jackson, 1953: 242).

Later, with the Norman conquest of Britain, the Welsh language was brought into contact with a new language, Norman French. The central Marches, the Vale of Glamorgan in the south, and nearly the whole of Monmouthshire in the southeast came under Norman control before the end of the twelfth century. The same is true of the lowlands of southwest Wales. In these areas the Welsh language came to be sustained mainly by the common people. In the western and northern highlands it remained the only language and was sustained by princely families. After consolidating their position the Normans were not prepared to attack these highlands, especially since their conquest offered them few advantages. Thus, at the beginning of the last century nearly six hundred years after the Norman Conquest, the "language divide" in South Wales still separated the Norman settlement areas (the Englishry) from the hilly north (the Welshry).

The Normans posed a lesser threat to the Welsh language than the Tudors, a dynasty of Welsh descent who came to the throne of England in the fifteenth century. For most of the time the Normans ruled through powerful but local families. The Tudors, faced with possible attack from abroad, pursued a very different, highly centralizing policy. They thought that a strong, united Britain was possible only by subordinating powerful, local families, creating a uniform, legal, administrative, and ecclesiastical system, and by permitting the use of only one language, namely English. The Act of Union provided that "no person or persons that use the Welsh speech or language shall have or enjoy any manner office or fees within this realm . . . unless he or they use and exercise the English speech or language." This meant the ambitious gentry's gradual alienation from the Welsh language, as well as the attenuation of the related culture. The use of Welsh was virtually proscribed in all prestigious contexts. Yet as one Welsh scholar complained, "if there be no learning, wisdom or piety in a language what better is it than the churn of wild fowls or the bleating of beasts" (Salesbury, 1547). Although the Welsh aristocracy transferred their preference to the English language, Welsh was still the native tongue of nearly all the common people of the principality. Even an English diocese, Hereford, was enjoined by Parliament to see that copies of the Welsh Bible and prayer book were available in the churches; and as late as 1660 there were complaints in the same diocese that the Welsh were not offered services in their own language.

With the Act of Union and the departure of the Welsh aristocracy for the Tudor court, the literary cultivation of Welsh and the tradition of education which had been prescribed by the Celtic bards went into a decline. The Renaissance and the Tudor dynasty exerted a different kind of influence from that of the bards and the gentry who had been their patrons. Many Welsh scholars were recusant Catholics who spent considerable periods in exile in France or Italy. They were well aware of the controversies which had exercised the minds of writers on the continent for many years concerning the use, the development, and "embellishment" of national languages and the "vulgar tongues." They argued the case for Welsh in much the same way as the case for Italian had been promoted by Dante and Petrarch a little earlier. The scholars saw the peril of Welsh losing its former status in the world of learning and scholarship and feared that English would be the sole medium for those purposes. "Do you suppose," asked one of the most prominent of these Welsh scholars, "that ye need no better words and no greater variety of expression to set out learning and to treat of philosophy and the arts than you have in common use in daily converse when you buy and sell and eat and drink . . . (Salesbury, 1547)?

But although Renaissance humanism and scholarship promoted the cause of a literary "embellished" Welsh, there was considerable native opposition to it. Of all nations one writer claimed "none is so indifferent or opposed to the preservation of its language as the Welsh. . . . Among the educated aristocracy and the learned leaders of the Church there is scarcely one in fifteen who is able to speak and write the language." This is not surprising, because education at all levels was available only in the English language. With the accession of the Tudors aristocratic parents sent their children to schools across the border. The less privileged used the new foundations in Wales itself which were almost invariably either near the border or in towns that were historical centers of Norman influence and were modeled on those in England. Not until the religious revival of the eighteenth century and the creation of Circulating Schools by religious organizations did the common people have an opportunity to learn to read and write their native tongue and so begin a new era of bilingual education.

(b) *Greek and Latin Bilingualism.* (i) *The Survival of Greek in Italy: Societal Bilingualism*—There were times when the Greeks appeared as serious competitors for the dominance of Italy, but between 272 B.C., when Greater Greece surrendered its power at Tarentum, and 148-146 B.C., when Macedonia and homeland Greece in turn were subjugated, their political power became moribund. It was this political power which had supported the spread of Greek and, in association with trade, maintained it overseas. Meanwhile the Romans began to exert their influence in the Mediterranean, and Latin penetrated the lands which they occupied. The Greek language continued to be spoken in certain parts of Italy, particularly in the South, for the Greeks made every effort to retain their tongue and never ceased to regard Latin as a barbarous language. Other nations learned Greek, and for that reason, among others, the Greeks never made any concessions to Latin. They despised it and learned it only when economic circumstances made it necessary for them to do so. The Romans for their part, in spite of Augustine's remark that "the victorious Romans imposed their own language upon the vanquished for the sake of peace," were completely under the spell of the Greek language. They made no effort to set up Latin in rivalry to it or to Latinize their political and military gains. This reluctance to undertake any degree of linguistic proselytization was due in part to a simple sense of their own superiority which induced them not to impose Latin and to consider its acquisition by foreigners a privilege to be sought, like citizenship. The inhabitants of Cumae for instance, had to request permission to use Latin in public affairs and in the pursuit of trade. For several reasons, therefore, Greek came to exert an increasing influence even in Rome itself. As early as the second century B.C. the city was permeated by Greeks, a large proportion of them slaves. The Greek-speaking Christians who formed a significant element in Rome carried the Greek language everywhere, and the highest ranking officers of the empire adopted Hellenistic models of culture and speech. For instance, Sempronius, father of the Gracchi, was able to deliver a Greek oration before a highly critical audience at Rhodes, and in 281 the Roman envoy addressed the people of Tarentum in their native Greek (Cicero, *Tusc.* IV. 4).

While this attitude was characteristic mainly of the aristocracy, it was not restricted to them, for the whole of Rome was drawn under the Greek spell. The language of serious life may have been Latin, but Greek was the language of pleasure, of frivolity and the lightest kinds of entertainment. The talk of the Scipionic circle, we are told, was full of Greek words. Words with a Latin root and a Greek termination, like *ferritribaces* "galled with iron," are found. Lucilius writes in Greek characters Greek words governed by Latin verbs, just as Ausonius does in the fourth century A.D.

It is significant in the history of bilingualism that Plautus expected his audience, which must have included a considerable popular element, to understand Greek phrases, as is the case in the "Bacchides." Juvenal declaims against women who irritate their husbands by talking Greek—"What can be more disgusting than to find that not a single woman considers herself attractive until she has been transferred from a Tuscan into a Greekling? . . . They talk nothing but Greek. . . . Greek is the language of their fears, their quarrels, their joys and anxieties. In Greek they pour out their souls."

It is not surprising, therefore, that in the Mediterranean areas Greek persisted as a parallel lingua franca with Latin for a considerable time, though as was to be expected, longer in the east than in the west. Latin was certainly regarded as the official language of administration, though in actual practice Greek was frequently used even in the courts of law. The Roman emperors after Diocletian endeavored to promote Latin as the language of imperial unity, and there is evidence that they attempted a strict enforcement of its use in official business and to promote its acquisition (Suetonius). But as time went on the numbers of Latin-speaking settlers in the east declined; the enclaves of Latin influence were submerged (Rostovtseff, 1959: 187). Though the Byzantines, for instance, were anxious to call themselves Romanoi, their education was bilingual and predominantly Greek. This was particularly true in the higher professions, such as law. In the fifth century the teaching of law was in Greek, but the students had in their hands copies of the Latin texts as well. The languages of the conquerors and vanquished continued to be yoked together in an uneasy partnership, and the empire in the east functioned to the very end as a bilingual or diglossic state.

(ii) *The teaching and use of Greek: Bilingualism in education*—In the light of what we have described it is no wonder that in the west, from the second century onward, Greek-Latin bilingualism was clearly reflected in the education of the young. This was true of the provinces, of Africa and of Rome itself, as Ausonius illustrates (*Epistles* XXII). Greek remained prominent for a long time after the true potential of Latin had been revealed by orators and writers like Cicero. Ennius, born in Messapia, had been brought up to be trilingual, which is hardly surprising, for his native city, Rudiae, according to Strabo, was still Greek two hundred years after Ennius' death. Italian by birth, Greek by education, Ennius used to refer to his "three hearts"—"Quintus Ennius tria corda habere sese dicebat quod logui Graece et Osca et Latine sciret" (Aulus Gellius). Some Roman children and young people were sent to Athens for their education, or to Massilia because of that city's Greek character. For those parents who could not afford to send their children away to school, there were the immigrant Greek teachers to whom Polybius (XXXI. 23) refers as "this tribe of teachers flocking over just now from Greece to Rome." Among these were Greek slaves like Livius Andronicus who, on receiving his manumission, set up a bilingual school (Jerome, 187a).

There were also Gallic bilingual teachers whom it was the custom of the Romans to employ because of the excellency of the Gallic schools. Juvenal writes "Gallia considicos docuit facunda Brittannos, de conducendo loquitur iam rhetore Thule." (Eloquent Gaul has trained Britons as lawyers and in Thule there is talk already of engaging a professor of rhetoric). There were popular wandering rhetors, and Aulus Gellius describes pupils accompanying the teacher from place to place. They were engaged by literary clubs where they perpetuated the methods of the bilingual rhetors—"rhetoricus sophista, utrius que linguae callens."

Such a provision of bilingual education prevailed for a very long time. As late as the fifth century the sons of aristocratic parents were still taught Greek, and some of them were taught entirely in Greek. So important was Greek that the nobleman Symmachus decided that "while my son is being taught Greek I will join him and like a young scholar share his labours" (Jones, 1960b: 937). Aemilius Paulus, father of the younger Scipio, was noted for the care he took to give his son a thoroughly Greek education. Cornelia, the daughter of the elder Scipio, provided her sons with the best Greek tutors of her day (Gwynn, 1926: 38). It is not surprising that Paulinus, the grandson of Ausonius, brought up by Greek slaves, is reputed to have been able to read Homer and Plato when he was only five years of age. And there must have been many children like Fulgentius, in Africa, who acquired a perfect Greek accent (Jones, 1960b: 987). In the fourth century, Greek was still part of the curriculum, not only of the aristocratic boys but of the middle-class student like Augustine, though it was not continued at a higher level under a rhetor. Even in the fifth century, boys from aristocratic homes still learned Greek. Sidonius Apollinarius read Menander to his son in the 60's of the fifth century.

Though the instances we have adduced must be only a very slight indication of the spread of certain types of bilingualism, it would be wrong to exaggerate the support for such bilingualism among the masses. The education which prevailed was based on an aristocratic way of life, and this meant a limited opportunity for any form of literate bilingualism for the vast majority. Greek was taught, as time went on, less as a "second language" for which there was a supporting background in the community, and more and more as a foreign language.

At the beginning Greek was not simply a subject in the curriculum but was regarded rather as the foundation and core of the child's education. It was taught before he was introduced to any formal instruction in his mother tongue, and this is illustrated by the case of the child Delmatius. He died at the age of 7, but though he had only begun to learn the Latin alphabet, he already knew Greek (Carcopino, 1956: 115). Such children were put in the care of Greek slaves or servant-tutors, and as Quintilian (*Institutio* l.i.4) remarked, the child's first step in education would be in the slave's speech. Cicero preferred Greek to Latin as the language of his son's instruction, and Quintilian advised that Greek lessons should begin as soon as the child could speak, and certainly before he gained any marked control of Latin (*Instit.* l.i.10, 12).

This early instruction in Greek was assumed to be at least as good a foundation of the child's intellectual development as his mother tongue could be. It had the advantage of ensuring the easy and firm acquisition of a necessary second language, and it was regarded as a satisfactory means of improving the child's control of his mother tongue. Naturally, every Roman child picked up Latin in the ordinary course of events, so that when he reached the age for attending school he was thoroughly bilingual (Quintilian, *Instit.* 1.i.10, 12), and could profit from formal instruction in both languages, though it was with Greek that such formal instruction began. The grammar classes were conducted in Greek and Latin, but the rhetoric classes were almost entirely in Greek. Later, parallel but separate Latin and Greek schools, rather than parallel instruction in both languages in the same school, became attractive. Cicero (*De Rhet.*: 2) remarked to Titonius that he remembered the first teacher of Latin, L. Plotius Gallus, and he regrets that older and more traditionally minded people interfered to prevent him from attending Plotius' very popular classes. Until a late period, then, Roman children were brought up as if they were Greeks but were instructed in Latin as well, though even so the Latin curriculum was modeled on the Greek course. It was for such schools that bilingual textbooks were prepared, the "Hermeneuamata Pseudo-dositteana." These contained a Greek-Latin lexicon arranged alphabetically as well as according to subjects and topics. Short, easily understood passages of prose were also arranged bilingually. Having acquired a firm grounding in the parallel short texts, the students were given the classics to read (Marrou, 1956: 263).

There was, of course, considerable antipathy to bilingualism, and especially to a bilingual education. The linguistic gaffs, mistakes in declension and gender, etc. in the conversations recorded by Petronius in "Cena Trimalchionis" are due, it has been suggested, to the author's wish to satirize the inept bilingualism of the Greek-speaking residents of Rome. Plutarch wrote that Marius the demagogue never learned Greek well or used it for any cultural or civilized purpose, thinking it foolish, as Plutarch continues, to learn a language that was taught by men who were themselves slaves. Of the same man's relatives, Cicero (*Letters* VII.i.3) wrote—"You care so little for all things Greek that you would not even use the Via Graeca to get home to your villa." The Romans themselves recognized some of the more pressing difficulties of their form of bilingual education. Quintilian noted that if formal instruction in the mother tongue were too long delayed in order to help the child consolidate his Greek, he might come to speak that native tongue with a foreign accent. And we know from other sources that this fear was not exaggerated. Cicero, for instance, took care to caution his son, who was being educated in Athens, not to neglect his Latin exercises. There is evidence that as a result of very early Greek instruction and the use of that language, educated Romans tended to introduce some features of the Greek tonic system into their Latin speech. The poor quality of the Latin spoken by bilingual Greeks who, apart from actually teaching Latin, would, as servants or child-minders, often provide the earliest models the Roman child would hear, is referred to by Quintilian (*Instit*, x. 5. 2-3). Then again, there is evidence that many felt that the acquisition of two languages simultaneously was an intellectual burden. A child's time and capacity are limited, it was argued; and even from the teacher's standpoint, it was thought quite impossible satisfactorily to keep instruction in the two languages going simultaneously. For many pupils, it was even more difficult and frustrating: Paulinus of Pella, the grandson of Ausonius, was in this predicament. He wrote

> Quae doctrine duplex sicut est potioribus apta
> Ingeniis, gemenoque ornat splendore peritos,
> Sic sterilis nimium nostri, ut modo sentio, cordis
> Exilem facile exhausit venam

> (To be asked to learn two languages is all very well for the clever ones, for they get a double glory. For the average school boy like me the need to keep up both languages is trying and exhausting.) (Quoted Haaroff, 1920: 226).

It was argued also that as a contribution to general education, apart from its value to men of letters, "Greek studies were barren and fruitless." Augustine (*Confessions* 1.13) criticized the futility of a system of bilingual education which imposed the exclusive use of the second language as the medium of instruction for the young, for this led to boredom and drudgery. It was unnatural: while Latin came to him in the course of nature—"inter blandimenta nutricum et ioca arridentium et lactitias alludentium" (with his mother's milk), Greek was a mechanical imposition. And this has been the burden of the remarks of many scholars to this day. Haaroff refers to thoughtless and unscientific pedagogy and to the teachers in this tradition "regarding the child as a receptacle for external and ready-made ideas (a kind of) spiritual militaris . . ." (Haaroff, 1920: 227). A contemporary classicist writes of the "well organized educational system of the Empire having for its main aim to teach the two literary languages and to inculcate in the minds of all its pupils the established methods and the desirability of imitation. . . . Among the reasons why the Empire failed we ought probably to number the intellectual failure of its educated classes. Hampered by their traditionalism and by the strict linguistic discipline which they imposed upon their minds, the members of that class could not solve their immediate problems." He concludes that "a smaller nation would not have been so prodigal of human effort" (Bolgar, 1954: 24, 59).

The social and educational dissatisfaction, and the Augustinian-type criticism of the practice, apart from other circumstances, made the continuance of Greek-Latin bilingual education impossible. As early as the fourth century competent teachers of Greek were hard to come by, certainly in the provinces. As Latin continued to realize its literary potential the impetus toward learning Greek for cultural purposes slackened. By the end of the fifth century its acquisition was a symbol of an outmoded tradition rather than a response to a realistic appraisal of educational need, or to the existence of social forces which at one time may have justified its position in the curriculum.

(c) *The Triumph of Latin.* (i) *Factors involved*—The diffusion and ultimate triumph of Latin in the west was the result of several factors, among which was the element of military conquest. The auxiliary regiments of the Roman armies were composed of provincials who had learned Latin. The "castella" which they usually built and inhabited were surrounded by villages and small towns— "canabae"—from which new recruits were drafted and which gradually assimilated Latin-speaking foreigners, mostly soldiers. They settled down there, organized a community of like-minded people and introduced Roman habits and the Latin language (Rostovtseff, 1959: 245). These settlements provided for administration, legal offices, schools, markets, and, by no means least in importance, places of amusement. The local people would acquire a sufficient facility in the new language to enable them to benefit from the amenities and services which were offered. Latin spread, gradually and thinly it is true, to more outposts and outlying hamlets, thus ensuring a degree of bilingualism.

But though military occupation was important in itself in spreading bilingualism, it was even more important in facilitating trade and commerce. During the civil wars several waves of Roman immigrants settled as organized groups in the conquered territories of Gaul, Spain, and Africa. Some groups were led by the instigators of the revolution, but others settled voluntarily as traders and as agents of the tax-gathering concessionaries. They were the necessary bridgeheads for the penetration of Latin into the vernacular areas. Many of these "negotiatores" followed the legions, but instead of returning to Italy they remained, occupying themselves in local affairs and becoming models of Latin behavior and speech, to be emulated by the natives.

The presence of the military, the promotion of trade and commerce, and, especially after the civil wars, stability and safety of communication along increasing numbers of good highways produced a high level of urbanization. The successors of Augustus encouraged provincials to migrate to the towns and cities, where they had to learn Latin in order to participate in the normal activities of urban life. Latin was, if not imposed, at least a superimposition, introduced more and more in a vulgarized form and in permanent conflict with the native language. Economic disintegration led to a more active bureaucracy and to an extension of education. A passage in the Digest of Ulpian mentions village schoolmasters (Auerbach, 1965: 251). The process of linguistic assimilation is not difficult to envisage: the highly developed public life, access to administrative and legal offices, markets and daily meetings in the streets, the places of amusement, theaters, public baths, gymnasia and palaestra (which were open to most inhabitants who wished to gather there), all these were sufficient incentives and provided opportunities to acquire Latin. Conversely, the need to trade with the provincials was an equally powerful motive for the Romans to acquire some proficiency in the local languages. There was a gradual intermingling of the two languages and an increasingly rapid diffusion of Latin into the countryside.

However, the rural population was in no way completely absorbed by the cities, and there was always a very extensive pool of proletariat monolinguals to ensure that the local language made up in strength what it lacked in prestige. The survival of the Gallic language into the third century is attested in a passage in the Digest of Ulpian (222-28). "Fideicomunissa quoqunque sermone relenqui possunt, non solum Latina vel Graeca, sed etiam Punica vel Gallicana vel alterius cujuscum cue gentis." St. Jerome's comparison of the language of the Treveri to that of the Galatians, and the inscriptions in the temples at Treves appear to indicate that Celtic was still in use in that area at the end of the fourth century. In the same period Postumanius in reply to a young priest who had apologized for the rusticity of his Latin in talking about St. Martin of Tours, said "Talk in Celtic or in Gallic so long as you talk about Martin." The diffusion of Latin, geographically and socially, and the retention of Gallic by the majority of the population ensured in every region a period of bilingualism during which the emphasis shifted from the vernacular to Latin.

(ii) *Impact of the Germanic tribes*—The Romans were not allowed to continue undisturbed in their assimilation of the Celts and their language, and the interruption ensured that there were in fact two periods of prolonged bilingualism, the second of which was due to the presence of a new linguistic element brought by the Germanic tribes (Meillet, 1951: 77). Their languages had for a long time influenced and been influenced by the Celtic languages. Germanic terms like "rik-a," "frei," "leder," "erbe" have a Celtic origin. The Celtic La Tène culture was responsible for the contribution to Germanic of the names of such materials as lead and iron. Similar and even closer contacts had been established between the Germans and the Romans. The latter made a practice of recruiting Germans into the army; others were made prisoners and slaves. The system of "laeti" allowed for the settlement of Germans who sought refuge in Roman territory, and in this way considerable numbers of Germans were born on Roman soil, spoke their own vernaculars, and learned Latin as well. There were as many as 14 such settlements in the cities of northern Italy, Apulia, and Calabria, and nearly half as many again in Gaul (Jones, 1960b: 620). In addition there were peaceful penetrations of Gallo-Roman settlements by German groups, while the promotion of commerce brought opportunities for close contact between the two linguistic groups.

Though the impact of the Germanic invasions elsewhere was considerable, in Italy itself the Germanic languages played an insignificant role, partly because of the relative fewness of speakers of Germanic dialects in the area, the disunity and fratricidal proclivities of the invading tribes, and the low prestige of the culture related to their languages compared with the culture of the Romans. Even so, the speakers of the Germanic dialects even in Italy were bilingual at some stages, and many of them must have remained so for long periods. The immigrants probably spoke their native tongue among themselves, but with the failure of the reinforcements necessary to the survival of Germanic in the invaded territories, the social and cultural pressure of Latin prevailed, and the shift to that language could not have been delayed beyond the second or third generation, about the tenth century. The Germanic dialects, for the reasons already given, were not strong enough to affect any radical changes in Latin. There is only very doubtful evidence of any influence on the phonetics of Italian, and the most identifiable effects were on the vocabulary (Pulgram, 1959: 230).

In Gaul the position was different, though it varied according to differences between the invading Germanic groups. Because the Burgundians had undergone a process of Romanization from as early as the fourth century, they were fairly easily and quickly assimilated and did not experience any lengthy period of bilingualism. This fact is reflected in the slight influence which their dialect had upon Gallo-Roman (Elcock, 1960: 224). There is every likelihood, too, that before the Visigoths settled in Aquitaine they had experienced a long period of Roman contact, so that the greater part of their nobility, although they spoke Gothic in ordinary intercourse, understood, spoke, and some even wrote Latin. The lower classes understood it less well in the early years of the settlement, but even they soon adapted to the new linguistic conditions.

The case of the Franks in the north was very different. In the first place their conquest was more extensive and their settlements more dense. Furthermore, unlike the Longobards of Northern Italy for instance, they were continually reinforced from their homelands. Unlike the Burgundians and the Visigoths, they had not hitherto been under any considerable Roman influence. For these reasons their language and Gallo-Roman contrived a lengthy period of coexistence, based on the numerical superiority of the one and the prestige and the cultural associations of the other (Meillet, 1951: 92). During the whole of the Merovingian and the greater part of the Carolingian periods the Germanic dialects were sustained. But with the coming of Christianity and its reception by the rulers, as well as the increasing attractiveness of the Gallo-Roman civilization, Latin became the common language. The conquerors found themselves obliged to use the language of the vanquished: there was a Latin secretary in the Burgundian court, and Theodoric the Visigoth was greatly drawn to Latin literature. Romans were used in administration and Romans of high rank became popular. The native nobility naturally followed the example of the courts. In spite of edicts to the contrary, intermarriage is known to have occurred. By the fifth century many of even the common people must have known Latin or they could not have worshiped and followed addresses from the pulpit. In the sixth century the majority of the Franks would be compelled by the necessities of day-to-day business to adopt the language of a population which immensely outnumbered them (Dill, 1926: 277-78).

The schools made their important contribution to the Latin-based bilingualism of this second period. Such schools as were established at Narbonne, Toulouse, Arles, Lyons, Autun, Trèves, Bordeaux, Vienne, and the other large towns were attended, generally speaking, by young noblemen, though inscriptions show that the trading classes were attracted to them as time went on (Pope, 1952: i). The schools were mainly interested in refining the language of the students. The sons of the Celtic nobility could learn the "correct" Latin of Rome itself, with standards which diverged more and more from the Vulgar Latin of traders and soldiers who were the ubiquitous tutors of the mass of the population. Their educational program was characterized by the distinctive methods of the bilingual Greek-Latin-speaking rhetors.

The schoolmaster of the west was the ally of the empire to the extent that he ensured the Romanization of the Gauls: and as more schools were built this Romanization of the Celtic and Germanic tribes was intensified. By the end of the seventh century many factors helped to sway the balance even more in favor of the Gallo-Roman dialect and facilitated the shift to what was now clearly emerging as Romance. One of the factors was the accentuation of very long standing differences between spoken (Vulgar) Latin, and the written language. The argument, previously accepted by most scholars, that the Romance languages developed as they did mainly because of the influence of the local languages on Latin is now largely discounted. Though it would be unrealistic to believe that the local languages did not have a material effect on the development of "Romance dialects" the "vulgar tongue" is now seen to be the result of a growing disparity between the spoken and the written variants of Latin. A second factor influencing the shift to the "vulgar tongue" was the consciousness of illiteracy among those segments of society to whom the rise of feudalism had given a new status. This was comparable, in its way, to the desire for literacy among the rising middle classes in England in the fifteenth and sixteenth centuries, a desire which promoted English in preference to Latin in the new grammar schools. This meant that though widespread or mass bilingualism was based on merely oral command of the languages, some were also literate in both languages. Although none of the superseded languages, apart from Gothic, provided a literature, the German dialects invited the attention of many of the clergy and some in the courts who would be well versed in Latin in any case. Because of such literate bilingualism the vocabulary, grammar, and to some extent the phonology of the successor languages came to reflect the contact of the several tongues (Ewert, 1959: 5). This phase of West European bilingualism left its mark upon the linguistic map, especially in France. Bilingualism or bidialectalism was a pronounced phenomenon for several centuries. As late as the sixteenth century, it has been remarked, bilingualism existed among a large number of Frenchmen, and the ancient vernaculars subsisted in familiar intercourse, especially among the less educated. The same thing is reflected in the way in which "le français commun" is even now spoken in the various provinces, for instance in Provence (Meillet, 1951: 101-2).

3. *The Byzantine Civilization and Slavic Contacts*

The concept of the Mediterranean as a culture unit and as a framework for coherent patterns of language contacts is exemplified in the contribution of Byzantine civilization to the history of bilingualism and bilingual education. Byzantium was the only center where Greek and Roman civilizations remained alive and where the respective languages were cultivated assiduously by large numbers of bilinguals. The Arab conquests of the seventh century, on the shores of the Mediterranean, because of the changes they precipitated in France and Italy, ensured that the remnants of the Roman Empire in the west in Romanized Gaul had little influence on their German conquerors: they were prevented from transmitting to them the Graeco-Roman literary and linguistic heritage. Charlemagne in the north did what he could to salvage something of what was left, but access to the source of Graeco-Roman civilization was barred by the Arabs, the Avars, and the Slavs who were holding Central Europe and the Balkans (Dvornik, 1949: 183). The Byzantines not only helped to safeguard what remained of the Classical world but constituted themselves consciously as the mediators between that civiliztion and the "barbarians." Economically and culturally the Greek cities on the north coast of the Black Sea in Classical and Hellenistic times linked the Greek world to the steppes of Western Eurasia. Those cities were then, as they were later to the Byzantines, outposts of Hellenism—"the hem of Greece sewn on the folds of the barbarians" (Cicero, *De Republica* 11.4).

Not only did the Byzantines safeguard an inheritance, linguistic in particular, and enable those with whom they were in contact to profit from it, they also expanded considerably the limited range of the Graeco-Roman influence of later centuries. "The world of Justinian's time was larger than that which the West knew in the Middle Ages. In Justinian's time men were acquainted with Scandinavia and could distinguish between Swedes and Norwegians. They used the trade routes through Russia to the Baltic. The peoples of Russia from Finns and Letts in the North to the Mordvins, Iranians and Altaic nomads were no strangers to the Byzantines. In Central Asia the Byzantines knew the great Turkic realm stretching from Persia to China. Byzantines visited West Turkestan and Sogdiana regularly (Haussig, 1971: 101). What Aramaic, Greek, and Latin had done to create a unity in the Mediterranean and to extend its influcne in the West, the Byzantines (using Greek but also the Slavic languages) did in bridging the West and East Mediterranean, and extending the Mediterranean influence northward and eastward of the Black Sea and throughout Central and Eastern Europe. The pattern of linguistic contacts so created was as complex as that of Western

Europe, and since it involved at least the fringes of what is now the Soviet Union it was vastly more extensive.

The Byzantine expansion depended on trading contacts rather than conquest, so that there had to be mutual respect for the languages of the participants. For instance, behind the conflict between Persia and the Byzantine Empire lay the struggle for access to the central Asian routes to China and the silk trade. The Byzantines depended entirely on trade: traders stayed in special quarters in cities—Turkic traders from central Asia, Persians in Cappadocia, in Caesarea. They also traded with the Altaic tribes in Russia and Siberia. Their communication network embraced the peoples of the Caucasus and West Turkestan. The Iberians in the Caucasus were stongly attached to Byzantium, while the Azeri and eastern Georgia generally were attached linguistically and by cultural influences to the Persians. But trade was not the only factor which promoted Byzantine Greek. In Armenia and the Balkans the Greek language was the instrument of political influence: in the former countering Arabic influences and in the latter forestalling Frankish and Latin papal overtures. In Italy Byzantine Greek was reinforced by three waves of immigration—consequent on the Slav penetration of Greece, from Syria and Palestine because of Arabic pressure, and from Greece, Asia Minor and Constantinople because of religious or "iconographic controversies." Whatever the reasons, Byzantine Greek influence spread.

The decline in the influence of Rome meant the shift of the linguistic, cultural, economic, and military center of gravity from Italy to Asia Minor and the provinces of the lower Danube. The language of trade, including the slave trade, was Greek. For slaves from Syria, Asia Minor, Egypt, and the Roman provinces of Africa, Greek was a common language, as it was among the traders. In the first half of the seventh century Latin was replaced by Greek as the official language of the Byzantine Empire, though Roman traditions remained strong and enclaves of Latin persisted for several decades in the east. However, even more important than the predominance of Greek over Latin was the eventual breakdown of the monopoly of both languages, brought about partly by the system of military command on the borders which gave a good measure of local autonomy, partly because of the establishment of new and important industries in the eastern provinces, but mainly because of the evolution of local Christian churches. These had begun as early as the third century when it became possible to speak of Anatolian, Syrian, Egyptian, and Roman churches, all distinguished by linguistic differences. There was a corpus of Syriac Christian literature at the beginning of the third century as well as Coptic (Egyptian) translations of the Bible.

It is the Byzantine relationship with the Slavs which introduces the principal new element into the history of bilingualism. Their precursors, the Antae, appeared about the third century when the Scythian and Sarmatian civilization was destroyed by the Goths. Even that antecedent Slavic culture was impregnated with Hellenistic influences, and those very early Slavs, the Antae, formed a link between the Hellenic-Scythian-Sarmatian civilization on the one hand, and that of ninth-century Kiev on the other. The Slavs, as we know them, advanced to the south, west, and north far into the eastern Alps and the Dalmatian coast. They possessed in time almost the whole of Greece. In Macedon up to Thessalonica, and even to Thrace, the Graeco-Roman provincial population held out only in scattered enclaves in towns of the lower Danube. The rest of the Romanized Illyrians in the face of the advancing Slavs retreated into the mountains until the end of the twelfth century when they settled as farmers and began the foundation of the Romanian nation. Most of the Greeks retreated too, and others fled to Southern Italy. By the ninth century the pattern in the area of present-day Yugoslavia and Bulgaria is a mosaic of peoples in which the Slavic element predominates. Baudel has called it an ethnic conglomerate. The Byzantines were ringed by Slavs from the Alps to the Black Sea and from the Adriatic to the Aegean, in Eastern Thrace, Thessaly, and Epirus. Furthermore these Slavs maintained their ethnic identity and their Slavic dialects, in some places within Greece up to the fifteenth century. Thessalonica, the native town of Constantine/ Cyril and Methodus, the Balkan missionaries, was a bilingual city in the ninth century. It received neighboring Slavs within its walls and had close contact with the Slavs of the surrounding countryside.

Although trade as well as political and military considerations entered into the Byzantine-Slav relationship, it was religion and especially the work of the missionaries which dominated the interlingual situation. On the eastern shore of the Black Sea the Lezgins and the Abazins were converted to Christianity in the sixth century by Byzantine missionaries, and it was their mediation which enabled the Greek language to penetrate Georgia and to influence the Iberians. The Byzantine renaissance of the ninth century provided the impetus for the Orthodox Church missionaries to carry the Greek language to the peoples of Central and Eastern Europe. Orthodox Christianity was a means of assimilating the Slavs culturally, and this was reinforced by the use of Greek as a liturgical language. Nevertheless, though in Greece itself Byzantine policy was Hellenization, elsewhere there was a remarkable degree of Byzantine tolerance of Slav dialects. Consequently linguistic conflict, between Slavic and Greek, but principally between Slavic and Latin, was expressed in arguments and practices concerning the liturgy.

The old Bulgar language was transcribed in Greek characters. The Bulgars had no script of their own, and the majority of transcriptions, even in the ninth century, were in the Greek characters so that Greek must have survived the barbarian invasions from the east. It was used as the official language of the Bulgar state in the first half of the ninth century. Young Bulgars were sent to Constantinople to school for a solid grounding in Greek secular education. It was from Bulgaria that the new written language, in Cyrillic, went out to become the Greek-rite ecclesiastical and educational language in Kiev and eventually became Russian Slavonic. By the introduction of the Slavonic liturgy into the Russian state, indirectly from the work of Cyril and Methodus, the Russian Slavs inherited the Old Slavonic literature bequeathed by the two missionaries to Moravia. As a result in the tenth, eleventh, and twelfth centuries Kievan Russia grew into the center of culture far ahead of anything similar in the Latin west at that time, partly because of the great inheritance the Byzantines transmitted, and partly because they were not simply willing but anxious to employ the Slavic languages as a means of transmission.

Thus Bohemia was biliturgical and its religious rites bilingual in the tenth century, and so far as Poland is concerned we may assume that besides Latin priests there came to Poland priests educated in the use of the Slavonic language. Even Wenceslas, committed to a westward Latin orientation, had no quarrel with Slavonic liturgy, literature, and language. The Slavonic language was centered on Prague, whereas it was at Budech, out in the country, that the Latin language was established in educational institutions. The same conflict of language affiliation is exemplified in the south. Slavonic was introduced into the rites of Dalmatian Croatia by the ninth century, and many priests were educated in Bohemia. At the same time the Latin bishop of Dalmatian Croatia was under the jurisdiction of Rome. Yet the favorable attitude to Slavonic was so strong that he showed no animosity to the use of Slavonic. The linguistic conflict worked out differently in Hungary. There the Byzantine influence was stronger than in Bohemia but from the tenth century to the end of the eleventh the dominant force was German with its Latin preferences.

4. *Jewish Bilingualism*

(a) *The Middle East.* The history of bilingualism we have attempted to trace has been governed by the interaction of one or another of three "imperial" languages (Aramaic, Greek, and Latin) on the one hand, and on the other many languages spoken in limited areas, like Phrygian or Lycian in the Middle East, the Italic languages, Celtic on the continent or in Britain, and the Slavic languages. The Jews have spoken or written Hebrew for well over 3,000 years and have been in close contact with the three "imperial" languages as well as very many of the "localized" languages in the Middle East, West, Central, and Eastern Europe. Hebrew is not an "imperial" or is it simply a local language: it has had an international provenance from very early times, but it has not had the political, military, or massive economic reinforcement which has enabled the imperial languages not only to survive for many centuries as Hebrew has done, but to dominate the local languages as well.

The extensive and varied bilingualisms which have characterized the Jews from the beginning of their history to the present time is not to be doubted or underestimated, but because of the unique status of Hebrew among Jews, together with their additional and intimate linguistic affiliations at various times and in different areas, the pattern of bilingualism among the Jews is both different from and far more varied than that of any other people. Furthermore, Hebrew-related bilingualism runs like a single, clearly identifiable strand through the texture of bilingualism in Europe, which is the limit of our present concern. Hebrew never died in any of the areas where Jewish communities were established, and for over 1,300 years it was the everyday language of the Israelites. Even when its status as the vernacular was undermined and it was replaced as a spoken language by Aramaic and Greek, after 200 A.D., Hebrew still remained a living language. From 500 A.D. onward written Hebrew was a vital means of secular communication within and between the Jewish communities of different countries, while remaining the sanctified language of study and religious observances. In some places it was also a spoken language, used either to emphasize separateness from the gentiles, or as a means of international communication among Jews from different areas of Europe. Consequently, Hebrew was the one stable or consistent element serving to ensure the continuity of the Jewish people. Nevertheless, while religious and historical literature, like Ecclesiasticus, Macabees I, Esther, and David continued to be written in Hebrew, it ceased to be their only or even their most frequently used language.

Aramaic became their dominant spoken language and gradually became a literary and even a cosanctified language. As Hebrew lost some of its familiarity for the Jews their scriptures had to be translated into Greek to be comprehensible to large segments of the population. Their late classical literature, for instance the last three books of Macabees, was written in Greek and even modeled on Greek genres. The protracted Greek rule in Judea, the patterns of the Ptolemaic and Seleucid regimes, the material achievements of the Hellenistic civilization in finance, agriculture, and city building combined to produce far-reaching changes in language affiliation among the Jews. Yet, Hellenization, normally supported by the Jewish aristocracy, the Greek princes, and Herodian rulers of Judea under Roman patronage, was resisted by the masses, so that Aramaic was able to coexist as a vernacular with Greek, together with Hebrew as a language of different status. The coexistence of Greek- and Aramaic-speaking settlements in Egypt was an important aspect of Jewish bilingualism at that time. The highest class was undoubtedly Macedonian and Greek, but there were many Jews whose influence was only slightly less (Sarton, 1950: 17). In the Herodian city of Caesarea there were Jews who read the *Shema* in Greek.

The rabbis knew Greek well, and as to the masses, though they were not favorable to Greek, their knowledge of that language was unlikely to be less than that which other nationalities in the Middle East possessed. The attraction of the cultured Jew toward Greek is suggested by the prohibition, expressed in rabbinic regulations, on the teaching of Greek, while the importance of the Maccabean revolt was as much linguistic as religious (James, 1920: 64, 65). The study of Greek was considered a prerequisite for leadership among the Jews of Palestine, since that task involved the needs and problems of the Hellenistic-Roman Jewish Diaspora and contact with gentile rulers and authorities. However, although elementary education in the Talmudic period points to contact between educational institutions of the Greek cities and the educational institutions of the Jews, the general Jewish school system for all Jews dealt with neither Greek culture nor with their language (Safrai, 1971: 148, 153). The great majority of the Jewish people lived in scattered towns and distant urban areas within and beyond the boundaries of the Roman Empire, in Persia, and in the Arab kingdoms along the Red Sea coast.

Meanwhile the Jewish affiliation to Aramaic became less firm with the rise of Arabic. Though many scholars have maintained that Aramaic remained as a spoken language among the Jews down to the eighth century, and others claim that dialects of Aramaic are still evident in Syria and Iraq, it is generally believed that most Jews ceased to use Aramaic as a vernacular after the fifth century and turned to Arabic. Great numbers of Jews worked in Arab academies and other educational institutions, and they took an active part in the cultural rebirth of the Orient (Keller, 1971: 145). About 300 years after the rise of Islam the Hebrew Bible had been translated into Arabic more than once, the tenets of the Jewish faith had been set forth in the language of Islamic theology, and the rabbinical law had been formulated with the aid of Muslim legal terms. Jews were intimately involved in the development of an Arabic culture. Simultaneously Judaism too developed in every respect, and the Hebrew language was cultivated, studied scientifically, and its proper usage established (Gottein, 1971: 170, 172).

(b) *Spain.* By the beginning of the High Middle Ages in Europe successive waves of linguistic influence had swept over the Jews—Hebrew, Aramaic, Greek, and Arabic. While these linguistic tides ebbed and flowed the speakers of Hebrew and Aramaic were in close contact with the Hittites, Phrygians, Thracians, Armenians, and many others. Educational influences originating in several different countries were experienced by them. For instance Egyptian pedagogic treatises—"Teachings"—exercised a marked effect on Jewish education under Solomon, whose need for increased numbers of trained scribes on account of the expansion of his bureaucracy caused him to turn to Egyptian practice and theory.

With the development of national languages in Spain, Italy, Northern and Eastern Europe the Jews were involved in even more and novel patterns of bilingualism. In Gaul the Jews were mixing with the native populations of Marseilles, called the Hebrew city, Narbonne, in the Auvergne, Arles, Orléans, and Bordeaux. They had been in Spain for centuries before the arrival of the Visigoths. In Northern Spain the headstone at the grave of a young Jewish woman named Miriam is inscribed in Hebrew, Greek, and Latin. With their long history of close relations with Arabs it is not surprising therefore that the Muslim invaders of Spain were supported by the Jews. Nor is it surprising that the Jewish system of education took Arabic into account while maintaining Hebrew. In Spain, no less than in France and Germany, the basis of Jewish education was a knowledge of Hebrew prayers, the Bible, and the Talmud. A knowledge of Arabic was presupposed in all the syllabuses, as was a knowledge of Latin later. The pedagogical program was discussed in Hebrew and Arabic writings. Two centuries after the Muhammadan conquest was a golden age for the Jews in Spain (Keller, 1971: 174), especially in Seville, Granada, and Toledo. Cordoba was the seat of an important Jewish academy with students from all over Spain and North Africa engaged in the study of Hebrew and Arabic, and acting as involuntary intermediaries between the literatures of the two languages, for instance the introduction of Arabic metrical forms (Keller, 1971: 181). It cannot be doubted that but for the use of Hebrew in worship that language would have been lost in Spain. There were complaints at the end of the thirteenth century that the younger generation spoke only the language of the country, and that the majority of male adults even could not speak Hebrew. In Sicily they spoke the local language, Greek, and Arabic. The Hebrew poets, grammarians, and Bible exegetes were indignant over the neglect of formal instruction in Hebrew and deplored the superficial knowledge of the language among the masses.

This was very different from the situation of Provencal Jews, although their influence in that area was derived very largely from Spain. "Provencal Jews were initially immersed head and shoulders in traditional learning . . . unlike their co-religionists in Muslim Spain, where in addition to rabbinic learning Jewish scholars welcomed and absorbed the culture of the Muslims and emulated them in poetry, comparative linguistics . . . the Jews of Provence were scarcely exposed to secular" influences (Ben-Sassoon, 1971: 195). Nevertheless it was Provence which provided the center for the transmission of Judeo-Arabic achievements in philosophy and philology. It was the clearing house and center for translations from Arabic, and its schools were involved in the dissemination of secular linguistic learning.

This was the result of the shifting of the Jewish center of gravity northward in Spain as a consequence of the transfer of political mastery in the Iberian peninsula from the Saracens to the Christians. Spanish was the tongue of the now dominant population, and Spanish was also the vernacular of the Jews in the reconquered areas, though as late as the fourteenth century the Jews spoke and wrote Arabic in Toledo. It is no wonder that of the Jews of Spain and Provence it was claimed "they knew Persian, Arabic, the languages of the Franks, Spaniards, and Slavs." But it was the Romance languages which the Jews cultivated as their secular native languages, and it is these languages which were referred to as "our language." Both Catalan and Castilian left their traces on the response literature. "As if prompted by a premonition of their destiny the Jews of the Iberian province adhered to their beloved language all the more tenaciously as the century of doom and exile advanced upon them. It became increasingly the language in which they formulated the statutes and regulations of their social and communal life. They also made it the literary medium of their lighter vein" (Neuman, 1969: 102). Meanwhile they preserved the use of Hebrew, and many continued to read Arabic.

(c) *Italy.* Jewish communities were to be found solidly established in many Italian cities when the empire came into being. The revolt against the Romans in Palestine and the fall of Jerusalem resulted in the enslavement of many thousands of Jews who were brought to Italy—97,000 to Rome alone. The increase in the Jewish population of South Italian cities, like Taranto, was enormous, and the cities north of the capital were also recipients of large numbers of Jews. About 96-100 A.D. Rabbi Mathea ben Hevesh was sent to organize the Italian communities, and he introduced an apparently new system of education which, while preserving the Jewish languages, also took account of local vernaculars. It is not surprising therefore that with increasing cultural and linguistic acclimatization an Italian vernacular literature makes its appearance among them. The language employed is evidence of the interaction of the Jewish and local languages, and the linguistic characteristics of this contact have been perpetuated in the Judeo-Italian language to the present day (Roth, 1946: 28).

In the eighth and ninth centuries it is obvious that there had been a remarkable revival of interest in Hebrew language and literature in Southern Italy. The Jewish scholars and educated lay members of the population were at all times in close contact with Palestine, partly because of commerce and pilgrimage interest. It is not surprising, therefore, that inscriptions in the Southern towns and in Rome itself are in choice Hebrew, displaying a wide knowledge of the literature and a scholarly acquaintance with the language (Roth, 1946: 59). In Southern Italy there appears to have been a prolonged cultural ferment. The Latin, Italian, Byzantine, and Muslim elements combined with the Jewish to keep in being a high level of intellectual excitement. The contribution of the Jews was important mainly because of their wide linguistic knowledge which enabled them to translate from Arabic, sometimes via Hebrew, to Latin. With the expulsion of the Jews from Spain, Sicily, and Portugal, this Jewish element in Italian intellectual life was greatly enriched. Italy was the only land in Christian Europe open to them. In Rome, in addition to the several old established Italian congregations and those maintained by immigrants from northern Europe, synagogues following the Castilian, Catalan, Aragonese, and Sicilian rites were established. A similar process occurred in the North, where in addition to a few Spanish refugees—Sephardim— there was a constant immigration from Germany and Central Europe, and, in the fifteenth century, from Rhodes. Holland experienced an influx of Ashkenazim from Germany so that the situation in Holland, as in Italy, reflected two types of Jewish linguistic characteristics—Spanish-speaking Sephardim who had been there for a long time, and German/Slavic-speaking Ashkenazim.

By the time of the full flowering of the Renaissance the Jewish population of Italy had been profoundly Italianized in both language and culture. Jewish immigrants from Spain, Portugal, and Northern Europe retained their former "national" and Jewish languages for some considerable time, but they too were assimilated like the Italian Jews. Together they constituted a rich and varied pattern of bilingualism, for though they would speak Spanish and Portuguese and would learn Italian, they also retained Hebrew, not only for use in their prayers and other aspects of worship, but for limited domestic purposes, in an archaic form. They also wrote Judeo-Italian in Hebrew characters, and an interesting corpus of Judeo-Italian literature has been preserved. This language (Italkic) was comparable in many ways to Yiddish (Judeo-German), and Judesmo (Judeo-Spanish). At the same time the linguistic interests of Renaissance scholars affected the Jewish attitude to Hebrew. The linguistic works of Elias Levitas, Solomon d'Urbino, and David de Pomi, most of them bilingual and thus available to the non-Jews, assisted in laying the foundation of Hebrew linguistic purity and so made the language available for non-Jews to study in the Renaissance, as they studied Latin and Greek.

The contribution of exiled Spanish and Portuguese Jews enriched the linguistic pattern of other areas than Italy. From 1450 onward they made a deep and lasting impression on the Levant. Judesmo, rich in Hebrew loanwords, displaced the Greek formerly spoken by the Jews of that area. In a more neutralized variety it became the lingua franca throughout the Near East. Thus a Spanish businessman, Gonzalo de Ilesiar, reported, around 1550: "The Jews have transplanted our language to Turkey. They have faithfully preserved it down to the present time, and speak it perfectly. In Salonika, Constantinople, Alexandria, Cairo, and other cities they employ Spanish alone in trade and otherwise. In Venice I met Jews from Salonika, very young people, whose Castilian was as fluent as mine" (Quoted, Keller, 1971: 272).

The influence of the Byzantines and of Germany, and later the Ottomans in the Slavic world, carried with it a Jewish component also. The immigrant Ashkenazim brought their language with them from Germany and established it in Poland. Yiddish became the lingua franca so that in time even among Jews long settled in Poland it gradually displaced their previous language, though not entirely. Indeed, next to Hebrew, Yiddish was considered virtually a sacred language. In the south Slavic areas and in European and Asiatic Turkey the Judesmo of the Sephardim from the Iberian peninsula became the prevailing language of the Jews.

A perusal of this very brief outline of the linguistic vicissitudes of the Jews will be enough to accept the proposition that the linguistic sophistication of their education had a considerable effect on the development of the Jews. On the one hand it led inevitably to what has been referred to as a "Levantization" of Jewish speech habits. On the other, Jews were induced very early to pioneer in comparative linguistics. Their familiarity with several languages may, indeed, have awakened their grammatical consciousness precociously, for they were among the first to know the "techne grammatice" of Dionysos of Thrax. The Masoretic obligation to preserve the accuracy of the Biblical text was a fundamental factor in all this, but there can be no doubt that their voluntary and involuntary acquaintance with so many languages also helped. They could not help noticing the differences between the various languages, and because of their knowledge of Arabic grammarians they were educated to elucidate texts in one language by comparisons with similar texts written in other Semitic languages. From here it was but a short step to comparisons with non-Semitic languages—the unrelated Berber, Persian, and other Indo-European languages. In the earlier Muslim era more intense contact with the Arabs promoted interest in linguistic analysis. Points of grammar became the subject of passionate debate among all educated persons. "Spanish Jews following a widespread fashion among their Arab neighbors heatedly debated philological minutiae in their social gatherings" (Baron, 1958: 3-4).

Conclusion: Some Implications

(a) *Language and Culture-Alliance.* An important characteristic of the successive phases of linguistic contact in Europe, as we have seen, is the overlap of several major languages. For many centuries there was an interpenetration of cultures and languages which extended from India to Rome and farther west.

Contacts between India and the Mesopotamian region had existed from the Sargonide period of Sumerian history (2500 B.C.). There was a historical, religious, and linguistic complex extending from the Nile Valley to beyond the Syro-Palestinian coastal strip, the table lands of Anatolia and Iran. Its influence, linguistic and cultural, irradiated from the east toward Greece and Anatolia. The overlap of languages ensured their would be no cleavage between east and west, but rather a pronounced continuity. "When Greek civilization comes into flower the Near East had thousands of years of history behind it," from which Greeks profited (Moscati, 1959: 314). In the second century B.C., when Greeks moved across to Bengal, the Romans established the Graeco-Roman civilization on the coasts of the Atlantic. Lingua francas allowed ideas and moods to sweep the area, so that the Mediterranean destiny was to provide coherence to our civilization—to establish a center and to connect epicenters with each other and epicenters with the center itself. Social habits became more and more alike; cities and the houses of upper classes had a similar appearance. Celtic forces, though they were submerged, except in Britain, made enduring contributions in Bohemia, Western Europe, and especially in Wales and Ireland. Celtic artist-craftsmen were sought after in the mature Graeco-Roman cultures of the south. The Celtic contribution to the Christian Church, whether in art (e.g., the eighth- and ninth-century illuminated manuscripts of Ireland) or in missionary work, has its own unique character. "The significance of the Celts in European civilization has no parallel in the early history of Europe" (Filip, 1960: 199). In the Eastern Mediterranean where the language remained Greek and education was based on Greek classics, centuries of Roman influence and the presence of Latin produced a network of institutions and established common ideals and assumptions regarding man and his work which were embraced by the Byzantines. The barbarians brought into the cities on the northwest of the Black Sea appeared as the outrangers of Hellenism. The consequent Graeco-Slav influence, linguistic and cultural, was to provide a channel for the transmission of Byzantine civilization to medieval Eastern Europe (Obolensky, 1971: 141).

All this was made possible by the intricate web of languages in contact and it was mediated by educational systems which, though highly selective, took account of those differences in language. In a very vital sense our concept of education, the *paedeua*, which, with all its faults, has promoted the advancement not of the Western world alone, derives very largely from the complex web of languages in contact. One language might be in contact with several others simultaneously, so that it is difficult to identify a period of history when important cultural consequences did not derive from a complex pattern of intertwined languages over vast territories. It is partly because of this that there has emerged a "European semantics," an expression of such contacts: "the common denominator of historical styles of semantic expressions of civilization which in the course of time have been superimposed the one on the other to make up the fabric of that semantic koiné which allows a person speaking one European language to master semantically any other" (Spitzer, 1948: 7). These are Aramaic, Greek, Latin, Celtic, and German. They constitute what Gilbert Murray (*Greek*

Studies, 66) referred to as "the inherited conglomerate." The phrase implies that the principle of linguistic and cultural interrelationships, such as we have described, is agglomeration not substitution. A new pattern of contact seldom effaces the old completely. These languages, because of their cumulative and interacting influences, have helped to ensure a fairly homogenous system of semantic reference, underlying whatever cultural differences there may be.

In the semantic overlap other linguistic traits have been diffused, helping to create what Trubetzkoy called a language alliance, a *Sprachbund* (Sommerfelt, 1954: 23). The disintegration of the various empires and the long period during which the smaller countries matured under varying conditions produced many European cultures, but because of the linguistic overlap and the complex contact situations we may venture nevertheless to speak of a European society and even of a European *Hochsprache* (Auerbach, 1965: 338). There is a linguistic alliance which in part provides the possibility of a consistent system of ideas and values we call our Western civilization. And though there is a widespread call for a transvaluation of Western values, those values and the Western system of education are influential throughout the world.

(b) *Education.* Different linguistic groups are increasingly determined to participate in a bilingual education. In 1962 a survey of six nations revealed that a majority of Dutch and Belgian adults claimed a speaking competence in one or more languages other than their native tongues. Of the German and French who were questioned, 25% and 33% respectively made the same claim (*Sondages,* 1963: 41). Russian is the second language of 16 million non-Russians. The same urge to establish communication outside one's own group is characteristic of less modernized peoples also. In Central Africa, it has been claimed, the natives set out consciously to extend their identity beyond their native villages by deliberately choosing to incorporate in their conversations a vocabulary other than that of their native dialect (Samarin, 1966: 199).

These facts illustrate the tendency of civilizations to increase progressively the radius of communication and point to important consequences for education. Lord Bryce saw this tendency in exclusively European terms. The new sort of unity being created among mankind, he contended, was the result of the dissemination of Western European languages and the culture and science related to them (Bryce, 1914: 2). But there is now no reason to believe that the world pattern of language contact of the kind that Bryce had in mind will be dominated by Western Europe: Russian, Arabic, and Chinese are increasing their range, and no doubt others will emerge into prominence. In the pattern of present and probably future bilingualism, it is likely that a few languages of this kind will enter intensively into complex contact situations and partnerships far beyond the areas where national territories have common boundaries. This development will affect not only the relatively small proportion of highly educated men and women but those whose professional or occupational interests bring them into immediate contact with speakers of other languages, professional soldiers for instance in integrated military organizations, as well as even comparatively low-grade industrial operatives employed by international industrial concerns. The introduction of a second language at lower levels of primary education in increasing numbers of school systems, and mass media of many kinds available to increasing numbers of young people have reduced the obstacles of mountain ranges, oceans, and rivers. Furthermore, these emerging contacts are not fortuitous, as they have been in the past, but planned and engineered as part of national and international social systems, mediated through educational institutions.

If there is one thing we learn from a historical study of languages in contact it is that the languages which appear to contribute most and survive longest, those which constitute the "adstratum" rather than the "substratum," are usually supported and reinforced by powerful institutions, of which the schools, monastic institutions, royal households serving an educational function, and specialized higher institutions like those to which the legal professions were attached, are among the most influential. But the fact that bilingual education has contributed so much in the past is due to its having been directly or indirectly a factor in the lives not only of the privileged classes but of the middle and lower classes also. They participated in the process of Romanization in the West and Hellenization in the East. Some of them wrote Latin or Greek. Though it is improbable that the urbanized workers or the isolated inhabitants of rural areas shared the education with which the others were provided, they could not fail to profit from their example. Nor can we ignore the experience of the most depressed class of all, the slaves. A considerable proportion of them, ten thousand in fourth-century Athens for instance, were absorbed into domestic service, and in many cases, apart from becoming the tutors of the children of the family, they became formally recognized teachers. Others were employed in a professional capacity as secretaries and bank managers (Jones, 1956: 185-99). Formal bilingual education might have been limited, but its influence spread among the total population.

The schools could not fail to provide a conservative influence in the fluid situations created by the social conditions which promoted bilingualism—"cette instabilité des habitudes ... qui est une caractéristique des régions et des milieux bilingues" (Malmberg, 1961: 74). It is through the schools that the vernacular can achieve the desired status once the demographic situation which makes its use necessary, in the attempt to integrate hitherto depressed elements in a nation, is recognized. The schools are also the means whereby the traditional values associated with a prestige language are made available to nourish the emerging vernacular. Nevertheless, a bilingual education should involve not only the survival of the habitual but the exploration of new modes of thought and feeling.

If a system of education is a necessary emollient in social-conflict situations, and a bulwark against the coarsening of the languages which are traditionally associated with education in any particular country when they come into contact with other languages, it needs also to be an insurance against the possibility that the survival of the traditional language does not create a chasm between a "refined" and a "vigorous consciousness." The Carolingian reforms in education were motivated by the awareness of the Latin compromises with the vernacular which pre-Carolingian texts reflected. But in attempting to preserve the traditional, the new system suffered from the same defects which had been revealed in the Roman system of bilingual education: the insistence on correct Latin (like the insistence on Greek) cut the feeble ties of communication between Latin and the vernaculars and between a sophisticated and a realistic education. Even "the leading classes of society possessed neither education nor books nor even a language in which they could express a culture rooted in their actual living conditions" (Auerbach, 1965: 254-55).

This is one of the prevailing problems of all bilingual education programs—how to ensure that the teaching of the language which encapsulates a traditional culture is not divorced from contemporary life. And at the same time, how to avoid such a commitment to the emerging vernacular that education does less than justice to the continuity of the great traditions or the "world of commanding forms." We are also unwilling to accept the fact that languages may be as exposed to natural laws of decline as human beings are. Many refuse to believe in the value of a pluralism which acquiesces in the coexistence of several languages among one people. It is for this reason, partly, that a historical study of bilingualism is needed to supplement what we have been accustomed to: it ensures greater objectivity and a perspective which enables us to detach ourselves from an ethnocentric stance. In most instances the history of one nation is very much the record of its contacts with neighbors, and the history of its language cannot be understood in isolation from an understanding of its contacts with other languages: "l'histoire de l'allemand en France nous semble être un complément nécessaire d'histoire du Français en France ... l'histoire linguistique de la France ne se limite pas à une simple histoire du francais en France" (Levy, 1950: vi).

Aarons, Alfred C., Barbara Y. Gordon and William Stewart (eds.). "Linguistic-Cultural Differences and American Education." *Florida FL Reporter,* 7 (1969), No. 1. Special anthology issue.

Adamesteanu, D. "Nouvelles fouilles a gela et dans l'arriere pays." *Revue Archeologique,* 49 (1957), 20-46 and 147-80.

Adams, E. *Bulletin of the Ulster Place Names,* 4 (1940).

Andersson, Theodore. "Bilingual Elementary Schooling: A Report to Texas Educators." *Florida FL Reporter,* 34 (1968), No. 6, 25.

–––. *Conference on Child Language.* Quebec: International Center for Research on Bilingualism, Laval University, 1971a.

–––. "Bilingual Education: The American Experience." *Modern Language Journal,* 55 (1971b), 427-40.

Andersson, Theodore and Mildred Boyer (eds.). *Bilingual Schooling in the United States.* Washington, D. C.: USGPO, 1970 (2 vols.).

Anon. *Bilingual Education for American Indians.* Washington, D. C.: Office of Education Programs, United States Bureau of Indian Affairs, 1971a.

–––. *Razon de Ser of the Bilingual School.* Atlanta: Southeastern Educational Laboratory, 1971b.

Armstrong, Robert G. "Language Policies and Language Practices in West Africa." In J. A. Fishman, C. A. Ferguson and J. Das Gupta (eds.). *Language Problems of Developing Nations.* New York: Wiley, 1968, pp. 227-36.

Atkinson, B. F. C. *The Greek Language.* London: Faber and Faber, 1952.

Auerbach, E. *Literary Language and Its Public in Late Antiquity and in the Middle Ages.* London: Methuen, 1965.

Augustine. *Confessions* I. 13. London: Dent (Everyman) 1954.

Aulus Gellius. *Noctes Atticae* XVIII. 17. Oxford: Clarendon, 1917.

Ausonius. "Exhortations to His Grandson." *Epistles* XXII. Oxford: Oxford Univ. Press, 1934.

Balkan, Lewis. *Les Effets du Bilinguisme Français-Anglais sur les Aptitudes Intellectuelles.* Brussels: AIMAV, 1970.

Baron, S. W. *A Social and Religious History of the Jews II* (2nd edition). New York: Columbia Univ. Press, 1967.

Baudel, M. *The Mediterranean and the Mediterranean World in the Age of Phillip II.* London: Collins, 1973 (2 vols.).

Ben-Sassoon, H. H. and S. Ettinger (eds.). *Jewish Society Through the Ages.* London: Weidenfeld, 1971.

Bloch, M. *Feudal Society* (trans. Manyon). London: Kegan Paul, 1961.

Boardman, J. *The Greeks Overseas.* Middlesex: Pelican, 1964.

CONSOLIDATED BIBLIOGRAPHY

APPENDIX 4

Bolgar, R. R. *The Classical World and Its Beneficiaries*. London: Cambridge Univ. Press, 1954.

Bosch-Gimpera, P. La formazione di popoli Spagna. *Revista di Studi Classici* (2) 1949, 97-129.

Bozman, A. B. *Politics and Culture in International History*. Princeton, N. J.: Princeton Univ. Press, 1960.

Brown, Roger W. and Marguerite Ford. "Address in American English." *Journal of Abnormal and Social Psychology,* 62 (1961), 375-85. Also in Dell Hymes (ed.). *Language in Culture and Society*. New York: Harper and Row, 1964, pp. 234-44.

Bryce, J. *The Ancient Roman Empire and the British Empire in India*. London: Oxford Univ. Press, 1914.

Bull, Wm. "The Use of the Vernacular Languages in Fundamental Education." In Dell Hymes (ed.), *Language in Culture and Society*. New York: Harper and Row, 1964.

Burns, Donald H. "Bilingual Education in the Andes." In J. A. Fishman, C. A. Ferguson and J. Das Gupta (eds.), *Language Problems of Developing Nations*. New York: Wiley, 1968, pp. 403-14.

Calder, W. M. "Corpus Inscriptionum Neo-Phrygiarum." *Journal of Hellenic Studies,* 31 (1911), 160-168.

Camejo, Antoni. *Documents of the Chicano Struggle*. New York: Pathfinder, 1971.

Carcopino, J. *Daily Life in Ancient Rome*. London: Routledge, 1956.

Cassano, P. V. "The Substrat Theory in Relation to the Bilingualism of Paraguay: Problems and Findings." *Anthropological Linguistics,* 15 (1973), 9, 406-426.

Cazden, Courtney B., Vera P. John and Dell Hymes (eds.). *Functions of Language in the Classroom*. New York: Teachers College Press, 1972; reprinted in Fishman, 1972d.

Cerny, J. "Language and writing" in Harris, J. R. (ed), 1971.

Chaytor, H. J. *From Script to Print*. London: Sidgwick and Jackson, 1945; reprinted 1966.

Chilver, C. E. F. *Cisalpine Gaul*. Oxford: Clarendon Press, 1941.

Chrysostom. "Homilia octava habit in ecclesia S. Pauli," in J. P. Migne (ed.), *Patrologiae Graeca*. Paris, Garnier, 1862, col. 507-8.

Cicero. *Tusculanas*. Berlin: Tauchnitz, 1869.

———. *Letters to His Friends* VII. i. 3. Oxford: Clarendon Press, 1958-65 (3 vols.).

———. *De Rhetoricus*. Chapter 2. Oxford: Clarendon Press, 1901-03 (2 vols.).

Cohen, Andrew D. *A Sociolinguistic Approach to Bilingual Education*. Rowley, Mass.: Newbury House, 1975.

Collingwood, R. G. and J. Myres. *Roman Britain and the English Settlements*. Oxford: Oxford University Press, 1931.

Cook, J. M. "Greek Settlements in the Eastern Aegean and Asia Minor." *Cambridge Ancient History,* II, Chapter 38. Cambridge: Cambridge Univ. Press, 1961.

Cooper, Robert L., B. N. Singh and Abraham Ghermazion. "Mother Tongue and Other Tongue in Kefa and Arusi." In M. L. Bender *et al., Language in Ethiopia*. London: Oxford University Press, 1976.

Das Gupta, Jyotirindra and J. A. Fishman. "Inter-state Migration and Subsidiary-Language Claiming: An Analysis of Selected Indian Census Data." *International Migration Review,* 5 (1971), 227-49.

Davis, Frederick B. *Philippine Language-Teaching Experiments* (Report No. 5). Manila: Philippine Center for Language Study, 1967.

Davis, Thomas. "Our National Language" in *Selections from Prose and Poetry*. London: Fisher Unwin, 1914.

Davis, William B. and F. J. Satterwhite. "Black Studies Programs: Problems and Prospects." *Issue: A Quarterly Journal of Africanist Opinion,* 2 (1972), No. 3, 51-59.

Diehl, E. *Inscriptions Latinae Christianae Veteris*. Bonn: Weber, 1912.

Dill, F. *Roman Society in Gaul in the Merovingian Age*. London: Oxford University Press, 1926.

Dillard, J. L. *Black English: Its History and Usage in the United States*. New York: Random House, 1972.

Dodson, C. J. *et al. Towards Bilingualism.* Cardiff: University of Wales Press, 1966. (See particularly Part II: "Early Bilingualism: An Experiment in the Early Presentation of a Second Language," pp. 17-77.)

Dunbabin, T. J. *The Western Greeks—The History of Sicily and South Italy,* etc. Oxford: Clarendon Press, 1948.

Dupont-Sommer, E. *Les Araméens.* Paris: Presses Universitaires de France, 1940.

Dvornik, F. *The Making of Eastern Europe.* London: Polish Research Center, 1949.

———. *Byzantine Missions among the Slavs.* New Brunswick, N. J.: Rutgers Univ. Press, 1970.

Elcock, W. D. *The Romance Languages.* London: Faber and Faber, 1960.

Entwistle, W. J. *The Spanish Language.* London: Faber and Faber, 1936.

Epstein, Erwin (ed.). *Politics and Education in Puerto Rico.* Metuchen, N. J.: Scarecrow, 1970.

Ervin-Tripp, Susan M. "Sociolinguistics." In Leonard Berkowitz (ed.), *Advances in Experimental Social Psychology IV.* New York: Academic Press, 1969, pp. 91-165; also in J. A. Fishman (ed.), *Advances in the Sociology of Language I.* The Hague: Mouton, 1971, pp. 15-91.

Essien-Udom, E. U. *Black Nationalism.* New York: Dell, 1969.

Ewert, A. *The French Language.* London: Faber and Faber, 1959.

Fellman, J. "Concerning the 'Revival' of the Hebrew Language." *Anthropological Linguistics,* 15 (1973), 250-57.

Ferguson, Charles A. "Diglossia." *Word,* 15 (1959), 325-40.

———. "The Role of Arabic in Ethiopia: A Sociolinguistic Perspective." *Georgetown University Monograph Series in Language and Linguistics,* 23 (1970), 355-70.

Filip, J. *Keltska civilisace a jeji dědictiví.* Prague: Czechoslovak Academy of Sciences and Arts, 1960.

Fishman, J. A. "The American Dilemma of Publicly Subsidized Pluralism." *School and Society,* 87 (1959), 264-67.

———. *Language Loyalty in the United States.* The Hague: Mouton, 1966.

———. "Bilingualism with and Without Diglossia; Diglossia with and Without Bilingualism." *Journal of Social Issues,* 23 (1967), No. 2, 29-38.

———. "Some Contrasts Between Linguistically Homogeneous and Linguistically Heterogeneous Polities." In Fishman, Ferguson and Das Gupta (eds.), *Language Problems of Developing Nations.* New York: Wiley, 1968, pp. 53-68.

———. "National Languages and Languages of Wider Communication in the Developing Nations." *Anthropological Linguistics,* 11 (1969), 111-35.

———. "The Politics of Bilingual Education." *Georgetown University Monograph Series on Language and Linguistics,* 23 (1970a), 47-58.

———. "Language Maintenance and Language Shift Revisited." In Fishman, *Language in Sociocultural Change.* Stanford, Cal.: Stanford University Press, 1972a, pp. 76-134.

———. *Language and Nationalism.* Rowley, Mass.: Newbury House, 1972b.

———. "A General Model of Bilingual and Bidialectal Education." *Conference on Child Languages.* Quebec: International Center for Research on Bilingualism, Laval University, 1972c.

———. *Language in Sociocultural Change.* Stanford, Cal.: Stanford University Press, 1972d.

———. *Sociology of Language.* Rowley, Mass.: Newbury House, 1972e.

———. "Enseignera-t-on encore les langues en l'an 2000?" *Le Français dans le Monde,* 100 (1973a), 11-41. In English in *Materials en Marcha* (1973a), December, pp. 12-15.

———. "The Phenomenological and Linguistic Pilgrimage of Yiddish." *Kansas Journal of Sociology,* 9 (1973b), 127-36.

———. "The Sociology of Bilingual Education." *Etudes de Linguistique Appliquée* (1974), pp. 112-24.

Fishman, J. A. and David E. Fishman. "Yiddish in Israel." In J. A. Fishman (ed.), *International Journal of the Sociology of Language.* The Hague: Mouton, 1974, No. 1, 125-46.

Fishman, Joshua A. and John Lovas. "Bilingual Education in Sociolinguistic Perspective." *TESOL Quarterly,* 4 (1970), 215-22.

Fishman, J. A. and Erica Lueders. "What Has the Sociology of Language to Say to the Teacher? " In C. B. Cazden, Vera John and Dell Hymes (eds.), *Functions of Language in the Classroom.* New York: Teachers College Press, 1972; reprinted in Fishman, 1972d.

Fishman, J. A. and V. Nahirny. "The Ethnic Group School and the Mother Tongue Maintenance in the United States." *Sociology of Education,* 37 (1964), 306-17.

Fishman, Joshua A., Robert L. Cooper, Roxana Ma *et al. Bilingualism in the Barrio.* Bloomington, Ind.: Language Science Monographs, Indiana University, 1971.

Frake, Charles O. "How to Ask for a Drink in Subanum." *American Anthropologist,* 66 (1964), No. 6, Part 2, 127-32.

Francisci, P. de *Primordia Civitatis* Rome: Studi Classici, 1959.

Gaarder, A. Bruce. "Organization of the Bilingual School." *Journal of Social Issues,* 23 (1967), 110-20.

———. "The First Seventy-six Bilingual Education Projects." *Georgetown University Monograph Series in Language and Linguistics,* 23 (1970), 69-76.

Glazer, Nathan. "The Process and Problems of Language-Maintenance: An Integrative Review." In J. A. Fishman, *Language Loyalty in the United States.* The Hague: Mouton, 1966, pp. 358-68.

Glotz, G. and R. Cohen. *Histoire Greque.* Paris: Presses Universitaires de France, 1955.

Gordon, C. H. *Before the Bible—The Common Background of Greek and Hebrew Civilizations.* London: Collins, 1962.

Gordon, Milton M. *Assimilation in American Life.* New York: Oxford University Press, 1964.

Gottein, S. O. "Jewish Society and Institutions under Islam." In H. H. Ben-Sassoon, 1971.

Greeley, Andrew M. "The Rediscovery of Diversity." *Antioch Review,* 3 (1971), 343-65.

Grenier, A. *La Guale Celtique.* Paris: Didier, 1943.

Grittner, Frank M. "Pluralism in Foreign Language Education: A Reason for Being." *Britannica Review of Foreign Language Education,* 3 (1971), 9-58.

Guldescu, S. *History of Medieval Croatia.* The Hague: Mouton, 1964.

Gwynn, A. *Roman Education from Cicero to Quintilian.* Oxford: Clarendon University Press, 1926, p. 38.

Haaroff, Th. *Schools of Gaul.* London: Clarendon Press, 1920.

———. *Strangers at the Gate.* London: Clarendon Press, 1938.

Hammond, N. G. L. The End of the Mycenean Civilization and the Dark Age—The Literary Tradition. *Cambridge Ancient History.* Vol. II, Chapter 36. Cambridge: Cambridge University Press, 1962.

Harris, J. R. (ed.). *The Legacy of Egypt.* Oxford: Clarendon Press, 1971.

Haussig, H. W. *A History of Byzantine Civilization* (trans. J. M. Hussey). London: Weidenfeld and Nicolson, 1971.

Heer, F. *The Intellectual History of Europe* (trans. Steinberg, 1966). London: Weidenfeld and Nicolson, 1953.

Heurgon, J. *The Rise of Rome* (trans. J. Willis). London: Batsford, 1973.

Hoben, Susan J. "The Meaning of the Second-person Pronoun in Amharic." In M. L. Bender *et al., Language in Ethiopia.* London: Oxford University Press, 1976.

Hocket, C. F. *A Course in Modern Linguistics.* New York: Macmillan, 1958.

Honnyer, Helen. "Some Observations on Bilingualism and Language Shift in Italy from the 6th to the 3rd Centuries B.C." *Word,* 13 (1957), 415-46.

Horace. *Satires,* I, 10, 30. Boston, Ginn, 1899.

Hymes, Dell. "Bilingual Education: Linguistic vs. Sociolinguistic Bases." *Georgetown University Monograph Series in Language and Linguistics,* 23 (1970), 69-76.

———. "On Communicative Competence." In J. B. Pride and Janet Holmes (eds.), *Sociolinguistics.* Harmondsworth: Penguin Books, 1972, pp. 269-93.

Imari, A. *Revolution and Nation Building.* Detroit: Songhay, 1970.

Isidore. *Etymolog.* XI. Oxford: Clarendon Press, 1911.

Jackson, K. *Language and History in Early Britain.* Edinburgh: Edinburgh Univ. Press, 1953.

James, J. C. *The Languages of Palestine and Adjacent Regions.* Edinburgh: Edinburgh Univ. Press, 1920.

Jerome. *Jerome Ep. ad Galat.* Oxford, Clarendon Press, 1929.

John, Vera P. and Vivian M. Horner. *Early Childhood Bilingual Education.* New York: Modern Language Association of America, 1971.

Jones, A. H. M. *The Cities of the Eastern Province.* Oxford: Clarendon Press, 1937.

———. "Slavery in the Ancient Worlds." *The Econ. Hist. Rev.,* 6 (1956), 185-199.

———. *The Greek City.* Oxford: Clarendon Press, 1960a.

———. *The Later Roman Empire II.* Oxford: Blackwell, 1960b.

Jungeman, F. H. "Structuralism in History." *Word,* 15 (1959), 3, 460-475.

Kazhdan, Hayyim, S. *Fun Kheyder un Shkoles biz Tsisho* (From the Traditional Elementary School and Russified School to Yiddish Secular Nationalist Schools). Mexico City: Kultur un Hilf, 1956.

Keller, W. *Diaspora—The Post Biblical History of the Jews* (trans. R. Winston). London: Pitman, 1971.

Kelly, L. G. (ed.). *Description and Measurement of Bilingualism.* Toronto: University of Toronto Press, 1969.

Kjolseth, Rolf. "Bilingual Education in the United States: For Assimilation or Pluralism." In B. Spolsky (ed.).

Kloss, Heinz. "German-American Language Maintenance Efforts." In Fishman, 1966, pp. 206-52.

Lambert, Wallace E. and G. R. Tucker. *Bilingual Education of Children.* Rowley, Mass.: Newbury House, 1972.

Lambert, Wallace E., G. R. Tucker and Alison d'Anglejan. "Cognitive and Attitudinal Consequences of Bilingual Education." *Journal of Educational Psychology,* 65 (1973), 141-59.

Lange, D. L. (ed.). *Pluralism in Foreign Language Education.* Chicago: Encyclopedia Britannica (*Britannica Review of Foreign Language Education,* 3), 1971.

Levenston, E. A. *English for Israelis: A Guide for Teachers.* Jerusalem: Israel University Press, 1970.

Levy, P. *La Langue Allemande en France.* Paris: Didier, 1950.

Lewis, B. *The Emergence of Modern Turkey.* London: Oxford Univ. Press, 1961.

Lewis, E. Glyn. "Migration and Language in the USSR." *International Migration Review,* 5 (1971), 147-59; also in J. A. Fishman (ed.), *Advances in the Sociology of Language II.* The Hague: Mouton, 1972, 386-412.

———. *Multilingualism in the Soviet Union.* The Hague: Mouton, 1972.

Lieberson, Stanley. *Language and Ethnic Relations in Canada.* New York: Wiley, 1970.

L'Isle, William. *Divers Ancient Monuments in the Saxon Tongue.* London: No publisher listed, n.d.

Liversidge, John. *Britain in the Roman Empire.* London: Cape, 1968.

Lorwin, Val R. "Linguistic pluralism and political tension in Belgium." *Canadian Journal of History,* 5 (1970), 1-23.

Mackey, William F. "A Typology of Bilingual Education." *Foreign Language Annals,* 3 (1970), 596-608; also in J. A. Fishmaan (ed.), *Advances in the Sociology of Language II.* The Hague: Mouton, 1972, 413-32.

———. *Bilingual Education in a Binational School.* Rowley, Mass.: Newbury House, 1972.

Macnamara, John. *Bilingualism and Primary Education.* London: Edinburgh University Press, 1966.

———. "The Effects of Instruction in a Weaker Language." *Journal of Social Issues,* 23 (1967), No. 2, 121-35.

Macnamara, John. "Bilingualism and Thought." *Georgetown University Monograph Series on Language and Linguistics*, 23 (1970a), 24-45.

———. "Comparative Studies of Reading and Problem Solving in Two Languages." *TESOL Quarterly*, 4 (1970b), 107-16.

———. "The Generalizability of Studies of Bilingual Education." Montreal: McGill University, 1973 (mimeo).

Magie, O. *Roman Rule in Asia Minor—to the End of the Third Century after Christ.* Princeton, N. J.: Princeton University Press, 1950.

Malherbe, E. G. *The Bilingual School.* London: Longmans, 1946.

———. *Demographic and Socio-Political Forces Determining the Position of English in the South African Republic: English as Mother Tongue.* Johannesburg: The English Academy, 1966.

Malmberg, B. "Linguistique Ibérique et Ibéro-Romaine." *Studia Linguistica,* 15 (1961), 2, 57-113.

Marrou, E. *A History of Education in Antiquity.* London: Sheed and Ward, 1956.

Meillet, A. *Linguistique Historique et Linguistique Générale II.* Paris: Societe de Linguistique de Paris, 1951.

Michel, John. "Tentative Guidelines for a Bilingual Curriculum." *Florida FL Reporter,* 5 (1967), No. 3, 13-16.

Modiano, Nancy. "National or Mother Language in Beginning Reading: A Comparative Study." *Research in the Teaching of English,* 1 (1968), 32-43.

Montet, P. *Eternal Egypt* (trans. Weightman). London: Weidenfeld and Nicolson, 1964.

Morain, G. "Cultural Pluralism." *Britannica Review of Foreign Language Education,* 3 (1971), 59-95.

Moscati, S. *The Semites in Ancient History.* Cardiff: University of Wales Press, 1959.

———. *The Face of the Ancient Orient.* London: Kegan Paul, 1960.

Murray, G. *Greek Studies.* London: Clarendon Press, 1948.

Nahirny, Vladimir and J. A. Fishman. "American Immigrant Groups: Ethnic Identification and the Problem of Generations." *Sociological Review,* 13 (1965), 311-26.

Nesborough, U. R. de A. *The Last Myceneans and Their Successors.* Oxford: Oxford University Press, 1964.

Newman, A. A. *The Jews in Spain.* New York: Octagon Books, 1969.

Noss, Richard. *Language Policy and Higher Education: Higher Education and Development in South East Africa.* Paris: UNESCO and the International Association of Universities, 1967.

Obolensky, Dimitri. *The Byzantine Commonwealth: Eastern Europe 500-1453.* London: Weidenfeld and Nicolson, 1971.

O'Huallachain, Colman L. "Bilingual Education in Ireland." *GUMSLL,* 23 (1970), 179-94.

Orr, J. *Words and Sounds in English and French.* London: Blackwell, 1953.

Osterberg, T. *Bilingualism and the First School Language.* Umea: Vasterbottens Tryckeri AB, 1961.

Pacheco, Manuel T. "Approaches to Bilingualism: Recognition of a Multilingual Society." *Britannica Review of Foreign Language Education,* 3 (1971), 97-123.

Pallatino, M. *The Etruscans* (trans. Cremona). London: Collins, 1955.

Palmer, L. R. *The Latin Language.* London: Faber and Faber, 1954.

Pedersen, Paul. "A Bilingual Alternative for Higher Education." *Culture and Language Learning Newsletter,* 3 (1975), No. 3, 8-10.

Pietersen, I. *De Friezen en Hun Taal.* Drachten: Laverman, 1969.

Pliny. *Naturalis historia* VI.5. Oxford, Clarendon Press, 1904.

Polybius. *Opera* XXXI. 23. Oxford: Clarendon Press, 1896.

Pope, M. K. *From Latin to Modern French.* Manchester: Manchester University Press, 1952.

Portal, R. *The Slavs* (trans. P. Evans). London: Weidenfeld and Nicolson, 1969.

Preaux, C. "Graeco-Roman Egypt." In J. R. Harris (ed.). Oxford: Clarendon Press, 1971.

Pryor, G. C. *Evaluation of the Bilingual Project of Harlandale Independent School District in* the First Grades of Four Elementary Schools During the 1966-67 School Year. San Antonio, Texas: Harlandale School District, 1967.

Pulgram, E. *The Tongues of Italy*. Cambridge (Mass.): Harvard Univ. Press, 1959.

Quintilian. *Institutio Oratoria*. Oxford: Clarendon Press, 1935.

Ramos, Maxino, Jose V. Aguilar and Bonifacio P. Sibayan. *The Determination and Implementation of Language Policy*. Quezon City: Philippine Center for Language Study, Alemar-Phoenix, 1967.

Richardson, M. "An Evaluation of Certain Aspects of the Academic Achievement of Elementary Pupils in a Bilingual Program, Coral Gables, Florida." Ph. D. dissertation, University of Miami, 1968.

Rojas, Pauline. "The Miami Experience in Bilingual Education." In Carol J. Freidler (ed.), *On Teaching English to Speakers of Other Languages*. Champaign, Ill.: National Council on the Teaching of English, 2 (1966), 43-45.

Rostovtseff, M. *Social and Economic History of the Hellenistic World*. Oxford: Clarendon Press, 1941, 3 vols.

———. *Social and Economic History of the Roman Empire*. Oxford: Oxford Univ. Press, 1959 (3rd ed.).

Roth, C. *The History of the Jews in Italy*. Philadelphia: Jewish Publication Society, 1966.

———. "Jewish Society and the Renaissance." In H. H. Ben-Sassoon, 1971.

Royal Commission on Bilingualism and Biculturalism. *Preliminary Report* (1965); *General Introduction, Book I: The Official Languages* (1967); *Book II: Education* (1968). Ottawa: The Queen's Printer.

Rubin, Joan. "Language and Education in Paraguay." In Fishman, Ferguson and Das Gupta (eds.), *Language Problems of Developing Nations*. New York: Wiley, 1968, pp. 477-88.

Rummel, R. J. "Understanding Factor Analysis." *Journal of Conflict Resolution*, 11 (1967), 444-80.

Safrai, S. "Elementary Education in the Talmudic Period." In H. H. Ben-Sassoon, 1971.

Salesbury, W. *A Dictionary in Welsh and English* (London, 1547). London: Welsh Cymmrodorion Society, 1877.

Samarin, W. J. "Self Annulling Prestige Factors among the Speakers of a Creole Language." In W. Bright (ed.), *Sociolinguistics*. The Hague: Mouton, 1966.

Sapir, E. *Selected Writings* (ed. Mandelbaum). London: Cambridge University Press, 1949.

Sarton, G. *A History of Science—Hellenic Science and Culture in the Last Three Centuries B.C.* Cambridge (Mass.): Harvard University Press, 1950.

Saville, Muriel R. and Rudolph C. Troike. *A Handbook of Bilingual Education* (revised edition). Washington, D. C.: TESOL, 1971.

Scherer, George A. C. and Michael Wertheimer. *A Psycholinguistic Experiment in Foreign-Language Teaching*. New York: McGraw-Hill, 1964.

Schermerhorn, Richard A. *Comparative Ethnic Relations: A Framework for Theory and Research*. New York: Random House, 1970.

Scott, Joseph W. "Ethnic Nationalism and the Cultural Dialectics: A Key to the Future." *The Review of Politics*, 34 (1972), 55-68.

Sibayan, Bonifacio. "Language Policy, Language Engineering and Literacy: the Philippines." *Current Trends in Linguistics*, 8 (1972).

Smith, S. *Cambridge Ancient History III*. London: Cambridge Univ. Press, 1937.

Sommerfelt, Alf. "Language, Society and Culture." *Norsk Tidsskrift for Sprogvidenskap*, 17 (1954), 5-81.

Sondages, No. 1 (1963), 41.

Special Subcommittee on Bilingual Education (U. S. Senate). *Bilingual Education: Hearings on S. 428*. (2 vols.). Washington, D. C.: USGPO, 1967.

Spencer, John. "Colonial Language Policies and Their Legacies." *Current Trends in Linguistics*, 7 (1969).

Spitzer, L. *Essays in Historical Semantics*. London: Cambridge University Press, 1948.

Spolsky, Bernard. "Speech Communities and Schools." *TESOL Quarterly,* 8 (1974), 17-26.
Spolsky, Bernard (ed.). *The Language Education of Minority Children.* Rowley, Mass.: Newbury House, 1972.
Stern, M. "The Amonean Revolt." In H. H. Ben-Sassoon, 1971.
Sturtevant, E. H. and E. Hahn. *A Comparative Grammar of the Hittite Language I.* New Haven, Conn. and London: Yale University Press and Oxford Univ. Press, 1951.
Suetonius. *De Grammaticis* Chapter 71. Oxford; Clarendon Press, 1911.
Swain, Merrill. *Bilingual Schooling: Some Experience in Canada and the United States.* Toronto: Ontario Institute for Studies in Education, University of Toronto, 1972.
Tabouret-Keller, Andrée. "Language Use in Relation to the Growth of Towns in West Africa: A Survey." *International Migration Review,* 5 (1971), 180-203.
Tarn, W. W. *The Greeks in Bactria and India.* London: Cambridge University Press, 1938.
– – –. *Alexander the Great.* London: Cambridge University Press, 1948.
Tovar, A. "Linguistics and Psychology." In Martinet, A. and U. Weinreich (eds.), *Linguistics Today.* New York: Linguistic Circle of New York, 1954.
Toynbee, A. J. *A Study of History VII.* London: Oxford Univ. Press, 1950.
– – –. *The World and the West.* London: Oxford University Press, 1953.
Tucker, Richard G. "An Alternate Days Approach to Bilingual Education." *GUMSLL,* 23 (1970), 281-300.
Twersky, I. "Aspects of the Society and Cultural History of Provincial Jewry." In H. H. Ben-Sassoon, 1971.
Valentine, Charles A. "Black Studies and Anthropology: Scholarly and Political Interests in Afro-American Culture." *Addison-Wesley Module 11960,* 1972.
Vanek, Anthony L. and Regna Darnell. "Canadian Doukhobor Russian in Grand Forks, B.C.: Some Social Aspects." In Regna Darnell (ed.), *Linguistic Diversity in Canadian Society.* Edmonton (Canada) and Champaign (USA): Linguistic Research, Inc., 1971.
Vasiliev, A. A. *Byzantium and Islam in Byzantium–* In Baynes, N. H. and H. Moss (eds.), *An Introduction to East Roman Civilization.* London: Oxford University Press, 1961.
Verdoodt, Albert. *Zweisprachige Nachbarn.* Vienna: Braumüler, 1968.
– – –. *L'Université Bilingue.* Quebec: International Center for Research on Bilingualism, Laval University, 1969. (Expanded in *Kölner Zeitschrift für Soziologie und Sozialpsychologie, Sonderheft 15,* 1971, 276-90.)
– – –. "The Differential Impact of Immigrant French Speakers: A Case Study in the Light of Two Theories." *International Migration Review,* 5 (1971), 138-46; also in J. A. Fishman (ed.), *Advances in the Sociology of Language II.* The Hague: Mouton, 1972, 377-85.
von Humboldt, C. W. *Collected Works* (ed. Leilzmann). Berlin: Behr, 1903-36.
Webster, T. B. *From Mycenae to Homer.* London: Methuen, 1958.
Weinreich, Uriel. "Research Problems in Bilingualism with Special Reference to Switzerland." Ph. D. dissertation, Columbia University, 1951.
Welbes, J. (pres.). *Plurlinguisme à l'Université.* Brussels: AIMAV, 1975.
Whatmough, J. *Pre-Italic Dialects of Italy II.* Cambridge, Mass.: Harvard University Press, 1933.
Woodhead, A. G. *The Greeks in the West.* London: Thames and Hudson, 1962.
Young Lords Party. *Palante.* New York: McGraw-Hill, 1971.
Zachrisson, R. E. *Romans, Kelts and Saxons in Ancient Briton.* Uppsala: Skrifter Utgiva av Kungl. Humanistika Vetenskaps-Samfundet; Uppsala, 1927.